"If World War 3 is fought with atomic weapons, World War 4 will be fought with sticks and stones."

Jacob Beser

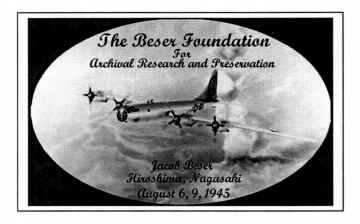

The Beser Foundation
For
Archival Research and Preservation

Jacob Beser
Hiroshima, Nagasaki
August 6, 9, 1945

The Rising Sun Sets
The Complete
Story of the Bombing of Nagasaki

Edited by

Jerome Beser

and

Jack Spangler

Compiled From Unpublished Documents
Provided by
The Beser Foundation
For Archival Research and Preservation

authorhouse®

AuthorHouse^{TM}
1663 Liberty Drive, Suite 200
Bloomington, IN 47403
www.authorhouse.com
Phone 1-800-839-8640

First published by AuthorHouse 6/12/2007

ISBN: 978-1-4343-1833-6 (sc)
ISBN: 978-1-431832-9 (dj)

Library of congress control Number: 2007904457

Printed in the United States of America
Bloomington, Indiana

This book is printed on acid-free paper.

Book cover Design by: Jack Spangler and Jerome Beser
Proof Reading by: Stefani R. Beser, Mark Ryan, Beryl and Lou Frank
Cover Photo: Trinity Test July 16, 1945
CD Cover Graphics by: Jaclyn A. Beser

"As in any war, our goal was—as it should be—to win. The stakes were too high to equivocate. We had to do what was necessary! Humane warfare is an oxymoron. War by definition is barbaric. I particularly feel a special sense of indignation at those self-proclaimed humanitarians that make an acceptable or intolerable distinction between the use of nuclear explosives or the use of conventional explosives and/or fire bombing or bullets as the means of killing the enemy. To try and distinguish between an acceptable method of killing and an unacceptable method is ludicrous. In my mind, to suggest that one specific act of war is barbaric and thereby illegal is to imply that other forms of slaughter are acceptable and consequently legal! If you have to die in warfare, what is the difference of being killed by a bomb or a bullet?"

"We do not claim that we as mortal men alone won the war. We do not claim that the thousands of men and women on the home front that designed and built the atomic bombs in record time won the war. A secret weapon far greater and far more powerful than the atomic bomb won the war - American ingenuity, industry and unanimity of purpose were the deciding factors."

Jacob Beser
October 1945

DEDICATION

Freedom is never really free

It is the most costly thing in the world

It is never paid for in a lump sum

Installments come due in every generation

All any of us can do is offer the generations

That follow a chance for freedom

This book is dedicated to

The valiant men of the U S Army Air Corps 509th

Composite Group

Whose selfless patriotism and devotion to duty

Contributed directly to maintaining the freedom

Of this great country

And especially to the memory of

My father Jacob Beser

Contents

Jacob Beser with his son Jerome and grandson Joshua enjoying leisure cruise of the Chesapeake Bay on his Bristol 34 sailboat.

Foreword

On December 7, 1941 over 300 carrier based airplanes clearly marked with the "Rising Sun" emblem of the Japanese Empire, initiated World War II in the Pacific by an unprovoked attack on the US Naval base at Pearl Harbor. The first wave hit the American airplanes on the ground. Most were destroyed. An inbound flight of B-17 bombers stumbled on the raid and several were destroyed. Ninety-four war ships lay at anchor and were attacked by dive bombers and torpedo planes. Almost all were destroyed or severely damaged. America was at war in the Pacific!

Japanese aerial photo of battleship row soon after the USS Arizona exploded

The overwhelming military power of the Rising Sun's army and navy followed up with irresistible drive and swept over Malay and the Philippines, then Java and finally Burma, conquering Southeast Asia in about a half a year. However, the Rising Sun reached its zenith in mid 1942 when its rise was halted at the Battle of Midway. From then on the Rising Sun began to set as the Japanese forces were forced to retreat as the Americans defeated them in the various land, sea and air battles in the South Pacific.

By the late summer of 1945 the war in Europe was over and Germany had surrendered. The war in the Pacific had been going on for almost four years and the world wanted to get it over with as soon as possible. Despite heavy losses on the ground and the destruction of their home island cities by the relentless fire bombing, the Japanese steadfastly refused to surrender. An invasion of the Japanese homeland would be required and was being planned. Men and material were being assembled in the area in preparation for a November invasion. Events of the months before August 1945 confirmed to Allied leaders that the Japanese would defend their homeland just as vigorously as they had defended Saipan, Iwo Jima and Okinawa. Casualties on both sides were expected to be in the hundred's of thousands if not in the millions.

The situation changed abruptly on August 6th. It was on this day that a single B-29 bomber from the Army Air Corps' 509th Composite Group based on Tinian Island and proudly displaying the name *Enola Gay* on its nose dropped the first atomic bomb on the Japanese City of Hiroshima. The explosive power of this bomb was greater than that of 2,000 B-29s flying with their maximum bomb loads. In an instant Hiroshima, the eighth largest city in Japan with a population of over 340,000 people, was obliterated. Still the Japanese refused to surrender even though they knew an invasion of their homeland was coming soon. They were hoping to get better terms if they could inflict heavy casualties on the Americans when the invasion occurred. Three days later, on August 9, another B-29 named *Bock's Car* dropped a second and more powerful atomic bomb on the city of Nagasaki. Now the Japanese knew that the Americans were serious and had more than one atomic bomb. In face of continued atomic bombing and the total destruction of their homeland, they surrendered nine days later. What had started as a day of unspeakable terror at Pearl Harbor ended with one blinding flash of light at Nagasaki!

Jacob Beser, my father, was the only man to fly as a crewmember on both the *Enola Gay* for the Hiroshima Mission and the *Bock's Car*[1] for the

---

[1] Editor's Note: *Bock's Car* or *Bockscar*, which is correct? We don't know! Jacob Beser as well as Colonel Tibbets, Major Sweeney, Cmdr. Ashworth and Capt. Beahan consistently used "*Bock's Car*" in their writings. However some historical writers use *Bockscar*.

The usual procedure was for the aircraft commander to select the name for his airplane so if Fred Bock said it was *Bockscar* then that name would be correct. But with Tibbets, Sweeney, Ashworth, Beahan, Beser and others thinking it was *Bock's Car* there must have been some reason for the confusion!

Most of the airplanes had names before the Hiroshima and Nagasaki missions based on what Tibbbets and others have written. This indicates that Capt. Bock's airplane was

Nagasaki Mission.   He witnessed first hand what happened on both missions.

In 1985 my father visited Hiroshima and Nagasaki and wrote his first book *Hiroshima and Nagasaki Revisited.*   In 1990 he was contemplating writing a second book to tell the complete and untold story of the Nagasaki mission.   Unfortunately he passed away in 1992 and was unable to fulfill this ambitious goal. However in 2006 Jack Spangler, a close family friend and I have attempted to complete my father's desire to tell the complete story of the Nagasaki mission and emphasize the horrors of nuclear warfare. We have used tape recordings from his radio and TV interviews, manuscripts and notes to tell his story in his own words and have included his personal opinions as he expressed them. At this point we should note that his personal opinions are blunt and in some cases opinionated. Anyone who knew my father knew him as a man who was not afraid to speak his mind and did so sometimes rather abrasively. But the message he preached until the day he died was always clear. War is immoral. If you are going to have a war its academic how you die. The lessons he learned from the atomic bomb missions speaks clearly "never again."   His hope was not only never again use weapons of mass destruction but never again to wage a war that would necessitate using such weapons.

This is more than just a simple rerun of the many stories that have been told for over half a century about the bombing of Hiroshima and Nagasaki. It is very easy to sit back in an easy chair today with a limited understanding of the conditions in 1945 and argue about what should have been done to end the war. But when you see it from the perspective of

---

probably known as *Bock's Car* certainly by Tibbets, Sweeney, Ashworth, Beahan and Beser.

The nose art on the B-29 clearly shows *BOCKSCAR* with the possibility of a small space between the "K" and the "S". Some documents indicate that the markings on the airplanes were removed before the Nagasaki mission for security reasons. Another document says the name *BOCKSCAR* was painted in black capital letters after the mission.

We have used my father's unfinished manuscript and his archived documents to complete his book. We have neither performed any extensive research to confirm the accuracy of what he said nor have we extensively edited his words or grammar. We have simply taken his unfinished manuscript; supplement it with what he said in other writings; personal conversations and interviews; and, stitched them together to complete his book more or less in accordance with his original plan. Since my father consistently used *Bock's Car* we have left the spelling in as he had written.

3

someone, such as my father, who was there and participated, you have a much better understanding about what took place. That is what my father did in his first book *"Hiroshima and Nagasaki Revisited "* and intended to do in his second book.

If you are looking for an apology for the bombing of Hiroshima and Nagasaki you won't find it here. Dad had absolutely no intent of ever apologizing for what happened during the later days of World War II. While he was against war in general and atomic warfare in particular, he was proud of his role in missions that ended World War II. He felt then and felt the same way until the day he died that what he and the other 1800 or so members of the 509th Composite Group did in August of 1945 saved the lives of millions of Allied and Japanese soldiers and civilians. He felt that way despite what revisionist historians say and would like people to believe. He also thought that Monday morning quarterbacking 45 years later is easy for people who didn't have to make the hard choices that had to be made in 1945 and get up on a soapbox and criticize the decisions of those whose job it was to win the war. But, as my father said *"Our job was to bring the war to a speedy end with a minimum number of casualties on both sides and we did our job in the best way we knew how."*

My Mission to Complete My Father's Work

My father spent his entire career from 1945 to 1985, with the exception of a short interval, in service to his country either in the Army or in defense work. As I said earlier, he held the distinction of being the only man to fly on both the strike aircraft that bombed Hiroshima and Nagasaki. At both Hiroshima and Nagasaki he saw first-hand the destruction caused by the atomic bombs. Later in his role as an employee of defense contractors, he had access to various weapon performance reports and study documents that further delineated the awesome destructive power of both the bombs dropped on Japan as well as the much larger bombs that have since been developed and tested. Based on his first-hand observation and the other information in his possession, he had more than just a casual observer's point-of-view of the opening of a new era where man's inhumanity to his fellow man had exceeded all previous assaults.

While chemists and physicists were utilizing the periodic table elements of uranium and plutonium to construct bombs, Dad also considered another element not in the chemical periodic table - the potential effects on humanity. Many times Dad said he was in total agreement that the use of the bombs was fully justified in 1945, but he was also firmly convinced that a better way must be found to settle future international disputes. Atomic bombs should never again be used in warfare! But, he was a willing participant and he had never regretted his part in the development of and the use of the first atomic weapons.

In 1985, my father retired 40 years after his Hiroshima and Nagasaki experiences. Based on his personal experiences in 1945 and what he had learned over the next 40 years from the test reports and studies, he felt he had a post-retirement mission to do as much as he could to better inform the public of the horrors of nuclear warfare.

In 1988, Dad published his first book, "*Hiroshima and Nagasaki Revisited.*" In this book, he related some of his experiences during the development and the delivery of the bombs as well as the results of his trip to Japan in 1985 for the 40th anniversary of the bombing of Hiroshima and Nagasaki. He faced head-on and bluntly answered questions of "revisionist historian" about his feelings regarding his wartime experiences. He also discussed in detail the response that he received from the Japanese people two generations later that were totally ignorant of World War II history. He even attempted to answer their questions,

"How could all of this ever happened?"

In 1990 my father outlined his second book. In this book, he planned to tell the unknown story of the Nagasaki raid. He also planned to answer some of the thousands of questions that had been asked over the past 40 years. Furthermore, he wanted to express his deep feelings that the world should never again have to experience the effects of atomic bombs in warfare. While preparing to write this book, Dad accumulated a vast archive of source material and renewed his effort to locate the voice recordings that he made while over Hiroshima, just minutes after the first bomb exploded. The contents of his document archive and the tapes would once and for all answer a number of questions and speculations that had plagued objective and revisionist historians for 40 years.

On June 17, 1992, my father passed away from melanoma cancer. As his illness progressed, unbeknownst to our family, he stored his archive of documents in his office at the family home. Unfortunately, after more than 40 years of searching, Dad never found the in-flight recording which he had made onboard the *Enola Gay*.

In 2004, the family home was sold. In the process of moving, my father's archives were discovered. Upon review of his documents, I found that they contained a wealth of historical documents. These documents included hundreds of unpublished private correspondence, lecture notes, interview recordings, mission planning, meeting agendas, summary reports and eyewitness debriefing transcripts as well as a number of private photos and films from crew members and military sources.

Reviewing my father's document collection revived my memories of our many conversations about his wartime experiences. It was then that I started my mission to complete the book my father had planned to write. At this point I renewed his search for the in-flight recording and also started restoring and digitizing his archived documents. In the process, I learned more about the true facts pertaining to the atomic bomb missions, the end of World War II, as well my father's life mission. My journey to complete his work has not been an easy one. In 2005, I was diagnosed with a large cell tumor mass that, due to its late discovery and pain, nearly caused me to come very close to ending my quest to finish his work. But, when my health failed, people stepped forward to pick up the torch. Friends like Jack Spangler and Robbie Jacobson and my immediate family, with both physical and emotional support, by working by my side as my health deteriorated and took over when it all became too painful.

This was particularly appreciated starting from the beginning of my diagnosis, during the time of my surgery, induced coma, recovery and rehabilitation. As a result of studying the documents in Dad's archives and with assistance, I have been able to complete my Dad's last mission.

Above all, Dad wanted my generation and generations beyond to recognize the true state of the world in 1945 and to be aware of the many thousands of lives on both sides that were saved by the use of the atomic weapons. He also wanted people to recognize that war itself was the immoral act, not just the weapons that were used. Dad stressed that we must study the mistakes of the past to prevent repeating them in the future.

My father was aware that many of the existing stories were misleading as to why Hiroshima and Nagasaki were selected as targets and continued to propagate myths of guilt and remorse from the soldiers who participated in these missions. My father wanted to correct these stories and myths with indisputable facts, not hearsay or propagandist material. In his manuscripts, lecture notes and other papers, he has quoted, with both written and spoken words of those that were there and participated in the target selection and the actual bombing missions.

The recording that Dad made immediately after the bomb exploded over Hiroshima were lost for more than 50 years, but has now been found. Also, *Enola Gay* crew interview transcripts made immediately after and 15 years later have been uncovered. The Hiroshima recording clearly disposes of the myth that Bob Lewis said, "*My G-d, What have we done?*" Neither was it found on the recordings that any of the crew members expressed any feelings or guilt or remorse. What was found on the recordings and also in the interviews was that some of the crew expressed sorrow for the Japanese citizens, but did not condemn what they had done. They instead expressed a belief that the bombings would bring a quick end to the war, thus saving the lives of an untold number of American and Japanese servicemen and civilians.

The members of the *Enola Gay* crew were all young men, many in their late teens through the late twenties. Fifteen years after the bombing, the same men were again interviewed. Again, there were no expressions of remorse or guilt for what they had done in 1945. Each and every man said that if the conditions existed today as they did in 1945 he would volunteer to do the same thing again! They still believed that this mission had helped bring a rapid end to the war and saved thousands of American and Japanese lives.

My father was a 1st. Lieutenant in the Army Air Corps 509th Composite Group. In addition to flying on both missions, Dad also participated in the Manhattan Project during the atomic bomb development and in the mission planning activities. In this capacity, his chain of command was Colonel Paul Tibbets, Commander 509th Composite Group; General Leslie Groves, Manhattan Project Manager; Henry Stimson, Secretary of War; and Franklin D. Roosevelt, President of the United States. In recognition of the importance of his service to his country, he was awarded the Silver Star, the Distinguished Flying Cross, the Air Medal, the Asiatic Pacific Service Medal, the American Campaign Medal and the WWII Victory Medal.

My father was a Jewish boy who grew up in Baltimore, Maryland. His grandparents had emigrated from Germany for political and religious reasons. His grandfather was from the area of Cologne and his grandmother was from Southern Germany. He still had close relatives in Germany and France that had been victims of the Holocaust. When the British entered World War II, Dad was a restless young man and wanted to withdraw from college and join the Royal Air Force "to kill some Nazis," but he complied with the requests of his parents and remained in college to finish his engineering degree. But, immediately after the Japanese attack on Pearl Harbor his parents, recognizing that he would eventually have to go to war anyway, relented and approved of his enlisting in the Army Air Corps. It was then that his superior performance at the Army communications, radar, and radar countermeasures schools enabled him to became one of the top rated radar countermeasures officers in the Army.

My father's experience as an amateur radio operator and his advanced training and knowledge of the new science of radar and electronic countermeasures, coupled with his college training as a mechanical engineer prompted the Army to select him to participate in the Manhattan Project. While with the Manhattan Project, he assisted Dr. Norman Ramsey and other civilian scientists at the Los Alamos laboratories in solving technical problems with the radar altimeter proximity fuse and the mechanical/ballistic configuration of the atomic bomb. In addition, his knowledge of the radar altimeter design and his advanced training in radar countermeasures made him an invaluable participant in the delivery of the atomic bombs.

Dad was small in stature, but was extremely strong in his opinions. Many would have described him as a feisty individual who did not let political correctness stand in his way in expressing his thoughts. This characteristic did not always make him popular with his fellow officers, who sometimes regarded him as a "cocky oddball," but respected his knowledge of radar. Some of his enlisted subordinates considered him a "longhair" because of his college education. But, Dad was an excellent interpreter of human nature. He once said that he saw *the Japanese, both civilian and military, as fanatic fighters, human certainly, but dedicated to the cause of a Japanese victory at all costs.* Dad never deviated from his opinions during his entire lifetime.

On the strike mission to Hiroshima, he utilized a lathe disk recording device connected to the in-flight intercom to record the verbal reactions of the *Enola Gay* crew after witnessing the deployment of the first atomic bomb. This recording was turned over to a news journalist after landing on Tinian. Soon after being broadcast on the WOR Network, the recordings disappeared.

After the war ended, Dad remained active in the 509th Composite Group's Alumni effort to document and preserve a record of the events and the processes involved in the planning and execution of the missions. Over the years, he became an authority of the history of the Manhattan Project and the resultant bombing missions on Japan. Unlike many of the members of the *Enola Gay* or *Bock's Car* crews, my father did not try to avoid the news media. He utilized his political and media connections to collect documents, photos, film, audio, eyewitness transcripts, government media reports, and correspondences that accurately and chronologically validated these historical events.

In 1985, Dad returned to Hiroshima and Nagasaki with "Good Morning America" and their television crew for the 40th anniversary of the bombing. Motivated by this experience and utilizing materials from his archives, he wrote his first book "*Hiroshima and Nagasaki Revisited.*" It was during this trip that he also visited Japanese World War II museums. The central theme in several exhibits was, "We must not dishonor our Veterans." Dad saw a kamikaze plane on display surrounded by the uniforms and letters left by some of the young kamikaze pilots. He said such an exhibit was understandable, but there should have been an explanation of why they did what they did other than loyalty to the Emperor. In short, he felt that in many cases the Japanese were advancing

9

the cause of peace activists who were determined to transform history into myth.

Other museum exhibits portrayed Japan more as the victim than as the aggressor. He often heard protesting Japanese extremists ask, *"Was the bomb truly dropped to save American lives that would have been lost in a bloody invasion?" "Was the decision tinged with racism, or was it simply a desire to send a signal to the Soviet Union?"*

Simply put, the message that Dad got from most of the Japanese citizens was that a war was on which was wanted only by the militarists in Tokyo and not by the Japanese people. An often-heard comment was *"You Americans did what you had to do to win the war and we did what we had to do to defend ourselves."* These words were repeated almost every day that he was there, even from folks that bore scars from the Hiroshima blast.

One of the men Dad talked with was an elderly Japanese citizen, perhaps a little younger than himself. As a young man, this man had been trained for a kamikaze flight. He too said, *"You did what you had to do and we did what we had to do to defend ourselves."* He went on to say that late in the war the call went out for volunteers 18 years or older and not the first born in the family to train as suicide airplane and submarine pilots to defend the Emperor. At the completion of a short flight-training period, he was given a scarf and a samurai sword. At the same time, clippings from his hair and finger and toenails were collected. When he completed his mission, which obviously he never did, these mementos would be returned to his family in a memorial box.

But what bothered my father most during his visit to Japan was hearing the American children, who were there for the 40th anniversary of the bombing, say they were ashamed of their country and viewed the atomic bombings as unwarranted and criminal acts. Japanese television also showed some American children viewing Hiroshima exhibits weeping and choking with remorse and shame for even being an American the nation that they felt had committed these war crimes. Some were even saying they thought the United States should pay compensation to the Japanese. These were children who had absolutely no understanding of what had taken place. None were aware of the actual atrocities that occurred during the war. Most of these children could not, or would not, even intelligently discuss the Japanese raid on Pearl Harbor or the Bataan death march, but in all fairness, neither could or would the Japanese

10

children.

It was my father's opinion that if one wishes to remember the personal sufferings of those who died at Hiroshima and Nagasaki in World War II, one must also ask why we ignore the millions of victims of Japanese atrocities. Yet thanks to contemporary "enlightened" historians, the primary victims - the victims of Japanese aggression across the Pacific - have been ignored while the secondary victims - the Japanese themselves - have been raised to a privileged public altar. It is as if the war in Europe were to be commemorated by yearly attention to German civilians who died in the bombing of Dresden and Hamburg, while the victims of Nazi aggression on the battlefield and in the death camps were completely ignored.

My father had no doubt that the atomic bombing of Hiroshima and Nagasaki helped to bring a speedy end World War II. While these bombs brought death and destruction on a horrifying scale, they averted even greater losses of American, English and Japanese lives that would have occurred if an invasion had taken place. No man can say what would have been the result if we had not taken the steps that we did in 1945 to achieve this end the war quickly.

As I said earlier Dad, in his second book, had also planned to address some of the more controversial issues and focus on the untold events that occurred during the Nagasaki mission as well as clear up some of the popular revisionist misconceptions that have been circulating for almost 50 years. In addition he specifically intended to address a number of other items:

(1) How much did the crew really know about the mission prior to flight time?
(2) Who was supposed to fly the first mission - Sweeney or Tibbits?
(3) Why were Hiroshima and Nagasaki selected as the target cities?
(4) Did an in-flight recording from the *Enola Gay* really exist and, if so, what happened to it?
(5) What problems really occurred on the Nagasaki mission?
(6) Did Bob Lewis really say, "My G-d what have we done"?
(7) Did the mission cause Claude Eatherly to go insane from guilt and remorse; and,
(8) Did any of crew members suffer from remorse as a result of the missions?

This all brings me to today. During the process of compiling this book using Dad's archives and other sources as reference material I became deeply involved in other projects including the search for and returning soldiers and sailors still missing in action from World War II and Korea. I found this very enjoyable and self-rewarding. It was then that I decided to continue and expand my efforts by bringing together a team of highly skilled individuals to create *The Beser Foundation for Archival Research and Preservation.*

It is the intent of the Beser Foundation to encourage others to become more engaged in locating, cataloging and preserving the records of the past. It is hoped that with my efforts and the efforts of the others with similar interests, we will be able to obtain and preserve materials that accurately validate historical events from the past up to the current times. The approach we are using is to make the talents of skilled individuals currently performing historical research available to mentor college students and teach them the methods and art of meaningful historical research with hands on experience. I want to do this not only for my children, grandchildren and myself but so that important historical information will be readily available for generations to come. Simply put "It is preserving the past for the benefit of the future."

Jerome Beser
January 2007

Introduction

Editor's Note: It is only fitting that I use my father's own words that he used over and over again in father and son conversations and many speeches to introduce this book. He says:

There has been hardly a day in the past forty-three years that I have not been approached by a friend, a colleague, or a member of my lecture audience with the following question: Would you do it again? You see, I had the unique experience of having been the only person in the United States Army Air Corps to have been aboard both strike aircraft that delivered the Atomic Bombs to Hiroshima and Nagasaki in August of 1945. Since then I have received many letters from people all over the world. I have been regarded at various times as an instant expert in Atomic Warfare, a National Hero, a Hired Killer, a Pariah, and even a War Criminal. I am none of these but was just a typical American College student who was thrust into the limelight by events of the time. If one finds this difficult to understand, one need only look at the voluminous stack of letters, newspaper clippings, or listen to the radio tapes or view the video tapes that have been amassed in my personal files over the years. This should remove any doubt from even the most casual observer's mind that such is the case.

When I wrote of my experiences in my first book, "*Hiroshima and Nagasaki Revisited*," I tried to show that by pure happenstance, a kid from the upper middle class Jewish suburbia in Baltimore Maryland, suddenly found himself right smack in the middle of one of the turning points in human history. To this day I often wonder what made me so lucky to be at the right place at the right time and for what real reason was I chosen for the task that I was called upon to perform.

As with all accounts that are based upon human recollection the passage of time has a way of modulating the recollection so that the details become melded into the whole, and what comes out is a composite of what the individual can best recall and human rationalization of the remainder. In other words, unless one is debriefed immediately after an event, or within a short interval of time thereafter, what he relates is what he thinks he recalls as the detailed description of the event. But there are exceptions to this. When the event that has occurred is of such uniqueness or of such a bizarre nature that it has been indelibly installed into the human memory system, and thus can be recalled forever exactly as it happened. Events that fall into this category are usually those that have some profound effect on the life or times of the viewer. My participation in the Atomic Bombings of Hiroshima and Nagasaki can be categorized as

13

having given me more than just a casual observer's view of the opening of this new era where man's inhumanity to his fellow man has exceeded all previous assaults. It has also placed me if not in the mainstream of discussion very close to it, and has provided me with an audience that I would otherwise never have obtained. It is the unique fall-out of my experiences that I have tried to capitalize upon for these many post-war years. I seldom, if ever, refuse an invitation to speak to students at any level, high school to college graduate, and share with them my views. These young people are the potential leaders of tomorrow, and although I do not claim to be THE authority in these matters, I know what I did, what I saw, and the impression it has made on me. Not only that, I react differently to their impact, real and potential, on matters of world affairs and international relations. I feel that my reactions are based upon my experience and intimate first hand knowledge of the devastating results of the primitive weapons that we used at the close of World War II, and my continuing association with the defensive arsenal of the United States over the ensuing years. In order that there be no misunderstanding, let me state at the outset, in the clearest way I know how, I was and still am in full accord with what we did in the final days of World War II, and I will never renege on this approval. There is no denying the fact that for every day the war was continuing during the late summer of 1945, 3000 Americans of our armed forces were becoming casualties. And, whether there was agreement or not at the various levels of command, an invasion of Japan was in the offing and another 1-3 million people on both sides would have become casualties.

We cannot redo the strategy of the war, nor can we deny the facts as they existed at that time. We can only judge the results of our actions and the impact that they have had on subsequent events. The fact is, that the Japanese, who were digging-in to resist the impending invasion that they knew had to come, were persuaded to alter their plans to resist and accept the terms of surrender that were evolving. In essence, the horrible effects of the Atomic Bombs that were dropped on Hiroshima and Nagasaki were sufficiently persuasive to change their minds.

Our retired Generals can argue until Hell freezes over that Japan was already beaten and several more weeks of conventional bombings and the results would have been the same. While there is no denying that Japan had suffered terribly under the onslaught of the B-29s, they had previously demonstrated a will to fight to the death. This had occurred in each of the

14

Island battles and there certainly was no reason to expect that they would do otherwise in resisting our invasion of their homeland. In what is to follow I will discuss with you my reader how I have come to my conclusions. These conclusions are based upon what I have seen, heard, and read over the past forty-three years and how all of this affects the manner in which I interpret the events that are taking place in the present time period {1988-89}.

Finally, a recent review of all that I have written and said in public, and even in private, indicates that from the moment we left the skies over the city of Nagasaki, I was hoping then and there that this will have been enough. As time went on, within months, I had firmly concluded that it was imperative that we find some other way to resolve disputes between nations.

I have saved many manuscripts of the talks that I have given over the years. There is a consistent refrain that appears in all of them. What we did in 1945 was right. We saved thousands of lives by shortening the war. We have established a general recognition of the futility of nuclear conflict and we are at that point in human history that says we must find another way of settling conflicts between nations or civilization as we have known it will perish. This refrain will appear many times in the following chapters.

Jacob Beser 1981

15

Part 1 The Road to Hiroshima and Nagasaki

The conditions that prevailed in 1945

The Manhattan Engineering Project

The atomic bombs were developed and built by the Manhattan Engineering Project. This super-secret project was one of the largest, if not the largest, projects ever undertaken by the United States Government at that time. It involved more than 130,000 people and included the best scientist and engineers available as well as the commitment of the full industrial manufacturing capacity of the United States.

According to Wikipedia, the free encyclopedia[2], the Manhattan Project refers to the project to develop the first nuclear weapons during World War II by the United States, the United Kingdom and Canada. Formally designated as the Manhattan Engineering District (MED), it refers specifically to the period of the project from 1942-1946 under the control of the U.S. Army Corps of Engineers, under the administration of General Leslie R. Groves, with its scientific research directed by the American physicist J. Robert Oppenheimer. On August 8, 1945 after the Hiroshima bombing the War Department made a three page public release to the news reporters assembled on in the Mariana Islands. A photocopy of this document is included in Appendix 2.

The 1930s decade was especially turbulent in Europe. Adolph Hitler had become the uncontested leader of Germany. By the later years of the decade his armies had overrun Europe and North Africa. His conquest of England had begun. During his build up of military and political power, Hitler's aggressive and inhumane treatment of certain people because of their racial or ethnic background had sent hundreds of thousands of people to the gas chambers. During the early and mid years of the decade, many of the brilliant physicist and mathematicians had fled Germany and immigrated to the United States to escape persecution by the Nazis. Dr. Albert Einstein was one of these refugees.

In 1939, just before the beginning of World War II, Dr. Einstein penned a letter to President Franklin D. Roosevelt in which he expressed the concerns of himself and several other scientists and mathematicians of the efforts in Nazi Germany to purify uranium. They believed that the Germans might use the fissionable U-235 isotope to build the ultimate weapon of war - an atomic bomb.

---

[2]See http://en.wikipedia.org/wiki/Manhattan_Project

Albert Einstein
Old Grove Rd.
Nassau Point
Peconic, Long Island

August 2nd, 1939

F.D. Roosevelt,
President of the United States,
White House
Washington, D.C.

Sir:

Some recent work by E.Fermi and L. Szilard, which has been com-
municated to me in manuscript, leads me to expect that the element uranium may be turned into a new and important source of energy in the immediate future. Certain aspects of the situation which has arisen seem
to call for watchfulness and, if necessary, quick action on the part
of the Administration. I believe therefore that it is my duty to bring
to your attention the following facts and recommendations:

In the course of the last four months it has been made probable -
through the work of Joliot in France as well as Fermi and Szilard in
America - that it may become possible to set up a nuclear chain reaction
in a large mass of uranium,by which vast amounts of power and large quantities of new radium-like elements would be generated. Now it appears
almost certain that this could be achieved in the immediate future.

This new phenomenon would also lead to the construction of bombs,
and it is conceivable - though much less certain - that extremely powerful bombs of a new type may thus be constructed. A single bomb of this
type, carried by boat and exploded in a port, might very well destroy
the whole port together with some of the surrounding territory. However,
such bombs might very well prove to be too heavy for transportation by
air.

The United States has only very poor ores of uranium in moderate quantities. There is some good ore in Canada and the former Czechoslovakia, while the most important source of uranium is Belgian Congo.

In view of this situation you may think it desirable to have some permanent contact maintained between the Administration and the group of physicists working on chain reactions in America. One possible way of achieving this might be for you to entrust with this task a person who has your confidence and who could perhaps serve in an inofficial capacity. His task might comprise the following:

a) to approach Government Departments, keep them informed of the further development, and put forward recommendations for Government action giving particular attention to the problem of securing a supply of uranium ore for the United States;

b) to speed up the experimental work,which is at present being carried on within the limits of the budgets of University laboratories, by providing funds, if such funds be required, through his contacts with private persons who are willing to make contributions for this cause, and perhaps also by obtaining the co-operation of industrial laboratories which have the necessary equipment.

I understand that Germany has actually stopped the sale of uranium from the Czechoslovakian mines which she has taken over. That she should have taken such early action might perhaps be understood on the ground that the son of the German Under-Secretary of State, von Weizsäcker, is attached to the Kaiser-Wilhelm-Institut in Berlin where some of the American work on uranium is now being repeated.

Yours very truly,

(Albert Einstein)

In theory an atomic bomb is very simple. An atomic nucleus is composed of elementary particles called protons and neutrons. The nuclear energy holding these particles together is thousands of times greater than the chemical energy binding atoms in molecules of conventional explosives together. For certain very heavy elements, uranium 235 and plutonium 239 in particular, the nucleus is almost unstable. When hit by a neutron, it will split into two smaller nuclei and more neutrons. When the nuclei fly apart the energy, that held them together, is released. If a "critical mass" of such an element is rapidly brought together as in a bomb, the average neutron cannot escape from the mass before it hits and splits another nucleus. This releases more neutrons, each of which repeats the process. The resulting "chain reaction" runs through the fuel in a few millionth of a second. The energy released by this reaction is enormous and is equivalent to that in many tons of conventional TNT explosives.

About the time of the Battle of Midway in 1942, laboratory experiments had confirmed that it was possible to split the U-235 atom and release tremendous amounts of energy. Based on these experiments it was suggested to President Roosevelt that America should prove whether or not it was possible to build an atomic bomb. If successful this new weapon could end the war immediately.

President Roosevelt's advisors cautioned that success could only be achieved if the full industrial and economic power of the United States was committed to the project. Even with this commitment it was felt that there was only a slightly better than 50% probability of success. But, it was a gamble that our scientific leaders felt should be made because they were suspected that Germany was probably working on a similar project. It would be a race between the scientific and industrial forces of the United States against those of Germany and Japan. The bottom line was that President Roosevelt was willing to accept the challenge if it would help bring about an earlier conclusion of the War.

Shortly thereafter, on limited study funding, the United States Government began the serious undertaking known as the Manhattan Project. Simply put, the initial focus of Manhattan Project was a jump ahead of the German scientific research. But based on the results of these earlier studies and experiments and the entry of the United States into World War II, the government expanded the scope of the Manhattan Project and committed a large percentage of the national wealth toward expediting research and production. Or stated otherwise, the Manhattan Project was committed to expedite atomic research and development and produce the atomic bomb!

The fact that the bomb was completed from initial concepts to a weapon in time to help finish World War II is remarkable. Most of the theoretical breakthroughs in nuclear physics that made it possible were less than twenty-five years old. Many of the fundamental concepts in nuclear physics and chemistry had to be confirmed by laboratory experimentation. The design and engineering difficulties that would be involved in translating theoretical concepts into working devices capable of releasing the enormous energy of the atomic nucleus in a predictable fashion were unknown. The industrial base created in less than five years is a tribute to American ingenuity and industrial base.

The atomic bomb project was originally conceived as a counter to the threat that Nazi Germany might develop one first. But it was not ready until after Germany had surrendered. Thus only by historical circumstance was the bomb deployed to avoid an even bloodier alternative namely the invasion of the Japanese homeland.

The Manhattan Project had a series of complicated chemical and metallurgical problems that had to be solved. The physicist had shown that U-238 is practically useless in making a bomb but by using the U-235 isotope a bomb could be built The typical uranium ore contained only about 0.2 percent uranium metal or which only about one percent was the U-235 isotope. The most complicated problem the scientist faces was the separation of ample amounts of U-235 uranium from U-238 to sustain a chain reaction.

Gaseous Diffusion Laboratory

Oak Ridge, Tennessee

Because of their similarity in chemical makeup, non-fissionable U-238 and fissionable U235 are very difficult to separate. There were no ordinary chemical means available to separate these isotopes. In order to solve this problem a three step process was developed consisting of an electro-mechanical magnetic process followed by gaseous diffusion and a gas centrifuge process to effectively separate the heavier non-fissionable U-238 isotope from the lighter U-235 isotope.

Because of the quantity of U-235 required for an atomic bomb and the difficulty in separating it from U-238, a massive laboratory was constructed at Oak Ridge, Tennessee. Engineers and scientist had to not only develop the process but also develop the materials required for implementing the processes. Uranium hexaflouride was used in the gaseous diffusion and gaseous centrifuge processes. This gas is very active and chemically corrosive. Some of the challenges include developing a material that would contain this gas. Teflon was one of the materials that resulted. The solutions to other challenges resulted in the development of very clean high vacuum diffusion pumps and high strength materials such as high strength aluminum.

The program consumed more than two billion dollars from its inception in 1939 to the successful production and explosion of three bombs in 1945. It was managed by General Leslie Groves with Dr. Robert Openheimer being a major driving force behind the scientific work. Dr. Openheimer was the overseer of the project and literally ran the show. Under his leadership, the formulae for refining uranium and separating the U-235 isotope were developed and the metallurgical materials required were developed at the various colleges and at Oak Ridge, Tennessee.

The program had two goals, first to create the engineering capability to accomplish the separation of the U-235 from the U-238, and second, to establish a facility to build a practical bomb that could be airlifted to a target. The facility at Oak Ridge was assigned the problem of U-235 separation and the Los Alamos Laboratory had the task building the bomb.

At Los Alamos the first and logical approach to achieving a critical mass of U-235 was to attempt to unite two sub-critical masses together to form a critical mass capable of sustaining a chain reaction. The obvious approach was to use a gun to fire a projectile of the material into a target of the same material at such a speed that the critical mass would be achieved before the two parts were blown apart by the chain reaction. Experiments were conducted to evaluate the concept. Eventually it was determined that a 5-inch gun barrel about ten feet long and a powder charge would provide the necessary velocity for the projectile to enter the target and "go critical". In the final design the target was surrounded by a mass of U-238 to act as a tamper and contain the explosion as long as possible. This was the "Little Boy" bomb that was used to attack Hiroshima.

At the same time the "Little Boy" bomb concepts were being developed another approach using a new element, Plutonium, not found in the natural state to build a different type of bomb.

Plutonium is also capable of fission but its natural neutron background was such that using the "gun barrel technique" would require exceedingly high velocities and would require a barrel almost 30 feet long. This did not appear to be a practical solution for an air transportable bomb.

Another and possibly a practical approach would be to squeeze a sub-critical mass together with sufficient force that it would become critical and thus generate and support a chain reaction. Although the idea seemed to have merit there also seemed to be no conceivable way of generating sufficient force to accomplish the required "squeeze" of a sphere of Plutonium the size of a softball to the size of a billiard ball.

Captain William S. Parsons U.S. Navy, a naval ordnance expert and Dr. John von Neumann[3] a theoretical mathematician came up with a solution. They concluded that it might be possible to generate, with the use of a properly designed high explosive system, a collapsing shock wave of such magnitude as to accomplish the force required to reduce the size of the Plutonium sphere to a critical mass.

Los Alamos perused this concept and the problems eventually solved with a design of a bomb that would fit in the bomb bay of a B-29 that ultimately would carry the bomb. This set the outside dimensions of the package at approximately five feet in diameter and ten feet long.

The secret of the Plutonium bomb was a method of making subcritical amount of Plutonium become critical by squeezing it together. The small core of Plutonium was surrounded by a sphere of conventional high explosive segments. These segments were shaped to focus the explosive shock wave inward. Each of the explosive segments had an electrical detonator. Each segment had to explode simultaneous with a tolerance of less than one microsecond. The resulting shock wave would compress a sphere of Plutonium about the size of softball into a sphere

---

[3]See http://en.wikipedia.org/wiki/John_von_Neumann

about the size of a billiard ball in order to achieve a critical mass and a resulting chain reaction. The theory had never been tested.

The test, code named "Trinity", came on the morning of July 16, 1945 in the desert of south-central New Mexico at a site located on a remote section of Alamagardo Air Base. At about 5:30 am the sky ignited with a light brighter than the noonday sun. A reddish-yellow ball of fire a quarter-mile in diameter was boiling and churning furiously on a tower over ground zero. The sudden released nuclear forces expanded with consuming fury its fireball reaching back to the ground as if the sun had suddenly came down on the earth. Then the fireball shot upward, sucking the desert sand beneath it into a column that within twenty seconds reached a mile into the sky.

Seconds after the flash the accompanying shock wave sent debris flying ahead of it. It was estimated that the core temperature at the instant of the explosion exceeded 50,000,000 degrees centigrade. The searing heat from the blast was sufficient to cause paint on buildings a few miles away to catch fire almost immediately and glass windowpanes to melt before the panes were broken or blown inward by the shock wave.

From the force measurements of the shock wave, the size of the fireball and the level of radiation in samples taken from the bomb's crater, it was estimated that the yield was equivalent to 20,000 tons of TNT. Incidentally this is where the number President Truman used when he announced that Hiroshima had been bombed came from.

Such an explosion certainly aroused the curiosity of the residents in the nearby towns of Alamagardo, Las Cruses, and Santa Fe, New Mexico and El Paso Texas. In anticipation of questions from the local residents a preplanned cover story was released by the Alamagardo Air Base Commander that said a remotely located ammunition dump containing a considerable amount of high explosive and pyrotechnics had exploded.

Trinity's aftermath is now history. The Postdam declaration to the Japanese to surrender or face prompt and utter destruction was rejected. The untested "Little Boy" U-238 bomb leveled Hiroshima on August 6, 1945. Three days later a duplicate of the Trinity Plutonium bomb was exploded over Nagasaki. A second Plutonium bomb had been shipped from Los Alamos in early August and was awaiting shipment to the war zone but it was never needed. Japan surrendered on August 14.

The fusing used in both bombs was essentially the same. Tail warning radars that were used in bombers to detect fighters attacking from

24

astern provided the basic element of the proximity fuse. In order to provide the desired height of burst of the bomb, the radars were modified and adjusted to trigger the fuse when a certain range to the ground had been reached.

Whereas the basic design of the "Little Boy" U-235 bomb lent itself to easy solution of the ballistic design problem, the basic spherical design of the "Fat Man" was a nightmare. To approach some kind of an acceptable ballistic shape it was decided to enclose the explosive sphere and the electronic components attached to it, inside an ellipsoid shaped case. Further, it was decided that the bomb should be protected from fifty caliber bullets should enemy fighters attack the delivery aircraft. This required a half-inch of special treatment steel formed into the ellipsoid shape, something that had never been done before by the armor plate industry. Small sections of the armor plate had to be formed into shapes with a compound curvature and then each section welded together to complete the case. Holding the proper shape during the welding process turned out to be an almost impossible job.

First, fins were tried to provide the stabilization in flight necessary to yield a reproducible trajectory, but without success. Wind tunnel test showed that perhaps a large box tail might solve the problem. But again, flight was erratic and reproducible trajectories were not achieved. At this point Captain Parsons suggested placing baffles in the box tail to provide a parachute effect. Tests showed that this was the answer. Time of fall was reduced significantly and reproducible flight achieved so that data could be obtained to calculate the bombing data inputs required by the Norden Mark XV bomb sight that would be used in the B-29.

During the winter of 1944 and the spring of 1945 tests of all the components of the bomb, both individually and in their final configuration, were conducted at the Army Air Corps base at Wendover, Utah. As it turned out the radar proximity fuse, which my father had helped design, gave the most trouble and testing continued right up until the date of the drop of the first bomb on Japan. As a rehearsal for the operation with the Fat Man bomb, a complete bomb without active material installed was carried out off the island of Tinian. This was the first time that the bomb in its final configuration had ever been dropped out of an airplane. The next day a Fat Man bomb was successfully dropped on Nagasaki. This was undoubtedly the shortest time between development and combat use of any ordnance in modern history.

The task of using the atomic bomb in the war was assigned to the Army Air Corps. However for security reasons this was a closely guarded secret. When the Army Air Corps officers visited the classified sites at Albuquerque, they would remove any military insignia that would indicate Air Corps personnel and replace them with Corps of Engineer insignia.

When it became reasonably certain that the Manhattan Project would be successful before the end of the war, the Army Air Corps proceeded full speed ahead to develop the means to deliver a bomb and to train flight crews in the tactics which would be required. This task was assigned to Colonel Paul W. Tibbets, Jr. He had been scrutinized by security agents to confirm that he had the right technical qualifications; the right mental attitude; absolute loyalty to the United States; and, that he would not unnecessarily divulge any information that should not be released.

Colonel Tibbets was a master of strategic bombing tactics and a veteran of the air war in Europe and North Africa where he had successfully lead a number of B-17 raids as well as flying General Mark Clark to North Africa and General Eisenhower to Gibraltar. For this new assignment he reported to the highest levels in the War Department and was given the authority necessary to implement the task to which he was assigned.

At the time it was not known how many missions would be required of Tibbets and his crew. In order to successfully complete the tasks assigned and maintain the utmost secrecy required Colonel Tibbets formed 509th Composite Group. All told, the 509th was an 1800 man mini-air force with 15 B-29 bombers along with all the flight crews; staff personnel; ground support personnel; security personnel; and, equipment necessary to support them as an autonomous and self-sufficient combat unit. The 393rd Bomber Wing became the basic cadre for the 509th Bomber Group in the spring of 1944. After training at Wendover, Utah and other locations in the United States, the unit was deployed to Tinian Island in the Marianas from where the operations against the Japanese homeland would originate.

On July 16, 1945 the first atomic bomb, a Plutonium device, was successfully detonated at Trinity Site near Alamogordo, New Mexico. Two days later the first atomic bomb, "Little Boy", was loaded into the bomb bay of a B-29 for transport to the war zone. After a refueling stop in Hawaii it was delivered to Tinian Island. By July 25, 1945 the

26

potential targets had been finalized and the decision had been at the highest levels in Washington and approved by President Truman to use the bomb. Orders were generated and a letter was sent from the War Department Office of the Chief of Staff to General Carl Spaatz, Commanding General United States Strategic Air Force directing the use of the bomb. This letter said in part:

> *"1. The 509th Composite Group, 20th Air Force will deliver its first special bomb as soon as weather will permit visual bombing after 3 August 1945 on one of the targets: Hiroshima, Kokura, Niigata and Nagasaki. To carry military and civilian scientific personnel from the War Department to observe and record the effects of the explosion of the bomb, additional aircraft will accompany the airplane carrying the bomb. The observing planes will stay several miles distant from the point of impact of the bomb.*
>
> *2. Additional bombs will be delivered on the above targets as soon as made ready by the project staff. Further instructions will be issued concerning targets other than those listed above."*

The Manhattan project's objectives had been completed and would soon be deployed.

Dawn of the Nuclear Age

Nuclear fire ball 0.025 Seconds after the first atomic bomb exploded in the New Mexico desert near Alamagado July 16, 1945

From a College Student to a Unique Place in History

Editor's Note: This text has been extracted from one of my father's 1966 radio interview.

Pearl Harbor was December 7, 1941 and I was a senior at Johns Hopkins University. On December 8, I withdrew from Hopkins fully intending to go into the Army Air Corps. I enlisted on December 8 and was immediately accepted into the cadet program but there was about a six months lag before the class was called up. So I went on active duty on the 4th of June 1942 and stayed on active duty until March 1946.

I went through the aviation cadet program at Scott Field and came out as a communications specialist, a second Lieutenant, in the Army Air Corps. From there I went to Radar School at Boca Raton, Florida. There I was in one of the first classes of Air Corps officers to be fully trained in this new field. From there I went to Orlando, Florida to the Air Corps school of Applied Tactics, where I taught for a while in the heavy bomb division. I took time out to go back for more training in electronics countermeasures. I was rated as a

Jacob Beser 1942

countermeasures observer. Incidentally this was the beginning of my undoing, the thing that got me into this program that later dropped the atomic bombs on Japan.

At that time the men who went through the countermeasures training had received the most advanced electronic training in the Air Corps. This was a brand new field and we were learning as we went. One of the requirements, or attributes they were looking for, was for people with an amateur radio background. I had been interested in ham radio since I was about eleven or twelve years old. They wanted someone who could improvise at the moment, as the need developed to build his own equipment in the field and to use the tools that he had and so forth. This wasn't a firm requirement but it helped.

In the spring of 1944, I went with a cadre that was moved out of Orlando to form a B-29 group. I had the assignment as the Group Electronics officer. Somewhere along the way I took leave and went to

29

Chicago and didn't make it back to the group on time. I don't recall all the events that lead up to that. But anyhow I got back and the Group Commander was more than a little perturbed and they put me in the 393rd Bomb Squadron as a disciplinary measure. The commanding officer of that squadron was a real fine fellow by the name of Tom Classen. I think Colonel Conley felt it would do me a good to get disciplined for awhile. Anyhow, I transferred over there with the understanding that for about a month to fill an opening that existed. This was the 504th in Fairmont, Nebraska. About a week or so after I transferred into the 393rd, a freeze order came down from the Second Air Corps that no one could be transferred into, or out of, the 393rd. It had been surveyed and was in the advanced stages of training of all of the squadrons that were being set up at the time and we were given real peculiar temporary duty orders. These orders required the whole 393rd squadron, complete with organizational equipment, to go to Wendover, Utah. This turned out to be a permanent transfer. The 393rd formed the basic cadre for the 509th Group that was the one set up for the Atomic Bombing missions.

I was the Group's Electronic Officer with a section of 45 men under me. I had in my group fifteen B-29s and was responsible for all the electronic equipment on them. In addition to which, I had these other duties with the project that included some special instrumentation equipment and some other assignments associated with the weapon. So, I had some little part to play in the design and operational planning as well as the delivery of the weapon.

When asked how and when he became associated with the Manhattan Project, my father's reply was: "I was quite anxious to get into it {combat}. I wanted to go to Europe. Classmates were there. I had family in Germany who had been chewed up already." I first got an inkling that something was up in the spring of 1944. I went to Washington with the expressed purpose of getting myself transferred to the 8th Air Force and to the good offices of a friend of my father, Major General Ulio the Adj. General. He had the authority to send me anywhere he wanted to. But much to the surprise of everyone, when the records came upstairs, he said "Sorry son I cannot touch you, I don't know why but go back where you came from. I am sure it will unfold."

Upon returning to Orlando, I went right to work getting myself assigned to the 9th Bomb Group. Rumors were flying about the 9th going to B-29s. This was the super fortress, the world's best bomber. What's more, every B-29 squadron was to have assigned to it one radar countermeasures officer.   Since this was an inside transfer I never discussed my experience {conversations with General. Ulio} in Washington and no one ever ask me about it.

That was in the spring of 1944.   In the late summer or early fall, I was transferred to the 393rd Squadron.   It was about a month later that the orders came down from Washington freezing all the personnel in the 393rd. - Nobody in and nobody out.   We were also alerted for a temporary move to Wendover Airfield.   They said take everything you own with you - all your trucks and your organizational equipment.   I thought this unusual {for a temporary move}!

The project plans and my expected role would soon be revealed. I was proud to be able to assist in furthering the technology needed to make this weapon a reality.

"Wars may be fought with weapons, but they are won by men. It is the spirit of the men who follow and of the man who leads that gains the victory."

General George S. Patton

The War in the Pacific

Editors Note: This chapter has been expanded utilizing current source material unavailable to my father.

In order to more fully understand what and why the nuclear bombings of Japan were necessary and justified in August 1945 one must be aware of what was happening on the battlefields in the Pacific; the atrocities committed by the Japanese prior to and during the war; their final fanatical resistance; and, the mood of the American people.

In short the American people would accept no less than unconditional surrender. This is not intended to be a history of World War II with Japan but instead I would like to summarize some of the prewar conditions and battles during the war that greatly influenced the mindset of the American people as well as that of our Allies in 1945. A lot of this kind of information is frequently left out of revisionist one point-of-view articles.

The true motivations and circumstances that led up to the invention and deployment of the first atomic weapon came from one of the darkest period of humanity. Without clear unbiased factual documentation and a society that understands the danger of allowing history to fade into the past, unfortunately the possibility of history repeating itself becomes a real danger to current and future generations. As my father said: **"If World War III is fought with atomic weapons, World War IV will be fought with sticks and stones."**

In 1853 Commodore Perry's unwelcome visit of four U.S. warships to Tokyo awakened Japan from an isolated state to one with a reckless quest for power and dominion over all of Asia. Now after hundred's of years of strict seclusion the Japanese people were exposed to western ideas, production techniques and military might. In the short period of less than 90 years of international relations, the nation of Japan changed herself from an ancient feudal state into a nation with an army and a navy trained and equipped to rival those of the European powers.

At the same time this was happening a master plan, "The Greater East Asia Co-Prosperity Sphere"[4], was being implemented to give Japan

---

[4] The Greater East Asia Co-Prosperity Sphere was a concept created and promulgated by the government and military of the Empire of Japan which represented the desire to create a self-sufficient "bloc of Asian nations led by the Japanese and free of Western powers". The sphere was to extend from the Kurile Islands southeast to the Marshall

domination of the whole of southeast Asia and all the Islands in the western Pacific irrespective of any Western resistance. Therefore, in order to implement this plan, the Western influence had to be completely removed at once and for all time.

Prodded by her military leaders in pursuit of this master plan, Japan launched in the early part of the 20th century an attack on China. The occupation of Manchuria began with the Russo-Japanese War in 1904-1905 which resulted in undisputed Japanese influence in Korea which was annexed in 1910 and the transfer to Japan of Russian railways along with considerable land and mineral development rights in Manchuria.

Anti-Western feelings developed in Japan in the same time period and intensified when, at the Washington Naval Conference, the Japanese Government was forced to agree to keep her navy smaller than those of Great Britain and the United States in a 5-5-3 ratio. The anti-western feelings were further intensified two years later when the United States passed an immigration act barring Japanese and other nationalities from immigrating to the United States.

In 1931 a group of mid-level Japanese officers, apparently with support and consent from higher-ups, staged a railway bombing in Mukden. Japan then used this incident as an excuse to "suppress bandits" and initiated a full-scale occupation of Manchuria. The official justification was the protection of natural resources -- Manchuria's coal, iron, and minerals -- crucial to Japan's economic health and strategic security.

The Japanese solidified the occupation of Manchuria on March 1, 1932 when they set up the Puppet State of Manchukuo. However the international community refused to recognize the legality of the Japanese occupation in accordance with a truce that had been negotiated in 1931. The League of Nations sent observers who condemned the invasion and sham-autonomy as an imperialistic land grab, whereupon Japan resigned from the League of Nations and began courting better relations with Germany and Italy.

The establishment of Manchukuo did not settle the question and border skirmishes between Japanese forces and various Chinese forces continued. The Japanese also increased their military presence in China's

---

Islands, west to the Netherlands East Indies, and in a great curve to India. This was one of a number of slogans and concepts used justify Japanese aggression in East Asia in the 1930s through the end of World War II.

treaty ports, *"in order to better protect Japanese nationals"* and their increasingly important business interests in China.

In spite of internal civilian and military reservations about full-scale operations in China, the opportunity to settle the ongoing border skirmishes was too good to pass up and the Japanese military proceeded to invade deep into China. They took a huge swath of northern China and the urbanized coast with remarkably little difficulty. What resistance they did meet they responded to with great brutality, including the atrocities at Nanking.

At the end of 1932 the Japanese Army invaded Chahar Province. The Chinese, armed only with spears and obsolete rifles, resisted the attack resulting in the War of Resistance at the Great Wall. The province fell to the Japanese. After the predictable victory, areas to the west of Beijing fell to the Japanese.

In 1933, Japan annexed Rehe using the security of Manzhouguo as a pretext. Consequently all areas north of the Great Wall and hence north of Beijing fell to Japan resulting in the establishment of several puppet governments in the area. The Japanese installation of various puppet governments was a deliberate attempt to annex the whole country of China by a nibbling process.

On July 7, 1937 a clash occurred between Chinese and Japanese troops near Peiping[5] in North China. When this clash was followed by indications of intensified military activity on the part of Japan, Secretary of State Hull urged upon the Japanese Government a policy of self-restraint. In a conversation of July 12 with Japanese Ambassador Saito, Secretary Hull elaborated upon the futility of war and its awful consequences, emphasizing the great injury to the victor as well as to the vanquished in case of war. He said that a first-class power like Japan not only could afford to exercise general self-restraint but also in the long run it was far better that this should characterize the attitude and policy of the Japanese Government; that he had been looking forward to an early period when Japan and the United States would have opportunity for world leadership with a constructive program like that proclaimed by the American republics at Buenos Aires in December 1936 for the purpose of restoring and preserving stable conditions of business and of peace.

---

[5] Peiping was the name of Beijing in China from 1928 to 1949.

On December 12, 1937 the Government and people of the United States were deeply shocked by the news of the bombing and destruction by Japanese aircraft of the United States gunboat Panay and three United States merchant vessels on the Yangtze River in China. The bombing and machine-gunning of the crews and passengers resulted in loss of life to citizens of the United States. This Government immediately sent a note to the Japanese Government stating that the United States vessels involved were on the Yangtze River "*by uncontested and incontestable right*", that they were flying the American flag, and that they were engaged in legitimate and appropriate business. The Government of the United States requested and expected of the Japanese Government "*a formally recorded expression of regret, an undertaking to make complete and comprehensive indemnification's; and an assurance that definite and specific steps have been taken which will insure that hereafter American nationals, interests and property in China will not be subjected to attack by Japanese armed forces or unlawful interference by any Japanese authorities or forces*".

This note was sent to Japan on the evening of December 13. On December 14 the United States Ambassador to Japan received a note from the Japanese Minister for Foreign Affairs stating that the Japanese Government regretted "*most profoundly*" the damage to these vessels and the casualties among the personnel; that it desired to present "*sincere apologies*"; that it would make indemnification's for all the losses; that it would deal "*appropriately*" with those responsible for the incident; and that it had already issued "*strict orders to the authorities on the spot with a view to preventing the recurrence of a similar incident*". Finally, the Japanese Government expressed the "*fervent hope*" that the friendly relations between Japan and the United States would not be affected by this "*unfortunate affair*". The Japanese Government later made full indemnification in accordance with the request of the United States.[6]

The Rape of Nanking also known as the Nanking Massacre was an infamous war crime incident committed by the Japanese military in and around the then capital of China - Nanking, after it fell to the Imperial

---

[6] See: U.S., Department of State, Publication 1983, "Peace and War: United States Foreign Policy, 1931-1941" (Washington, D.C.: U.S., Government Printing Office, 1943)

Japanese Army on December 13, 1937. The duration of the massacre is not clearly defined, although the violence lasted well into the next six weeks, until early February 1938.

During the occupation of Nanking, the Japanese army committed numerous atrocities, such as rape, looting, arson and the execution of prisoners of war and civilians. Although the executions began under the pretext of eliminating Chinese soldiers disguised as civilians, a large number of innocent men were intentionally identified as enemy combatants and executed—or simply killed outright—as the massacre gathered momentum. Thousands of victims were beheaded, burned, bayoneted, buried alive, or disemboweled.

The extent of the atrocities is debated. The Imperial Japanese Army claims that the death toll was military in nature and that no such atrocities ever occurred. However, an overwhelming amount of evidence contradicts this claim. The West and other nations outside Japan have generally tended to adopt the 1938 estimates of 300,000, with many sources now quoting 300,000 dead. This is partly due to the evidence of extensive photographic records and archaeological evidence of the mutilated bodies of women and children.

The Rape of Nanking by James Yin and Shi Young (ISBN 0-9632231-5-1. Copyright © 1996, 1997 by Innovative Publishing Group, Inc.) estimates that between December 1937 and March 1938 at least 369,366 Chinese civilians and prisoners of war were slaughtered by the invading troops. An estimated 80,000 women and girls were raped; many of them were then mutilated or murdered. The savagery of the killing was as appalling as its scale. As Japan steadily claimed more land and cities in China, it left a lasting legacy of cruelty and barbarism against the Chinese people.

On October 29, 1929 Wall Street collapsed and an economic recession began in the United States that carried negative repercussions around the world. It came to be known as the "Great Depression." Countries that relied on imports of raw materials and natural resources suffered the most. Japan was one of those countries. Japan also knew that the Dutch East Indies and parts of Asia contained over fifty percent of some of the world's most important raw materials. They were also looking for more land so the people of their overpopulated country could have more space to live. At the time there were approximately 2,900 Japanese people living on every square mile of usable farmland, and Japan, being the most advanced country in the area, believed it had a right to these areas of resource. The Japanese people believed it was their "Divine Mission" to fully implement the "Greater East Asia Co-Prosperity Sphere" master plan.

Many of the people who believed that Japan had the right to these resources were young military officers. They attributed the problems in Japan to corrupt Japanese politicians. Most of the Japanese people tended to agree with these officers. In March 1931, a mob of Japanese civilians, armed by the Japanese military with about 300 bombs, planned to storm and blow up the buildings housing the Japanese Parliament. Amidst the chaos, the Japanese military would step in and take control, establishing a military dictatorship. At the last moment, the coup was called off. The political turmoil in Japan was such that six prime ministers were assassinated prior to WWII. Any politician in power who believed in expanding Japan through a peaceful means was killed. Eventually, the Japanese army put political leaders in power that saw things the way the military did. Although there were still politicians in positions of power, they did what the military told them to do. At one point Admiral Yamamoto was sent to sea for his own protection. He was one military man speaking out against an attack on the U.S. He knew that in the end Japan could not defeat the United States ability to mass-produce.

In 1940 the Roosevelt administration opened the possibility of imposing economic sanctions against Japan. Since a large percentage of Japan's raw materials came from the United States, it was hoped that the Japanese government would re-think its foreign policy in China. Although Japan wanted to avoid a confrontation with the United States, it was unwilling to pull out of China. On September 27, 1940, Japan, Germany, and Italy signed the *Tripartite Pact*[7]. If the United States decided to challenge Japan or Germany this pact would ensure a two-ocean assault on American shores. With this threat looming over President Roosevelt, Japan hoped he would not interfere.

---

[7] The Tripartite Pact, also called the Three-Power Pact, Axis Pact or Three-way Pact or Tripartite Treaty was a pact signed in Berlin, Germany on September 27 1940 by Saburo Kurusu of Imperial Japan, Adolf Hitler of Nazi Germany, and Galeazzo Ciano of Fascist Italy entering as an alliance and officially founding the Axis Powers of World War II that opposed the Allied Powers. The agreement formalized the Axis Powers' partnership, and can be read as a warning to the United States to remain neutral in World War II or become involved in a war on two fronts.

A critical stage in the relationship with Japan was reached in July 1941 when the United States clamped a total embargo and froze all Japanese assets in America and caused a run on Japanese banks. Negotiators were sent to Washington to try and settle the disagreements between the two countries. During the negotiations, Japan's war party completed it plans to attack the United States. If the negotiations failed, Japan would attack Pearl Harbor. When the decision was made to attack, to the best of his abilities, Yamamoto planned the attack on Pearl Harbor.

The United States was certain there would be a Japanese attack on an American facility. The exact location was uncertain. Admiral Harold Stark was alerted that Guam, Thailand, Borneo or the Philippines would be the most likely targets. Because of the great distance between Japan and Hawaii, Pearl Harbor was never considered a possibility. In the other four places, the United States Military began to make preparations for the possibility of an assault.

On December 7, 1941 over 300 carrier based airplanes clearly marked with the "Rising Sun" emblem of the Japanese Empire, initiated World War II in the Pacific by an unprovoked attack on the U.S. Naval base at Pearl Harbor. The first wave hit the American airplanes on the ground. Most were destroyed. An inbound flight of B-17 bombers stumbled on the raid and several were destroyed. Ninety-four war ships lay at anchor and were attacked by dive bombers and torpedo planes. Almost all were destroyed or severely damaged.

Only a few hours after the Pearl Harbor attack, Emperor Hirohito issued a formal declaration of war.

"We, by grace of Heaven, Emperor of Japan seated on the throne of the line unbroken for ages eternal, enjoin upon you, our loyal and brave subjects: We hereby declare war on the United States of America and the British Empire."

Tragically, amid the burning battleships and thousands of seriously wounded sailors and unrecognized corpses at Pearl Harbor, America was at war. On December 8th President Roosevelt addressed a joint session of congress where he said:

"Yesterday, December 7, 1941—a date which will live in infamy—the United States of America was suddenly and deliberately attacked by naval and air forces of the Empire of Japan.

The United States was at peace with that nation and, at the solicitation of Japan, was still in conversation with its Government and its Emperor looking toward the maintenance of peace in the Pacific.

Indeed, one hour after Japanese air squadrons had commenced bombing Oahu, the Japanese Ambassador to the United States and his colleague delivered to the Secretary of State a formal reply to a recent American message. While this reply stated that it seemed useless to continue the existing diplomatic negotiations, it contained no threat or hint of war or armed attack.

It will be recorded that the distance of Hawaii from Japan makes it obvious that the attack was deliberately planned many days or even weeks ago. During the intervening time, the Japanese Government has deliberately sought to deceive the United States by false statements and expressions of hope for continued peace. The attack yesterday on the Hawaiian Islands has caused severe damage to American naval and military forces. Very many American lives have been lost. In addition, American ships have been reported torpedoed on the high seas between San Francisco and Honolulu.

Yesterday the Japanese Government also launched an attack against Malaya.

Last night Japanese forces attacked Hong Kong.

Last night Japanese forces attacked Guam.

Last night Japanese forces attacked the Philippine Islands.

Last night the Japanese attacked Wake Island.

This morning the Japanese attacked Midway Island

Japan has, therefore, undertaken a surprise offensive extending throughout the Pacific area. The facts of yesterday speak for themselves. The people of the United States have already formed their opinions and well understand the implications to the very life and safety of our nation.

As Commander in Chief of the army and navy I have directed that all measures be taken for our defense.

Always will we remember the character of the onslaught against us.

No matter how long it may take us to overcome this premeditated invasion, the American people in their righteous might will win through to absolute victory. I believe I interpret the will of the Congress and of the people when I assert that we will not only defend ourselves to the uttermost but will make very certain that this form of treachery shall never endanger us again.

Hostilities exist. There is no blinking at the fact that our people, our territory and our interests are in grave danger.

With confidence in our armed forces—with the unbending determination of our people—we will gain the inevitable triumph—so help us God.

I ask that the Congress declare that since the unprovoked and dastardly attack by Japan on Sunday, December 7, a state of war has existed between the United States and the Japanese Empire."

War was immediately declared with only one dissenting vote in Congress.

The Japanese strategy was to neutralize the U.S. Pacific Fleet so they could immediately initiate a full-scale offensive in the Pacific. By mid-December the military forces of the Empire of the Rising Sun had invaded Malaya, Hong Kong and the Philippines. The U.S. forces tried to reorganize but were unable to effectively resist the onslaught of the overwhelming Japanese armies. The next six months would be especially painful for the United States and our Allies in the Pacific. During this period the overwhelming military power of the Emperor's Rising Sun army and navy followed up with irresistible drive as they swept over Malay and the Philippines, then Java and finally Burma, conquering southeast Asia in about a half a year.

On December 8, Philippines time, December 7, Washington time, Japanese forces began an air attack on the Philippines. December 22, 1941, Japan landed 43,000 troops in the Gulf of Lingayen, which is 120 miles north of Manila. The next day American and Filipino troops were forced to pull back to the Bataan Peninsula. They kept the Japanese at bay until mid February of 1943. Homma, the Japanese commander of the forces in Luzon, was only given 50 days to take Luzon and his 50 days had passed. Over 7,000 of his men were dead or wounded. They were also suffering from Malaria, Beri Beri, dysentery or Dingue fever. Homma

41

pulled his army back and asked Tokyo for reinforcements. The pull back lasted almost two months. In those two months, hunger and disease were wearing down the American and Filipino troops. In addition to that, there were also entire Japanese platoons sneaking past the lines. They would go through one or two at a time, regroup on the other side, and launch well coordinated attacks that killed many American and Filipino soldiers. If the Japanese captured any of the troops, they would execute them. It was not unusual for a soldier to wake up and see the man sleeping next to him stabbed to death. Eventually, Homma was re-supplied with fresh troops. American and Filipino troops had to choose between surrender and slaughter. They chose surrender and the surrender led to the "Bataan Death March."[8]

Also on December 8, 1941, the attack on Guam began. 427 U.S. Marines were defending Guam, a small portion of navy men, and 247 native troops. The 674 men were armed with about 170 rifles, a few W.W.I vintage machine guns, and some Browning automatic rifles. Two days after the attack began, on December 10, 1941, 5,400 Japanese marines and infantry troops invaded the beaches shortly after midnight. Before dawn the Japanese troops reached the Governors Palace. A short firefight took place, and at 5:45 a.m. Navy Captain George McMillin, who was in command of the island, surrendered to a Japanese officer. The officer ordered McMillin to strip down to his under shorts simply to humiliate him. At this point the only piece of land the U.S. held between Wake Island and the Philippines was lost to the enemy[9].

JAPANESE PROCLAMATION

"We proclaim herewith that our Japanese Army has occupied this island of Guam by order of the Great Emperor of Japan. It is for the purpose of restoring liberty and rescuing the whole Asiatic people and creating the permanent peace in Asia. Thus our intention is to establish the New Order of the World.

You all good citizens need not worry anything under the regulations of our Japanese authorities and my (sic) enjoy your daily life as we guarantee your lives and never distress nor plunder your property. In case, however, when use demand you (sic) accommodations necessary

---

[8] See http://en.wikipedia.org/wiki/Battle_of_the_Philippines
[9] "The Defense of Guam - 1941: Fateful and Tragic Year" compiled by Tony Palomo

for our quarters and lodgings, you shall meet promptly with our requirements. In that case our Army shall not fail to pay you in our currency.

Those you conduct any defiance and who act spy (sic) against our enterprise, shall be court martialled and the Army shall take strict care to execute said criminals by shooting!

Dated this 10th day of December 2601 in Japanese calendar or by this 10th day of December, 1941. By order of the Japanese Commander-in-Chief."

Wake Island was the other American held island in the Pacific that was attacked on December 8, 1941. The Japanese strafed and bombed the airstrip on Wake Island. At the time of this attack, 447 Marines and 75 Naval and Army signal Corps personal defended the island. There were 12 Grumman Wildcats, three batteries of two 5-inch guns each and twelve 3-inch antiaircraft guns. In the jungle beyond the beach several machine guns stood guard. There were no radar air-raid alarm systems. The men fired three shots in the air when they spotted a plane. After midnight on December 11, 1941 a Japanese invasion force of three light cruisers, six destroyers, two patrol boats and two transports appeared off the coast. While four miles out, they began bombarding the beach but caused no damage to any of the big guns. The Americans waited until the Japanese ships moved within range of the coastal defenses when they opened fire. Almost immediately three shells hit the Japanese cruiser Yubari. Another shell hit the magazine of a destroyer. That destroyer blew up and sank. Five-inch shells hit two more destroyers and a troop transport. At the same time the aircraft were dropping 100-pound bombs on the ships. One plane scored a direct hit on the depth charges stored at the back of the destroyer Kisaragi. It blew up, sank and there were no survivors. In the end, two destroyers were sunk and about 500 Japanese killed. The U.S. lost one man. The Japanese forces retreated and headed back to Kwajalein. But on December 23 Japan sent a second and much larger task force consisting of 2,000 marines, six heavy cruisers and two of the aircraft carriers the Soryu and the Hiryu that attacked Pearl Harbor. The Americans were out numbered, but they fought hard. On one of the landings 70 marines stopped an invasion of 100 Japanese marines, killing almost every one of them. In the end Japanese forces overwhelmed the Island defenders and the Americans had to surrender.[10]

By January 2, 1942 the Japanese had captured Manila, "the Pearl of the Orient" with the forces of General MacArthur tenaciously defending the island fortress of Corregidor. President Roosevelt recognizing that the Japanese had superior strength in this area and that the United States could not re-supply our forces, ordered General MacArthur to leave the Philippines and go to Australia. On May 6, 1942, the Japanese forces prevailed despite the courageous stand by the American and Filipino forces on Corregidor and other Island forts in the Philippines and General Jonathan Wainwright surrendered.

On February 1, 1942 the remaining U.S. Pacific Fleet attacked the Japanese bases in the Marshall and Gilbert Islands. However the Forces of the Rising Sun continued their advances in Southeast Asia. On February 8 they invaded Singapore which fell by February 15th. On February 14th the Japanese parachutist attacked Sumatara and on the 19th Port Darwin on Australia's northern coast and on March 7, 1942 the Japanese landed troops in New Guinea. On March 9, 1942 the Allies capitulate to the Japanese and surrendered 100,000 troops.[11]

February 23, 1942 - First Japanese attack on the U.S. mainland as a submarine shelled an oil refinery near Santa Barbara, California. This incident was not the only successful attack on U.S. soil. These facts are often obscured by revisionists who would like current generations to believe the U.S. mainland was out of reach from our foes.

On April 18, 1942 Colonel James Doolittle led a group of U.S. bombers on a lightning air attack on Tokyo and other Japanese cities. The planes launched from the aircraft carrier *Hornet* 600 miles off the coast of Japan did little damage but the psychological victory was enormous.

On May 8, 1942 the American Navy got its first taste of victory in the Pacific in a fierce naval and air battle in the Coral Sea that checked the Japanese advance toward Australia. This was the first time in naval history that enemy ships did not face each other instead they served as launch pads for carrier based airplanes that carried out the attacks. The fighter airplanes were so effective that the Japanese retreated before the American ships even advanced on them.

---

[10] See http://en.wikipedia.org/wiki/Battle_of_Wake_Island
[11] Newspaper clipping dated February 15. 1942. Newspaper identity unknown.

In this 5-day engagement the Americans succeeded is stopping the Japanese from landing at Tulagi in the Solomons and Port Morsby on New Guinea. In this battle the Japanese were dealt their first serious setback of the war. The American force was overwhelmingly victorious. The United States lost the aircraft carrier Lexington, a tanker, a destroyer and about 60 carrier based planes while the Japanese lost two carriers, two destroyers, numerous miscellaneous vessels and over 100 planes. Casualties on the Japanese side were estimated at 3500, while American casualties numbered at 540.[12]

The tide of the war turned in favor of the Americans in early June of 1942 at the battle of Midway. In four days of savage fighting on the sea and in the air the invading task force was forced to withdraw. It was clear that the Japanese wanted more than the island of Midway. Hawaii is only 1300 miles away. This battle began on the same day that the Japanese planes raided Dutch Harbor and seized Kiska and Attu in the Aleutian Islands and set up military bases.

June 4, 1942 the battle of Midway began. Yamamoto thought that no American carriers would show up to challenge his own carriers and his ships would be safe. On May 26 the U.S. carrier Hornet and Enterprise were in Pearl Harbor. Yamamoto received false information that these two American carriers were operating somewhere near the Solomon Islands. He also received information that the Yorktown was sunk along with the carrier Lexington in the battle of the Coral Sea. The Yorktown was receiving repairs in Pearl Harbor. Also on May 26 America received intelligence reports that Japanese forces were on their way to Midway Island. On May 30th U.S. task forces 16 and 17 headed towards Midway.

At dawn on June 4, 1942 the attack began with Japanese airplanes bombing and strafing Midway. The last Japanese plane to bomb and strafe the island radioed back that a second attack would be necessary since the runway and antiaircraft weapons were still very much operational. Vice Admiral Chuichi Nagumo had nearly all his torpedo bombers rearmed with bombs to aid in the attack on the runway and antiaircraft weapons on the island. At 8:20 a.m. one of his search planes reported, "*Enemy carrier appears to be bringing up the rear.*" Nagumo ordered all torpedo bombers to be rearmed with torpedoes. Precious time was taken and the crews carelessly left bombs sitting in the open on the

---

[12] Newspaper clipping dated May 8, 1942. Newspaper identity unknown.

deck of the carriers. Before he could launch his torpedo bombers his planes that attacked Midway returned. They were shot up and low on fuel. They requested to land on the carriers immediately. Nagumo had the crews move all the torpedo bombers off the deck so his returning planes could land. He next ordered the launch of all the torpedo bombers after the returning planes landed but what he did not know was that 67 dive bombers, 29 torpedo planes and 20 fighters had left the Enterprise and the Hornet at 7:02 a.m. Two hours later, 12 torpedo bombers, 17 dive bombers, and six fighters left the deck of the Yorktown. When the Japanese fleet was discovered the torpedo bombers came in to launch their torpedoes. Several torpedoes were launched but none hit their targets. At the same time Japanese Zeroes wreaked havoc on the American torpedo bombers. Of the 200 planes that left the American carriers that morning only 54 were left. Nagumo's fleet had survived the attack. Not one of his ships was hit with anything serious and only had some strafing damage. At 10:24 a.m., with his Zeroes flying at very low altitudes protecting the fleet from American torpedo bombers, the first Japanese bomber was launched off the Akagi's deck. This was going to be Japans turn to attack the American carriers. About the time the first bomber left the Akagi, American dive-bombers appeared overhead. Because the Zeroes protecting the fleet were down low, the American dive-bombers were unopposed. They scored numerous direct hits that devastated the Japanese carrier fleet. The bombs that were left on deck during the changing from bombs to torpedoes were also exploding. In the end, four Japanese carriers were sunk: the Kaga, Soryu, the Akagi, and the Hiryu. They also lost one cruiser, 322 planes and 3,500 Japanese fighting men. This also included about 100 of their top rated fighter pilots. The American losses were not as severe. They lost the carrier Yorktown, the destroyer Hammann, 150 planes, and 307 lives. The Japanese Navy never recovered from this battle.[13]

Guadalcanal was the first stop on the road to Tokyo for the American offensive. On August 7, 1942 the U.S 1st Marine Division landed on Guadalcanal and the islands of Tulagi, Tanambogo and Gavutu across Savo sound. Sharp fighting on Talagi and its neighboring islets continued for three days before the Japanese were overpowered. On Guadalcanal however, the airfield was captured with comparative ease.

---

[13] "Battle of Midway: 4-7 June 1942" Department of the Navy -- Naval Historical Center, 805 Kidder Breese SE -- Washington Navy Yard Washington DC 20374-5060

On the night of August 9, 1942 the naval battle of Savo Island took place. As the battle unfolded three U.S. cruisers were reduced to swimming wrecks. The U.S. picket destroyer Ralph Talbot blundered into the Japanese path and was given an unhealthly large dose of fire. Burning and listing, only a rain squall at the right time saved the little ship from becoming another victim. The dawning of the new morning saw the vicinity of Savo littered with wrecks. The Vincennes had slipped under already, with her surviving crew being rescued from the shark-infested waters. The Astoria had looked as if she were salvable, and energetic efforts went into her, improving her watertight integrity and keeping fires down, but uncertainty rose with regard to her ammo lockers, which were presumed to have not been flooded - correctly. Thirty minutes past midday, the Astoria accompanied the Vincennes and Quincy, having already sunk to the bottom of Iron Bottom Sound.

The Canberra, burning fiercely in her interior was ordered to be scuttled. With lots of fires raging around the boilers but none in a position to power the ship's engines, rudders, or even pumps the ship was sunk by U.S. destroyer Ellet.

The combination of near flawless execution of a well-exercised operation by the Japanese, and the problematic layout of command and control arrangements on the Allied side led to the defeat of Savo; the worst naval defeat ever suffered by the U.S. Navy.[14]

Determined to regain the airfield, the Japanese counter attack by land, sea and air. Reinforcements were rushed in from Rabul. Night after night Japanese warships bombarded the American position. On November 13-15 1942 the tide of the battle turned in the Naval Battle of Guadalcanal when 11 Japanese troop ships crammed with men, 2 battleships and 2 destroyers were sunk.

According to the Department of the Navy -- Naval Historical Center World War II in the Pacific --Guadalcanal Campaign, Aug. 1942 - Feb. 1943 *"The long fight for Guadalcanal formally opened shortly after 6 AM on 7 August 1942, when the heavy cruiser Quincy began bombarding Japanese positions near Lunga Point. In the darkness a few hours earlier, what was for mid-1942 an impressive invasion force had steamed past Savo Island to enter the sound between the two objective areas: Guadalcanal to the south and, less than twenty miles away,*

---

[14] http://www.navy.gov.au/spc/history/general/savo.html

47

Tulagi to the north. These thirteen big transports (AP), six large cargo ships (AK) and four small high-speed transports (APD) carried some 19,000 U.S. Marines. They were directly protected by eight cruisers (three of them Australian), fifteen destroyers and five high-speed minesweepers (DMS). Led by Rear Admiral Richmond Kelly Turner, this armada was supported from out at sea by three aircraft carriers, accompanied by a battleship, six cruisers, sixteen destroyers and five oilers under the command of Vice Admiral Frank Jack Fletcher, who was also entrusted with the overall responsibility for the operation.

The great majority of these ships (9 AP, 6 AK and most of the escort and bombardment ships), with Marine Major General Alexander A. Vandegrift and the bulk of his Leathernecks, was to assault Guadalcanal a few miles east of Lunga Point. Tactically, this part of the landing went very well. There were few enemy combat troops present, and these were some distance away. The first of the Marines came ashore soon after 9AM at "Red" Beach, a stretch of grey sand near the Tenaru River. By the afternoon of the following day they had pushed westwards to seize the operation's primary object, the nearly completed Japanese airfield near Lunga Point. The surviving Japanese, mainly consisting of labor troops, quickly retreated up the coast and inland, leaving the Marines with a bounty of captured materiel, much of which would soon prove very useful to its new owners.

While the Marines consolidated their beachhead and began to establish a defensive perimeter around the airstrip, the landing of their supplies and equipment proceeded less well. Typically for these early amphibious operations, arrangements were inadequate to handle the glut of things brought ashore by landing craft. Mounds of supplies soon clogged the beaches, slowing the unloading of the ships offshore. A series of Japanese air attacks, which forced the ships to get underway to evade them, didn't help, and when the catastrophic outcome to the Battle of Savo Island and the withdrawal of Vice Admiral Fletcher's carriers forced the big transports and cargo ships to leave on 9 August, none of them had been completely unloaded. Though the Marines had taken their objective, supply shortages would plague them in the coming weeks, as the Japanese hit back by air, sea and land in an increasingly furious effort to recover Guadalcanal's strategically important airfield."

The six-month battle for Guadalcanal in the Solomon Islands ended February 8th 1943 with the withdrawal of the Japanese forces from

Guadalcanal and New Guinea. The conquest of Guadalcanal and its airstrip put the American forces within striking distance of Rabaul a major Japanese base.

On May 10, 1943 the American forces landed on Attu in the Aleutian Islands which had been held by the Japanese since June 1942. On July 1, 1943 General MacArthur launched the Allies offensive in the Pacific.

In October 1943, in a surprise attack, the U.S. Pacific Air Fleet raided Rabaul and destroyed 177 Japanese airplanes and 124 ships.

The invasion of the Gilbert Islands began on November 20, 1943. On the island of Butaritari in the Makin Atoll the Japanese defenses numbered 798 men. The U.S. forces numbered 6,470 along with two tank companies of the 193rd Tank Battalion and three batteries of the 105th Field Artillery. The numbers on the enemy's side were so low that the battle was expected to be over very quickly. General Holland Smith expected that the island could be taken on the first day. Irritated, General Holland Smith went ashore on the afternoon of November 21 to see why things were going so slowly. He suggested to Admiral Turner that the 165th's 3rd Battalion be sent to Tarawa to help his Marines. His suggestion was rejected. This irritated "Howlin' Mad" Smith even more. Two days later, on November 23, 1943, word came through the radio that "Makin was taken." This battle cost the Americans 66 dead, and 152 wounded. The Japanese casualties were 550 dead and 105 prisoners. All but one of the prisoners was a labor troop. Because the battle on Butaritari took much longer than expected, the American escort carrier Liscome Bay was forced to stick around until the end of the battle. As a tragic consequence of this delay, on the last day of the battle, a Japanese submarine torpedoed the Liscome Bay. The bombs and ammunition she was carrying exploded. The ship sank in 23 minutes. Over 600 men lost their lives. This was ten times more than the men who were killed in battle on the island.

On the same day the invasion of Butaritari began there was a much more savage battle beginning on Betio Island in the Tarawa Atoll. (Betio Island is a little over one mile long and about a half-mile wide at its widest point.)

The Japanese had made the coral island of Betio the heart of its defense of Tarawa Atoll. It was so heavily defended that the Japanese commander is reported to have said *A million men cannot take Tarawa in a hundred years.*

Before the invasion, the Navy and American planes began bombarding the tiny island. The battleships Tennessee, Maryland and Colorado along with five cruisers and nine destroyers fired 3,000 tons of shells at the island. It was an average of about 10 tons of high explosives per acre. At one point, they were shooting over one hundred shells per minute. Navy personal, as well as the Marines who were going in on the invasion, believed that there was no possible way for anything to be left alive on the island. The bombardment was supposed to continue until just before the Marines hit the beach, but because of the dust and smoke obscuring their vision it was feared that the landing craft might be hit. Eighteen minutes before the Marines landed, the Navy quit shelling and the planes flew away. As the landing boats and amtracs (amphibious track-driven vehicles) made their way to the beaches, the Japanese began firing with heavy artillery. The boats and amtracs began blowing up in the water. Marines were jumping overboard. Also, due to bad judgment on the water's depth, the landing boats were hanging up on the coral reef, unable to make it all the way to the beach. Marines were forced to wade toward the shore with bullets flying at them. Some Marines fell one at a time, and some fell in rows. Due to the heavy equipment they were carrying, many Marines drowned in impact craters under the water. About half of those that made it to the beach in the first wave were either wounded or killed. Out of 700 men in the 3rd Battalion, 2nd Marines, who had left the transport vehicles to land on Red Beach 1, only 100 were ashore, about 250 of them were hung up in boats on the reef's edge, and the rest were dead or wounded.

The first wave of Marines was virtually slaughtered on their way into the beaches. Heavy fire was coming from an 8-inch gun located in a well-reinforced blockhouse. The USS Maryland scored a direct hit with a 16-inch armor piercing shell on the ammunition room of the blockhouse. The resulting explosion killed hundred of Japanese soldiers and destroyed the gun emplacement and thousands of enemy shells.

On November 23, 1943 three days after the invasion began Betio Island was declared secured. Out of the 4,836 Japanese and Korean laborers on the island, only 17 Japanese soldiers surrendered along with 129 Korean laborers. Over 4,700 Japanese soldiers were killed. In that 76-hour battle, out of 12,000 Americans that invaded the island, 1,027 Marines were killed, or missing, along with 29 Navy officers and enlisted men. Most of the Navy personal were medics. 2,292 men were wounded but recovered. Betio was a costly battle, and the U.S. Military gained some valuable lessons from those high losses.

Some of the hardest fighting of World War II in the Pacific occurred during the Bougainville campaign between the first of November 1943 and the last of August 1945 on and around the Island of Bougainville. Bougainville, at that time, was part of the Australian territory of New Guinea, although geographically part of the Solomon Islands chain. Bougainville was occupied by Japanese forces in 1942, who constructed naval air bases at Buka in the north and Buin in the south, as well as a naval ship base in the nearby Shortland Islands. The Japanese bases provided security for their major base at Rabaul, New Britain and supported their forces operating at other locations in the Solomon Islands.[15]

In November 1943 the U.S. Marines landed on Bougainville and established a beachhead. The intent was to only establish a beachhead within which an airfield would be built and not capture the entire Island. An attempt by the Japanese Navy to attack the U.S. landing forces was defeated in the Battle of Empress Augusta Bay, on November 1 and 2, 1943. A subsequent attempt by Japanese land forces to attack the beachhead was defeated in the Battle of Koromokina Lagoon. Protracted and often bitter jungle warfare followed, with many casualties resulting from malaria and other tropical diseases.

The U.S. forces defended the beachhead against a major Japanese counterattack in March 1944. The counterattack was defeated with heavy losses for the Japanese, who then withdrew the majority of their forces into the deep interior and to the north and south ends of the island. After the defeat of the Japanese counterattack, the forces of the two adversaries settled into an informal, but mutual truce in which neither side attempted major attacks against the other. The Japanese isolated and cut off from outside assistance concentrated on survival while the American forces concentrated on constructing three airfields from which they conducted fighter and bomber operations over Rabaul and other Japanese held islands in the South Pacific area. Combat operations on Bougainville ended on August 21, 1945 after the Japanese surrendered.

By the end of January 1944 General MacArthur's Island-hopping campaign was in high gear with air raids and landings on various atolls in

---

[15] See http://www.answers.com/topic/bougainville-campaign

the Marshall Islands. In February aerial bombardment of the Admiralty Islands begun of the Japanese strongholds on Momote and Loarengau Islands as well as Wewok in New Guinea. Once the sea channels were opened General MacArthur rushed troops to the Admiralties via fast destroyers rather than the usual landing craft. MacArthur personally witnessed the landings and said "the conquest isolates 50,000 Japanese on the Bismarck Archipelago and clears the way to push to the Philippines 15,00 miles to the north".[16]

Earlier in February and in another arena in the Pacific the American bombers raided Guam. The assault also hit Japanese Naval and air bases on Saipan and Tinian. It was reported that 135 Japanese planes were destroyed and 11 ships sunk or seriously damaged. The Japanese could do little to stop the raid but managed to down six American airplanes.

Editor's Note (Jack Spangler): Throughout the war rumors of Japanese war crimes and atrocities persisted. By the end of the war, more details of the Japanese mutilations of live prisoners; chemical and biological experiments using humans as guinea pigs; and, the other inhuman treatment of prisoners of war became known. To this day, many do not believe these accounts, but they have been documented in official records.

On April 10, 1942 the Bataan Death March began at Mariveles. Troops were forced to march from Bataan to Manila, a distance of about 100 kilometers. During the march, if a soldier were too weak to continue, he would either be bayoneted or shot. In one case six ill soldiers were forced to dig their own graves before they were buried alive.

Any troops who fell behind were executed. Japanese troops beat soldiers randomly and denied them food and water for many days. Anyone who dared ask for water was executed. On the rare occasion they were given any food, it was only a handful of contaminated rice. When the prisoners were allowed to sleep for a few hours at night, they were packed into enclosures so tight that they could barely move. Those who lived collapsed on the dead bodies of their comrades. Many Bataan Death March survivors are reluctant to talk about the atrocities they were forced to endure. I was in the army in the early 1950s. One of my

---

[16] Newspaper clipping dated February 29, 1944. Newspaper identity unknown.

commanding officers was a Death March survivor and occasionally he would tell of some of the horrible incidents that he had witnessed.

Almost 60 years have passed since I have talked with him but I can recall to this day his account of being forced to march for long hours in the hot sun without food or water. If a man fell out of rank from exhaustion he was executed on the spot and his body left to rot in the sun.

Another story involved three American soldiers that tried to escape by hacking their way through the jungle. They took with them bolo knives and enough food and rice to survive about three days in the jungle. They were caught just outside the camp and staked in full view of the rest of the prisoners. They were wearing only shorts and were never given any food or water. For several days they cooked in the sun. Their sunburned skin blistered and cracked. Hordes of flies swarmed around their oozing sores. After a few days the men begged to be put out of their misery. Finally about a week later the Japanese did put them out of their misery, but they assembled all the prisoners and forced them to watch the execution. It was horrible as they watched the bullets make dents where they entered the men's bodies and their blood drained out[17].

Of the 25,600 American POW's captured by the Japanese at the beginning of the war, 10,650 were dead by the end of the war. Of these 5,135 died in the Philippines and 3,840 died on Japanese "Hell Ships"[18].

---

[17] For more such stories see the book "The Emperor's Angry Guest" by Ralph M. Knox, ISBN 99-I9069. Knox was also a Death March survivor and described a similar and possibly the same event in his book.

[18] Hell Ships: As early as the spring of 1942, the Japanese began moving prisoners of war by sea out of all the areas they had conquered - Singapore, Hong Kong, the Philippines, Java, and other places, and sending them to slave labor camps. Thousands of these prisoners were transported on dozens of Japanese Hell Ships. They were crammed into stinking holds, filthy with coal dust, congealed sugar syrup or horse manure left over from previous voyages. To make matters worse they were given little or no water or food. The prisoners were so crowded that they couldn't even get air to breathe. Some went crazy, cut and bit each other through the arms and legs and sucked their blood. Some of the cruelty they experienced was extraordinary and unparalleled even for prisoners of the Japanese. Many thousand perished from murder, starvation, sickness and neglect - or were killed when the unmarked ships on which the Japanese forbade Red Cross markings to identify them as carrying American POWs were attacked unknowingly by friendly forces. Also see World War II Seminar", University of San

The struggles on the battlefields of all the Pacific islands were horrible. As the Americans advanced northward toward the Japanese Home Islands the resistance became fiercer. The outer defensive perimeter around the Japanese Home Islands started at Saipan in the Marianas. The Japanese military leaders were optimistic that they could successfully defend the island with the 30,000 soldiers on duty there.

The U.S. Marines started the landings on Saipan on June 15, 1944 and had 20,000 men ashore by nightfall. In a running fight, the battle was over by June 20. Except for a group of caves, the island was in Allied hands. Saipan was declared secure on June 22.

But on the night of July 7, 3,000 Japanese soldiers remaining on the island charged in the largest suicide rush of the war. Stunned, the Americans fell back, but quickly recovered and wiped out the Japanese in an all-night fight.

All but 1,000 of the 30,000 Japanese defenders on Saipan were dead, along with 22,000 civilians. Many of the civilians had been pushed or pulled many over cliffs by the soldiers, but most had committed suicide by jumping themselves or by holding onto grenades in the caves. American casualties numbered 16,525.

By early 1945 the advancing American forces invaded the Islands of Iwo Jima and Okinawa from where they could launch air attacks on the Japanese home islands. Newspaper articles from 1945[19] show that intensive bombing of the Japanese Empire started in February when 1200 carrier based planes hit Tokyo in the morning followed by a B-29 raid that afternoon. These air raids were followed by a fire bombing in March by 300 B-29s and still another B-29 raid in May. The Japanese government estimated that the fire-bombing raid on Tokyo alone killed more than 100,000. However, these raids did not demoralize the Japanese but stiffened their will to resist and they fought back on the ground and at sea with kamikaze attacks from the air and human torpedoes from the sea. In an attempt to hold Okinawa, the *Yamato*[20] the largest battleship ever built

Diego, Spring 1999 by Elizabeth Himchak.

[19] See "Chronicle of the 20th century", Clifton Daniel, Editor in Chief

[20] Editor's Note: The *Yamato*, and her sister, *Musahri* were the largest battleships ever built, even exceeding in size and gun caliber of the U.S. Navy's abortive *Montana* class. She carried nine 18.1-inch main battery guns, which could fire 3200-pound armor piercing shells and were the largest battleship guns ever to go to sea. Commissioned in December 1941 the *Yamato* served as flagship of the Combined Japanese Fleet during the naval battles of 1942. During the following year, she spent most of her time at Truk,

carrying nine 18-inch guns, was assigned to take part in the suicidal "Ten-Go" Operation, a combined air, sea and kamikaze effort to destroy American naval forces supporting the invasion of Okinawa. The *Yamato* was accompanied by a light cruiser and eight destroyers but with no protective air cover. So badly depleted was the Japanese fleet by this time, the *Yamato* was reported to carry only enough fuel for a one-way trip to Okinawa. Her mission was to beach herself at Okinawa to avoid being sunk in deep water and fight until eliminated. On April 7, 1945, while still some 200 miles north of Okinawa, the *Yamato* was attacked by a massive force of U.S. carrier based fighters, dive-bombers and torpedo planes and sunk with the loss of several thousand elite Japanese sailors.

As the U.S. Forces got closer to the Japanese homeland, the more fanatical the fighting became. Approximately one third of the American Pacific War casualties occurred between April and August 1945. The price paid for Okinawa was dear on both sides. The final toll of American casualties was the highest experienced in any campaign against the Japanese. Total American battle casualties were 49,151, of which 12,520 were killed or missing and 36,631 wounded. Army losses were 4,582 killed, 93 missing, and 18,000 wounded. Marine losses, including those of the Tactical Air Force, were 2,938 killed and missing and 13,708 wounded. Navy casualties totaled 4,907 killed and missing and 4,824 wounded. Non-battle casualties during the campaign amounted to 15,613 for the Army and 10,598 for the Marines. The losses in ships were 36 sunk and 368 damaged, most of them as a result of air action. Losses in the air were 763 planes from 1 April to 1 July 1945.

The cost of the battle to the Japanese was even higher than to the Americans. Approximately 110,000 of the enemy lost their lives in the attempt to hold Okinawa, and 7,400 more were taken prisoner. The enemy lost 7,800 airplanes, 16 ships sunk, and 4 ships damaged. More important, they lost about 650 square miles of territory within 350 miles of Kyushu.

---

as part of a mobile naval force defending Japan's Central Pacific bases. Torpedoed by USS *Skate* in December 1943, the *Yamato* was under repair until April 1944, during which time her anti-aircraft battery was increased. She then took part in the Battle of the Philippine Sea in June and the Battle of Leyte Gulf in October. During the latter action, she was attacked several times by U.S. Navy aircraft, and fired her big guns in an engagement with U.S. escort carriers and destroyers off the island of Samar.

In June and July, B-29s fire bombed Kobe and Honshu resulting in heavy Japanese civilian casualties. During the same time period carrier based planes destroyed the Japanese naval base at Yokusuka and

American Cemetery on Tinian Island

essentially destroyed the remaining Japanese navy. In addition the U.S. Pacific fleet began the first heavy naval bombardment of the Japanese home islands. On July 26, 1945, an ultimatum was sent to Japan. Unless she surrendered immediately, Japan would face "prompt and utter destruction." In this ultimatum, President Truman said, "If the Japanese leaders do not now accept our terms, they may expect a rain of ruin from the air, the like of which has never been seen on this earth."

From visual observations over Japan post war assessments concur that these firebombing raids caused more death and destruction than anything else in the war including both atomic bombs. These raids continued for six months, destroying dozens of cities. The Japanese could not stop them, yet they refused to surrender.

Despite the losses from the increasing number of air raids; the losses on Saipan; Iwo Jima and Okinawa; the prospects for a lot more from future air raids; and, an invasion of their homeland the zealous Japanese military leaders chose to continue the war and fired back a defiant refusal turning down the U.S. surrender ultimatum. Even though they may have recognized that defeat was possible, they ordered their soldiers in the field to hang-on and never suffer the disgrace of being taken alive.

The war had now been going on for almost 4 years. By August 1945 the war with Germany had ended and the American people wanted the war with Japan over as soon as possible. According to records in the National Archives 16,112,566 Americans served in the armed forces during World War II. Of these 291,557 were killed and 670,846 wounded. With a population of 131,028,000 this meant that one out of ever 136 people in this country had either been killed or wounded in the war. Almost every family in the United States was affected personally in one way or another by the war![21]

On August 3 American mines sealed off Japan closing all main harbors. Then on August 6 and 9 the promised destruction arrived in the form of a one-two punch with atomic weapons dropped on Hiroshima and Nagasaki. The Japanese government put the toll at 60,000 dead in Hiroshima, 10,000 in Nagasaki with 120,000 wounded and offered to surrender on August 10. However they did not stop the fighting or the kamikaze and manned torpedo attacks on American targets. On August 13, about 1000 U.S. aircraft resumed the air assaults on Japan. Two days later on August 15 Emperor Hirohito went on the Japanese radio and finally spoke to his people.

> *"I cannot bear to see my people suffer any longer. It pains me to think of those who served me so faithfully, the soldiers and sailors who have been killed or wounded in far-off battles, the families who have lost all their worldly goods and often their lives as well. The time has come when we must bear the unbearable. I swallow my tears and give my sanction to the proposal to accept the Allied proclamation."*

It had taken the almost instantaneous destruction of a second Japanese city and the threat of the same fate to at least four other major cities to finally get his attention! He then ordered his armies to accept the inevitability of surrender and appealed to the kamikazes to give in. On September 2 Japan officially surrendered on battleship Missouri.

Editor's Note: My father's opinion reflected in virtually every interview was consistent. The following was extracted from a 1966 radio interview:

---

[21] See http://www.fas.org/sgp/crs/natsec/RL32492.pdf

"As in any war, our goal was—as it should be—to win. The stakes were too high to equivocate. We had to do what was necessary!

Humane warfare is an oxymoron. War by definition is barbaric. I particularly feel a special sense of indignation at those self-proclaimed humanitarians that make an acceptable or intolerable distinction between the use of nuclear explosives or the use of conventional explosives such as fire bombing or bullets as the means of killing the enemy. To try and distinguish between an acceptable method of killing and an unacceptable method is ludicrous. In my mind, to suggest that one specific act of war is barbaric and thereby illegal is to imply that other forms of slaughter are acceptable and consequently legal! If you have to die in warfare, what is the difference of being killed by a bomb or a bullet?

As for the question of morality that has existed ever since 1945, volumes have been written to support each side of the controversy. Unfortunately, there has been a notable lack of objectivity by a number of revisionist historians who prefer to sift through old records to find fragments of evidence to back up or support their own moral preconceptions. The examination and re-examination of events such as these make careers in history. Although the atomic bombings happened almost fifty years ago, contemporary researchers examine every archive, every recollection, and every possible motivation surrounding the events. I'm sure that truly professional and objective historians would never discount the observations of people who were there. If nothing else, they have a far better sense of the tenor of the times then trying to reconstruct it through documents.

Over 45 years later, in today's culture, certain groups of people dispute the need for the bombs. I take issue with those that view the Japanese were defeated before Hiroshima and were willing to surrender. They also claim the bombs were unnecessary because a naval blockade or an invasion of Japan would have been a better alternative. Some even say that the United States was the aggressor nation and violated the Geneva Convention rules of conduct. As I will show later eyewitness accounts from both sides do not support these claims.

As Patrick Henry said in his March 23, 1775 speech in the Virginia House of Burgess and I think it is appropriate here:

"No man thinks more highly than I do of the patriotism, as well as abilities, of the very worthy gentlemen who have just addressed the House. But different men often see the same

58

subject in different lights; and, therefore, I hope it will not be thought disrespectful to those gentlemen if, entertaining as I do opinions of a character very opposite to theirs, I shall speak forth my sentiments freely and without reserve."

I agree that history can be viewed from more than one perspective. However, I totally disagree with "enlightened or sophisticated" educators, politicians, religious leaders and anyone else who would deny history, or water down, change or make up "facts" to preserve their private morality issues or to further their private agendas.

PART 2 Preparations for the Final Blow on Japan

"Then conquer we must for our cause it is just"
Francis Scott Key

Enola Gay on Tinian Island August 1945

"As with any human endeavor, perfection comes with great difficulty and is seldom achieved. Colonel Tibbets made us practice until we got it right every time."

Jacob Beser

Training At Wendover

Editor's Note: This chapter has been complied from several TV and radio interviews and personal conversations with my father. However we have written this and some of the following chapters as if he were speaking to you the reader.

Returning now to my personal experiences. The bulk of the 393rd personnel traveled from Fairmont, Nebraska to Wendover by troop train. If you have ever been involved in a large troop movement by train you are certainly aware that the creature comforts were minimal but Uncle Sam provided good food and if the cooks didn't ruin it, you ate reasonably well.

It was mid September, as I remember, when we arrived at Wendover[22]. I had never been to Wendover before. The first things I saw was a gas station with an attached restaurant; several other little stores; and, little else. An airfield and a collection of assorted barracks and shops were at the base of the mountain. There were also several large hangers and a

Base Housing Wendover Air Field

---

[22] Editor's Note: Military records show the 393rd Bomb Squadron was constituted 28 February 1944 and activated 11 March 1944 at Fairmont Army Airfield, Geneva, Nebraska as part of the 504th Bomb Group (VH). The primary mission was to train combat crews for the B-29 Superfortress.

On September 10, 1944 the 393rd was ordered to transfer to Wendover Army Airfield, Utah. They arrived on September 14. The facilities at Wendover were not ready for B-29s, and there weren't any there yet, so Colonel Tibbets gave most of the men a ten-day furlough beginning September 21.

When they returned the ramp was fenced in and everyone had to wear special badges to be admitted. More personnel were arriving daily to form support units and the 509th Composite Group which, for the record, was organized and activated in December 1944 for the specific purpose of delivering certain special bombs when these bombs become available. It is now anticipated that the first of those bombs will be available for delivery in August 1945. When the airplanes began arriving; everyone knew that their mission was special, by the configuration of the planes and special security procedures required.

chapel. My first impression of this place has been with me for over 40 years. If the North American continent ever needed an enema, the tube would be inserted here at Wendover.

We saw a lot of strange faces from the start, officers and enlisted men. I staked out a space and an office in the Engineering hanger to set up our electronics facility. Since our equipment was classified, it would require a twenty-four hour guard. It was assigned a post number with the guard duty being performed by a routine interior guard. My men began setting up test benches and equipment racks. Within a week we had our sections operational.

By the middle of our first week the strangers had become numerous. No one seemed to know who they were or where they were coming from but soon we would learn a little but not very much.

On Monday, September 25th, Colonel Tibbets called us all into the base auditorium {for a briefing}. There he told us that the group had been selected for a special mission. Those of you who stay will be going overseas and will take part in an effort that will win the war. But, secrecy was of the utmost importance and we would never find out the details of the mission until the day it is pulled so just have faith. It is going to be a rigorous training program and we were his staff to help him build a new group to perform the mission. He then sent virtually everyone else home on leave with the exception of about a half dozen of us. There was where I first met Paul Tibbets.

So after the meeting with Paul broke up, I was signaled out and invited into the inner sanctum. There I met with Paul and Dr. Brode from the University of California. I got asked the usual questions about my background and experience just like I was being interviewed for a job, which I was. Then they ask me about my attitudes towards the war; towards flying; and, would I object to flying combat. Well, I had my wings and was pretty young and cocky at the time. My answer was sure I would fly combat - which is what I have been trained for. Dr. Brode said, "you wouldn't want me giving you the impression that we are conducting experiments over the enemy. We have some people in our group that are trained to do the job {we have in mind} but they are too valuable to risk." At this point in time I could see the cost of my life insurance going up. It really didn't register with me as something particularly odd. We had just been told that it was a special secret mission. What are you going to do? You are out in the middle of the desert, you are wearing an army uniform and you have been trained to fly combat so I guessed one way or another it was going to happen.

I was excused from the room and about 10 minutes later invited back and everybody shook my hand and congratulated me. I'd been hired but what for? Nobody was saying, but I was now part of the crowd but I didn't know what I was part of.

Several days later I was told to be on the flight line at seven the next morning and be packed for three or four days travel. I said, Where are we going? "You'll find out when we get there." That's interesting. And do I take warm clothes or summer clothes or what? "Take 'em both." They wouldn't give me the slightest clue.

I crawled in the airplane. I didn't know the rest of these fellows too well. But I did know the pilot and I said, "Arthur, where are we going?" He said, "I don't know but when we get near we'll find out. All I know is I filed a clearance for a place called Y. The letter Y. I've never been there before."

Our destination turned out to be Los Alamos where I would be escorted by Colonel Tibbets and Navy Commander. Frederick Ashworth. Before we left for our destination the security officer had me remove my Air Corps insignias and replace them with the castle insignias of the Army Corps of Engineers.

We went {from the flight line} right to the office of Dr. Norman Ramsey, who was a young Ph.D. from Columbia University. He ran the fusing and firing section and gave us a briefing but never mentioned the words atomic bomb. He just called it a weapon. Ramsey said that they wanted this weapon to burst over the ground at a precise altitude and they had been working on the problem but they weren't nearly as far along as they should be.

We had lunch at the lodge. Names like Nils Bohr, Enrico Fermi, and Hans Bethe were bandied around. It all began to add up. Then in conversations with Ramsey one day he pretty much filled me in without ever saying words like atomic bomb. He talked about fundamental forces of the universe. He hit all around it and it "spelled mother" to me.

The importance of the fusing mechanism and the devices used to trigger them at the correct altitude cannot be overstated. It had to be reliable and fool proof. It had to detonate at the correct altitude. Safeguards had to be incorporated to prevent premature denotation and we needed to minimize its susceptibility to outside {radio or radar} interference. I had to know its workings inside and out. This is where my training in electronic counter measures training came in handy.

Redundant trigger mechanisms were included - the radar altimeter, the barometric pressure sensor and the impact sensor. Each had its place as well as its limitations. The scientist wanted the weapon to explode at 1890 feet above the surrounding terrain. This left out the impact sensor as being the primary device. Not precisely knowing the altitude of the target as well as the local barometric pressure placed limitations on the barometric sensor. However the radar proximity could, if properly working, detonate the weapon the precise altitude.

The fusing used in both bombs was essentially the same. Tail Warning Radar functioning as radar altimeters provided the basic elements of the fuse. Four were used to achieve the desired reliability. Each radar set was modified and adjusted to trigger when a certain altitude above the ground had been reached in order to provide the desired height of burst of the bomb. The fusing system was connected so that any two could actuate the detonators.

The radar sets were modifications of the standard APS-13 tail warning radar (410 to 420 MHz). Their directional antennas were mounted around the circumference of the bomb pointing forward to ensure that as the weapon rotated during its fall, one set of antennas was always pointing at the ground. As a backup for the radar fuses there was a barometric fuse set to the same altitude. In case neither the radar nor the barometric fuses functioned properly the bomb carried mechanical impact fuses in the nose and tail to set it off when it struck the ground.

Radar in the mid-1940's was new and crude by today's standards. Developing a reliable radar altimeter was a daunting engineering task. Achieving perfection in any engineering endeavor comes with great difficulty and is seldom achieved. But in our case the lives of the crew as well as the performance of a two billion-dollar weapon was at stake and it was absolutely necessary to achieve perfection.

Needlessly to say nothing is more unsettling to the pilot and crew than a premature explosion of a bomb under your aircraft. Achieving these goals set for the radar altimeter did not come easily and required lots of experiments, redesigns and tests. Some of these resulted in memorable incidents and accidents. The results of our initial tests were not encouraging. Sometimes the damn thing worked, sometimes it didn't. Some test models even exploded the test bomb under the aircraft almost immediately after it was released. The bottom line was that perfecting the altimeter remained a nightmare right up to the day the bombs were dropped.

Several safety factors were also designed into the bomb firing system. First, it was necessary to insure that the bomb could not be accidentally detonated close to the airplane and damage or destroy the plane. While the bomb was secured in the bomb bay electrical power was provided from the aircraft electrical supply through an umbilical cord. Upon release of the bomb the umbilical was disconnected and power for the bomb's electronic components was provided by storage batteries contained within the bomb.

After the bomb was released, fail safe separation timers were provided. These devices were started when the umbilical cable was released. Until these timers were started, all internal power to the bomb electronic components was cut off so that nothing could cause a premature detonation. About fifteen seconds after release of the bomb the timer closed the power circuits and activated the bomb fusing and firing circuits. For reliability, as I recall, nine clocks were used. Any three could close the appropriate switches.

Second, since the altimeters were radar devices, it was recognized that they could easily be jammed if the enemy were to broadcast jamming signals on the correct frequency. Therefore it was necessary that the altimeters start radiating at the latest possible time to reduce the vulnerability to jamming. Barometric switches were provided that would start the altimeters radiating at about an altitude of eight thousand feet. Again, there were nine of these switches so arranged that any three could start the process. I had telemetry signals relayed back from the bomb to tell me of the fusing mechanism progress throughout the bomb flight.

Throughout the design, test and operational phases I got any piece of equipment I thought might be of use to perform my mission. All I had to do was quote "Silverplate", the Army Air Corps' code-name for the operation, and I got anything I wanted!

For the protection of our airplane I had a mix of APT-1, APT-4 and ARQ-8 jammers, for use if we were engaged by radar-laid anti-aircraft fire. However my main task during the bomb run was not to ward off possible Japanese ground fire, but to ensure there were no enemy radar sets in the target area at the time of bomb release whose radiation might prematurely trigger the bomb's radar air-burst fusing system.

From previous intelligence information and from my previous twelve flights over enemy territory, I knew the Japanese had no radar sets operating on the frequencies in the 410 MHz band which might directly interfere. But there remained the possibility that harmonic signals from an enemy radar operating in 205 MHz band might be strong enough to trigger one of the altimeter fuses during the bomb's fall and prematurely detonate the weapon. If that happened there was a serious risk that the airplane would be incinerated in the fireball from its own bomb. To overcome this possibility my task during the bomb run was to monitor the four frequencies used by the bomb's altimeters and ensure there were no signals present. At any time up to bomb release I could switch off some or all of the bomb's altimeter fuses if necessary and, as a last resort, leave the detonation of the weapon to the barometric or impact fuses.

For the next several months, I continued working with scientists at Los Alamos in perfecting the design and testing of the radar altimeter proximity fuse and some other tasks. This necessitated making several trips from Wendover to the highly secret site Y. No one other than Paul knew where we were going and no flight plans were filed when we made one of these mysterious trips.

The training program at Wendover was intensive and in the process I got to know Paul Tibbets very well. I even baby sat with his kids on Christmas of 1944 so he and his wife could go out together. I developed some admiration for him as a pilot, as a co-worker in a cause, but never as an exceptional leader or commander. I saw him as an egocentric, hard driving and selfish individual who played favorites, and was unwilling to share himself with anyone other than his close associates from the European Theater of Operations. He had a low tolerance level for incompetence or insubordination. He had priorities for his mission and backup if needed at the highest levels of the Army to get what he wanted or needed. He demanded and got absolute security and perfection from the men who served under him. He made us practice until we got it right every time. But as a pilot, he was the type of man I would want to fly with in combat and get me home alive!

Our aircrews were given extensive training in the drop and breakaway procedures[23]. A lot of this was done while we were still

---

[23] Editor's Note: I have often heard that the bombs were dropped attached to a parachute to give the airplane time to escape the blast. This is a myth. In reality the objective was to have the bomb hit within a 500-foot circle centered on the aim point to

developing the ballistics characteristics of the bomb and trying to solve the many technical problems with the proximity fuse. Engineering test flights were combined with training flights. We literally wore out one set of B-29s.

In January 1945 I went along with the flight crews to Batista Field in Cuba for long distance over water night navigation training and to continue our high altitude bombing practice. Prior to leaving for Cuba Tibbets gave us all a strong warning. "The same rules apply to Havana that apply here. Don't ask nor answer questions but just do your job! Your performance on this training exercise will determine who will participate in the upcoming historic mission."

Who could resist leaving the cold winter temperatures at Wendover for a few days of temporary duty in the Caribbean? I had never been to Cuba but had heard legends about the wild bars and the nightlife to expect. But I would have one serious problem if I were to fully enjoy the nightlife in Havana. My personal "bodyguard" who would also be going along so I had to figure out a way to lose him in Havana at least for a few days.

Perhaps at this point I should explain why I was the only one in the 509th to have a personal "bodyguard." It all began on my first trip to Los Alamos. As I was about to board the aircraft to leave I was approached by a "civilian" and told to remove all my Air Corps insignia. He handed me a set of Corps of Engineers brass to put on. I thought this rather strange procedure but after noticing that Colonel Tibbets had undergone an insignia change I thought no further of it.

Security was of absolute importance on the project and maintained from the very beginning. I would be working with the scientists at Los Alamos supporting the radar altimeter proximity fuse design. Furthermore I was aware that this was an atomic project with the objective of building a bomb. It would be my responsibility to determine that there was no electronic radiation present over the target that would interfere with the operation of the proximity fuse. I also had been told

---

minimize casualties in the civilian communities surrounding the military target. This accuracy requirement could not be achieved using a parachute. The parachute myth has its origin from Japanese eyewitness accounts of seeing a parachute at Hiroshima before the bomb exploded. The parachute they saw was attached to an instrumentation canister to record the blast effects and not to the bomb. The breakaway procedure required the B-29 to execute a 155-degree diving turn in order to achieve a sufficient distance from the bomb blast to avoid destruction of the airplane.

that I would fly with each one of them until such a time that the medics said that I had had enough. No one would venture a guess at that point in time how many of the weapons were planned for use.

On my second night at Los Alamos despite all of the precautions that had taken to disguise my military affiliation, I went to the Post Exchange with Mr. Sheldon Dike, a mechanical engineer who at one time worked for the Martin Co. in Baltimore. While standing at the counter waiting to be served a beer, a WAAC standing alongside me whispered to her friend "that little fellow is wearing a "40 mission hat" if ever I'd seen one." Both of us realized that in the attempt to disguise my service affiliation a change of hat was in order, since no other branch of service would tolerate the Bancroft Fighter hat. Needless to say, we left the PX at once and returned to the guest lodge where I was staying. After I told the story to Ashworth I was assigned an escort to be my shadow at all times whenever I left Wendover, except for the times I would travel with Colonel Tibbets. It was his job to make sure that I did not meet or talk with anyone about what we were doing. A real problem on a date! And, yes I lost him a few times. With the passage of time, my escort became a bodyguard. By the time Hollywood acquired the story and produced the movie *"Enola Gay"* even I found the story a little far fetched and incredible; this despite the fact that I had tried to convince the producer and writers to tone it down.

In Havana we were housed in a separate compound from the other American servicemen at Batista Field. Our compound had 24-hour guards and no outsiders were allowed to enter. We had no problem impressing the others that we were a special group. We had a round the clock chow line supplied with the best food available on the Island.

Probably my most memorable event in Cuba was finding a place in Old Havana where I could get plenty of good whiskey at about a quarter of what we paid in the states. It was no problem pooling our money and purchasing a truckload. But before I could pick it up I had to find a way to lose my bodyguard. I took up the challenge and on the designated night I whisk him off to a bar where I fed into him about eight drinks in less than an hour. By this time he would not miss me and I made my escape to the motor pool and using Silverplate priority signed out a truck. Buying and loading the booze went fine but I encountered a problem with a Military Police who wanted to see what was in the truck before he would let me enter the compound where our B-29s were parked. Resorting to my rank of Lieutenant, I stood the MP at attention and asked what his security clearance level was. He quickly admitted that he did not know and I told him "you had better find out quick" and sped through the gate.

After circling around the compound for a few minutes to be sure I was not being followed I went to the flight line where the crews were waiting to unload my cargo of booze and safely stowing in the airplanes. I returned the truck to the motor pool and as I went through the gate the MP saluted and waved me through.

I must admit that this escapade was typical of some of the things we did during the three weeks we were there. In fact we developed a reputation as a bunch of hell raisers. When the local military authorities tried to intervene our operations officer used the Silverplate code to get our men out of a jam. Hence we became known as "The untouchables."

Even late in the training program Colonel Tibbets was still making frequent trips to the Pentagon. I accompanied him on some of these trips to a Target Committee meeting. On one trip I had been tipped off by either Commander Ashworth or Dr. Doll that radar was not being considered as a primary bombing aid if the target was obscured by weather. That bothered me no end since our crews had been subjected to a number of practice drops using radar as the aid. I envisioned this meeting as an opportunity to get my feelings heard.

As it turned out the decision to not allow a radar drop had been cast in concrete at an earlier committee meeting that I had not attended. What was up for decision at this meeting was the use of Loran beams from submarines off the coast of Japan in case weather obscured the target. I don't remember the Admiral's name that was making the presentation but his approach didn't impress me as being a practical solution. I summarized my feelings by stage whispering "Bull S--t" to Colonel Wright who was seated next to me. General Groves overheard me and said: "What did you say Lieutenant?" I repeated my observation. Colonel Tibbets groaned and I was given the opportunity to go to the chalk board and point out why I thought the tactic would not work. Among other points I specifically addressed the geometry of the problem and the accuracy required. I don't believe you can hold a submarine steady enough to meet the accuracy requirement. Tides and ocean currents will pull it off track. What is more the submarine must be on the surface for Loran to work. It is my opinion that there is no way a submarine could remain surfaced three miles off the Japanese coast and not come under attack.

Not knowing that radar had been ruled out in the previous meeting, I went on to explain how I could do a much better job using the AN/APQ 13 radar set on my B-29.

General Groves, who was chairing the committee meeting, closed the matter by saying: "Those seem to be good enough reasons not to use Loran so lets move on."

Little did the people in that room know that several months later a distressed B-29, not wanting to jettison it's atomic bomb, would be led to the environs of Nagasaki by an A/N APQ-13 airborne radar operated by a GI and interpreted by an Air Corps Navigator and a Navy Commander.

The outcome of the meeting was that neither submarine Loran beams nor airborne radar would be used but at least I got to put in a plug for using radar if the need arose. Later I ask Tibbets how did I do? His answer was a terse "Bull's eye."

Editor's Note (Jack Spangler): In a 1985 radio call in show interview Jacob was asked several questions about the training program at Wendover. One caller asked: "The movie last night emphasized that you were the only man in the 509th to have a bodyguard. Why did you have this guard and did you ever manage to "lose him"? Jacob responded: "Security was of absolute importance on the project and maintained from the very beginning. I had been working with the scientist at Los Alamos and was aware that this was an atomic project with the objective of building a bomb. The word "atomic" was taboo. Because of my support of the radar altimeter proximity fuse design and association with the scientist at Los Alamos, I knew we would be carrying an atomic bomb."

Lieutenant Morris Jeppson

During the development of the radar proximity fuse I worked with Dr. Edward Doll who was in charge of the weapon electronics. The same electronics was used in both the Hiroshima and Nagasaki weapons even though they were different types of bombs. I helped with the development of the electronics in the fusing system as well as flying with them when the bombs were deployed. Radar was very critical. In order for the bombs to have maximum blast effect they had to be detonated above the ground, at about 1500-1800 ft. At 1500 ft above the ground, you only have about one and a half seconds for proximity fuse to react and detonate the bomb when it's supposed to.

The words "nuclear" and "atomic" were never permitted to be spoken outside of Los Alamos. They were never spoken at Wendover. As far as I know the other members of the *Enola Gay* crew who knew we would be delivering an atomic bomb were Tibbets, Parsons, and Morrie Jeppson the assistant weaponeer.[24] I think Ferebee also knew. I don't think Lewis and van Kirk knew. The radio operators, the gunners and the radar operators didn't know. It was a closely held story. On the Nagasaki trip, we took another crew. I was the only one of the *Enola Gay* crew who made the second run. Fred Ashworth, he's a Rear Admiral now, knew. He was Parson's right hand man and Phil Barnes, the assistant weaponeer at Nagasaki knew. The weaponeers were really not part of the 509th, but were a hand picked bunch of boys who grew up with the thing. They knew the workings of the apparatus inside and out. I had to learn some of it, to understand it, in order to understand what they wanted me to do, in order to do the test work.

We had a midnight briefing prior to the Hiroshima mission. The purpose of this briefing was to show the crews what an atomic explosion really was but as I recall the word atomic was not used. For security reasons this briefing was limited to the crews of the three aircraft involved in the actual Hiroshima strike. The first time I recall the word atomic being used openly was after we had dropped the bomb and Colonel Tibbets announced that you have

Admiral Ashworth

---

[24] Editor's Note: A "weaponeer" was not an official B-29 flight crew member. But General Groves wanted to be sure that the officer making the final judgments during a mission was thoroughly familiar with the atomic bombs and responsible for the success of the mission. To identify these members of the flight crew, Captain Parsons made up the title "Weaponeer". Later, as the Air Force developed their capability for the delivery of atomic weapons, this member of the crew was called The Bomb Commander".

just witnessed the first atomic bomb or words to that effect. This was confirmed by interviews with the *Enola Gay* crew members 15 years later.

Another caller asked the question: *"Why were you the only man to fly on the strike aircraft for both missions?"* To this question Jacob responded: "I could be facetious and say I was the best man for the job but I won't. My job in the Group was Electronics Officer which was a staff position. I had a crew of about 45 people in my section. Probably some of the radar men could have been trained to perform the job on the flights but that would have presented more security problems. But, I was the only man in my group that had worked with the design of the proximity fuse and knew the thing inside and out and how it was supposed to work and what radar interference it could and could not tolerate. Of course there were civilians there that could have done the job equally as well but they were "too valuable" to risk on a combat flight."

Another not so obvious security measure taken during our training at Wendover was not to initially allow all of the crews to execute the violent 150-degree diving turn escape maneuver. This was not a conventional bombing technique. I suspected at that time, and later learned, that this was for security reasons. To avoid speculation on the subject, only Colonel

Left to right: Dr. Ramsey, Navy Capt. Parsons, Colonel Tibbets, Dr. Doll, and Unknown Navy Officer

Tibbets and Major Sweeney executed it under the cover story of checking the airplanes stability to make such a turn at altitude. Colonel Tibbets' background as a B-29 test pilot made this explanation acceptable. Of course all pilots were trained to perform this maneuver as time progressed.

Tinian Operations

Editor's Note: As for war stories, my father always had an ample supply. When he described his Tinian experiences he had lots of interesting things to tell to anyone willing to listen. Unlike many war stories told by others 40 plus years later when the fact and individual memories have faded, my father's stories could almost always be confirmed as fact from official government records. This even includes calendar dates although sometimes they may have varied by a day or two.

Following about six months of intensive training at Wendover with the exception of a break of about two weeks for some long range over water flight training in Cuba, the 509th was ordered to deploy to the island of Tinian in May of 1945. The island of Tinian is 125 miles north of Guam and approximately 1450 miles southeast of Tokyo. It is shaped like a pork chop about 10 miles long and 3 miles wide, and has a gently rolling terrain. Prior to our occupation, approximately 95% of its area was planted in sugar cane. Tinian has two major airfields, North Field and West Field, the larger being North Field with four 8500-foot landing strips directed into the prevailing easterly winds. West Field has two 8500 foot landing strips also directed east and west. It had been captured the previous July and would be the staging area for the delivery of the new weapon, now code named "the Gimmick" to Japan.

On Sunday June 17, 1945 I received my special orders to depart for an overseas assignment. The next two days were spent clearing post. I was accountable for a wide assortment of junk {government property} as well as highly classified documents. Property had to be turned in and the appropriate classified documents forwarded to my new address. Also any outstanding police citations or bills at the Officer's club had to be cleared. Certain programs as well as training and medical had to be certified as being up to date.

Most important of all were my pay records. Pay due as of the date of departure had to be collected as well as any per-diem advances that had been authorized. Needlessly to say I had a busy day collecting all 20 signatures that were required! The last step was to go the Base Adjutant who signed off that I was free to go.

On the morning of June 20 all fifteen of us who were to depart that day met at the flight line. We left Wendover early that morning for Hamilton Field California where we were on the ground for several hours where the plane got a 50 hour inspection and the flight crew got a mandatory 8 hours of sleep. From there we went to Hawaii and on to Johnston Island where we spent about an hour and then headed for Kwajelein. It was about two a.m. as we approached Kwaje and all of a sudden anti-aircraft fire erupted all around us. The pilot explained that Kwaje was still in the hands of the Japanese. Shortly after this episode we landed at Kwajelein.

About an hour later we were on our way to Tinian where we landed at about 10:00 am local time or nineteen hours and fifteen minutes after leaving Hawaii. The whole trip had taken almost three days with over 34 hours of it spent in a C-54 four-engine transport plane. Certainly not first class accommodations by today's standards!

Our arrival at Tinian had been anticipated by lots of folks, including some of my colleagues of the old outfit, the 504th. With all of the security attached to our move orders, it was a mystery to me how this came about. My old friend Bill Stallings in the 504th was on the line to meet me when our airplane rolled to a stop on its hard-stand in the 393rd revetment area. Bill had with him Chief Warrant Officer Karl Pendray. I hadn't seen either one of these fellows since I left Fairmont, Nebraska, over a year earlier. They were bubbling over with all kinds of news about the various fellows in the old group. Stallings, whom we called Shorty had inventoried the available nurses on the island and informed me that there were at least two "nice Jewish girls from Chicago."

But his curiosity about the 509th mission was getting the better of him and he finally asked me the question, "What are you guys up to?" He as much as said that the whole immediate world in the 313th Wing would give their eyeteeth to get their hands on our airplanes. Ours were the most up-to-date that had been seen out there as of that time. Our B-29's had new fuel injected engines, Curtis electric reversible pitch "Paddle Blade" propellers, pneumatic bomb bay doors, engine mounted front collector rings, and other smaller mechanical improvements with all of the armor and guns removed except for the tail guns.

I told him flat out that even if I did know our mission, I could not tell him.

To my surprise, I came across fellows that I had not seen since high school days. I ran into other Army school classmates. Here again I was able to benefit from their experiences, both on the ground as well as in the air. By the end of the month some of my peers in the tech area were beginning to give me advice as to what I should be doing on any practice missions, if I get to go. Unbeknownst to them, it was already a known fact of life at I would fly with the "Gimmick", if and when the time came that was declared operational.

Once I got through the "greeters", there were more mundane things that had to be done. These included, signing into the squadron so that I could be picked up on the Morning Report and continue to draw pay. I

Tent City Tinian

also had to be assigned quarters, and check to see that the work area and Quonset Hut assigned to my people was adequate for the job that we would have to do. Along the way I stopped in at the Group Mess to get caught up with some food, and a short visit with my friend Charley Perry, our Group Mess Officer. My most important chore of all was to determine if my people had drawn a vehicle for our section, and if they had where was it. I had some visiting I wanted to do, and some sights to see.

My first living quarters were in a tent area, This was temporary lodging until our permanent quarters were ready. Later, we were fortunate enough to take over a compound that the Navy Sea-Bee's had built for themselves. It consisted of Quonset Huts at the foot of a hill on the edge of a bluff overlooking our airfield. They were oriented so that the prevailing winds supplied natural air conditioning. The wash areas were behind the huts and were designed to take advantage of the elements. Water barrels doubled as cisterns, collecting fresh rainwater each afternoon. The abundance of tropical sun kept it nice and warm, so that taking a shower was a comfortable and refreshing experience.

But as for the other necessary facilities, what can one say in praise of "eight-holers"? Ours seemed to trap flies the size of B-29s, that delighted in nipping your under parts in the course of your daily constitutional. They were well vented with stove type chimneys that raised the vapors into the prevailing air stream and carried them away from the camp. Needlessly to say the Navy Sea-Bee's had really taken care of themselves when they built their living quarters and were the best available under the circumstances!

Later I had a refrigerator in the X-5 building where we had support ice and mixes for adult beverages we served to our distinguished guests. This is documented in numerous pictures of our screened in patio The most fun I had was to hop into a jeep, drive to the X-5 building, get a drink with ice and sit in our screened in porch.

My responsibilities on Tinian were twofold.   I was the sole proprietor of a complete electronics maintenance Quonset on the flight line. As everyone who had been in the military knows that the Army cannot operate without orders, paperwork and lots of red tape.   This being the case I had loads of administrative details and paperwork to attend to. My enlisted men were able to draw out most of the equipment we needed but it was up to me and Lieutenant Homa to inventory the equipment, sign for it and have work benches built and the equipment installed.

My other duties were associated with the weapon they took me to a special secure facility that had been set up specifically for this mission. It was known as the "509th Technical Area." This was the place where the technicians and project people would assemble the weapons or "gimmicks" as we affectionately called them.

It had been decided that despite our training back in the states that all of our flight crews would still go through the lead-crew training in the Island. Here the experienced people would bring everyone up-to-date on their experiences over the Empire.   For pilots, navigators and bombardiers this may have been on a formal basis.   But for Radar Countermeasures people it was very informal and usually conducted in someone's Quonset hut. Since I was the new kid on the block they chose my place to get together and talk things over. I suspect the real reason for choosing my place was to look over my equipment to see if I had anything new that they could beg, borrow or steal and secondarily to try to find out something about the real mission of the 509th. Talking with these fellows was a real satisfying experience even though I could not lend them any of my new equipment or tell them anything about our mission. I learned a lot about the Japanese tactics that I could not get elsewhere from people that had been going there several times a week. Intelligence reports are no substitute for getting the information directly from the "horse's mouth."

In off duty hours there was much to see, and many people to meet. I liked to explore the jungle and caves on the Island looking for war souvenirs. On one of these expeditions I had an encounter with one of the Japanese soldiers who was still on the Island. This encounter was grossly exaggerated by a scene in the movie "*The Enola Gay.*" My part in the movie was played by Billy Crystal.

Editor's Note (Jack Spangler): One of the myths about Jacob's experience on Tinian was his experience finding and shooting a Japanese sniper in a cave as was depicted in the movie "The Enola Gay." Jacob and I were at the movie studio in Culver City, CA and along with the movie producer viewed a version of the film before it went to the final editing process. One of the scenes depicted Jake with his 45-caliber pistol hunting for Japanese holdouts and shooting a Japanese soldier in a cave on the island of Tinian. Jake voiced his objection to this scene, as it did not accurately tell what really happen. We were told that yes they realized that but as is the case of many movies it was included to add some more war time excitement into the movie.

I have not found any written account of his encounter with the Japanese soldier but later he told me what really happened. This is how I remember this story:

It seems that one of the favorite pass times for the marines on Tinian was to go into the jungle and mountain caves and search for Japanese holdouts. Jake had traded a quart of good whiskey for a carbine and persuaded a marine patrol to take him with them on one of these nighttime hunting exercises.

The marine sergeant in charge had explained to him the hunt rules. First we surround the area where we think the Jap soldier is hiding.

77

Then we work inward and squeeze him into an area of a few square yards and illuminate the area as best as we can with flashlights. Then we try to convenience him to surrender.

Jake ask the sergeant "and what if he don't?" The marine responded "wait and see."

Two or three times the patrol followed this procedure on suspected locations but found no Japs. They continued to move higher up on the mountain when suddenly the front man stopped. The sergeant ordered Jake to get down on the ground and deployed his men to encircle the suspicious area. Jake released the safety on his carbine and wondered what he would do if a Jap soldier appeared in front of him. He had never killed a man and he wished he had stayed back at the Quonset and played poker.

At this point he heard one of the marines call out in Japanese "You are surrounded. Come out with your hands up."

Moments later he heard a movement and a human grunt. Out of the undergrowth and directly in front of him appeared a Japanese soldier with his hands up. The marine flashlights were all directed on to the soldier's eyes blinding him. The marines came forward to take the soldier prisoner and proceeded to search him. The prisoner then said in English: "Cigarettes please."

Jake gave the man a pack of cigarettes and the prisoner gave him a silver cigarette case in return. In broken English the soldier explained that he had taken it from a dead American soldier in New Guinea. A couple of marines walked beside the prisoner holding his arms behind him to prevent him from trying to escape and took him back to the base.

Now back to Jacob's words.

Now we were really getting ready for the mission we had trained to do. In order to do my job as best as I could I felt it absolutely necessary that I become as familiar as possible with the characteristics of the Japanese radar and other equipment that may radiate radio frequency signals that could interfere with the proper operation of the bomb's radar proximity fuse. I had developed an operational plan that I discussed with Dr. Edward Doll who was my technical contact with the {Manhattan} project. In particular I wanted all the flight crews to know that if I were assigned to their crew I would be adding several antennas and about 300 pounds of equipment to their airplane. Number 2, I wanted as much exposure to the Japanese electronic environment as I could get and as rapidly as I could get it, and Number 3, I wanted to assure myself that I had the procedures that I planned to employ on the mission well thought out and tested.

I also discussed my plans briefly with Colonel Tibbets, and in detail with Colonel Tom Classen, his deputy. Within a week of my arrival on Tinian, Major Hopkins issued orders for me to begin executing my plan.

Editor's Note (Jack Spangler): This brings up an interesting question. The Combined Chiefs of Staff had approved a policy regarding security measures to prevent personnel having knowledge of the details of the future operations from being unnecessarily exposed to risk of capture. According to these orders "such personnel should not participate in flights over the battle zone except in instances of absolute operational necessity." Jacob was the only one in the group to have a personal bodyguard which he attributed to the fact that he had detailed knowledge of the weapon and especially the proximity fuse (which he helped design and test). Therefore, it is logical to assume that this order applied to Beser as well as Tibbets and certain others i.e. Parsons and Ashworth. Why was Jacob allowed to make these flights? Did he convince his superiors that it was an absolute operational necessity that he participated in flights over the battle zone?

The relationships between the 509th and the other groups were not a perfect world. It quickly became obvious that, even though our group had been out here only a short time, we were the butt of many jokes and were being subjected to some ridicule by the rest of the Wing. As time went on there was a lot of sniping and sneering by the other units envious of the special treatment we appeared to be getting. We had better housing accommodations as well as better food and even though we had newer and better planes than they did, we were not flying the dangerous fire bombing missions they were ordered to fly.

One of the local poets expressed his feeling in this little poem that was printed and distributed on the Island:

> *Into the air the 509th crew rose,*
> *Where they're going, nobody knows.*
> *Tomorrow they'll return again,*
> *But we'll never know where they've been.*

Don't ask them about results or such,
Unless you want to get in Dutch.
But take it from one who is sure of the score,
The 509th will win the war.
When the other groups are ready to go,
We have a program for the whole damned show.
And when Halsey's Fifth shells Nippon's shore,
Why shucks, we hear about it the day before.
For MacArthur and Doolittle give out in advance,
But with this new bunch we haven't a chance.
As they tell us we'll be home in a month no more,
For the 509th is winning the war.

At times the show of disdain became more vocal and even some of the crews from other units on their way to the flight line resorted to throwing stones on our tin Quonset huts at night to let us know that they were on their way to the Empire.

Military politics and turf fighting was also obvious from the very moment we arrived on the Island. Generals LeMay and Groves had crossed swords over who would be in charge once the bombs arrived on the Island and were ready for combat use. LeMay 's position was it was "my baby" once it was ready to deliver to the target. Groves thought otherwise. LeMay could not understand why Washington would even consider trusting the new weapon to a unit that had not been fully tested in combat! To assign the responsibility for delivering this 2 billion-dollar bomb to someone else was more than he could swallow. But that was what he was told to do and he had little choice other than to gripe.

Once we got on the Island there was an effort to break up the 509th and reassign the flying and ground crews to other battle seasoned groups that were already on the Island. They cited as their reasons the 509th fliers would benefit from working along side veterans; they needed to plug gaps in crews that had lost men over Japan; and, the ground crews were needed to help keep the flow of flight worthy bombers moving. It appeared to me that reasons cited for breaking up the 509th were more or less excuses. In reality there was a little "military style back stabbing" and meddling by some who felt they were being denied their rightful role in this historic operation fearing "outsiders" were going to get all the credit and recognition for ending the war. I have even been told that at the highest levels our commanding officer, Colonel Tibbets, was challenged and attempts were made to relieve him of his command and responsibilities. I was told that Tibbets really did not want to have to resort to Washington to settle the argument. Instead he challenged LeMay to let him prove his and his crew's proficiency. LeMay accepted Tibbets' offer and assigned his Operations Officer, Colonel Blanchard to go along on a training flight. According to Tibbets, "Blanchard got the thrill of his life when I did the 155 degree diving turn escape maneuver." Blanchard did not speak until he got his feet firmly planted on terra firma and commented "Ok you have proved your point." After this demonstration no one on LeMay's staff challenged Tibbets' or his crew's capabilities.

It was also a known fact that some high ranking officers in the Pacific Theater of Operations, including General MacArthur, were caught by surprise and were miffed that they had not been briefed in advance and allowed to get their "two cents worth" into the mission strategy, planning and execution. After the very successful Hiroshima mission, some of those that had been left out, at least wanted to be photographed with the *Enola Gay* to imply they were participants in the missions that would bring Japan to its knees!

During July we started dropping pumpkins filled with conventional explosives on selected targets in the Japanese held Islands. These hit and run missions gave the pilots, bombardiers and navigators experience they would need when it came time to drop the real thing. The pumpkins were filled with black powder and were not only destructive but also easy to spot the explosion from the air. I went on twelve of these missions moving my equipment around from plane to plane. Since the bombs employed radar proximity fuses I needed to learn as much as I could about the electronic environment over Japan. I also was able to observe and interpret the radar images of the land and city features which came in handy on the Nagasaki mission.

Porter Richardson, a T/Sgt. in Jacob's Radar Section tells the following story about the task of finding a clear range of frequencies to operate the atomic bomb radar proximity fuse:

"Jake Beser had the job of ascertaining a clear range of radar frequencies in which to operate the atomic bomb controls without enemy radar interference. He did this with missions in the "Porcupine B-29" the plane with antennas sticking out all over. Installed in the plane were three radar signal receivers covering the entire range of frequencies used. After every "seek" mission our Radar Countermeasures guys

pulled all three receivers and checked them on the mock-up. Since we figured he was actually interested in scanning a narrow band of frequencies that were designated for the bomb, he would only be using one receiver for the job. Each receiver had a butterfly tuner that was rotated with a small motor. When it passed a signal it could be stopped and made to go back and forth over a tiny range.

The tuner was driven by a metal disc with a little rubber wheel to turn it. How the cloak and dagger part! We took the discs off the receivers and black-smoked them with a candle thus we could tell where the wheel rubbed on the disc.

After the next mission we found that two receivers were not being used at all, and the third only a narrow portion of its bandwidth.

We knew the frequency range with which the bomb would be controlled although we were not supposed to. After that we only checked the unit he was using and with the others still in their racks we logged them as being inspected.

A beneficial side effect of the pumpkin missions was to get the Japanese homeland air defenses use to seeing two or three bombers flying over a target area during daylight hours and dropping only one bomb which did not do the widespread damage caused by mass attack. The tactic seemed to work since they seldom sent up fighter planes to intercept us and their anti-aircraft shells could not reach us at 30,000 feet. In fact they did not send up any fighters for the Hiroshima raid."

In a February 1960 interview Jacob was asked the question: Have you flown any other missions before this one (the bombing of Hiroshima)?

His answer was "Yeah, I did. The Group took its place in a line. We didn't fly with the Twentieth Air Force. We began to practice the maneuver that that would be used for the A-Bomb delivery. We used a different type of bomb but used the same tactic. I flew, oh I've forgotten how may now. I don't know. I had enough to get battle stars."

The interviewer followed up with another question: Five?

To which Jacob replied: "I had more than that."

The next question was: "Were you flying with Tibbets at the time?"

To which Jacob replied: "No. I flew with Ralph Taylor and with, let's see, mostly with Taylor and one mission with Buck Eatherly

During another interview in September 1985 Jacob was asked: "You mean that you evaluate the radar operator—whether he was getting the right--?"

His response was whether he was the guy to do it. See? And on this crew these guys hadn't done a hell of a lot of flying. See, all the rest of us had gone up—Hiroshima was my 13th trip. I had more trips than anybody did because every day the group flew, I moved all my junk on to another airplane because I wanted to be able to do my job right when the time came. And I wanted to get fairly familiar with the electronics environment over Japan. That's what I was there for.

And still in another interview in 1985 Jacob was discussing the Nagasaki mission. During the interview he was quoted as saying: "I had been on about 13 other flights testing and re-testing my electronic equipment. I had more trips than anybody in the Group because every day the 509th flew, I moved all my electronic equipment onto another airplane because I wanted to be able to do my job right when the time came. And I wanted to get familiar with the electronic environment over Japan as well as the radar signatures of ground features. That's what I was there for. I had compared the radar images of the ground features with maps and visual observations. With this experience and my confidence in the advanced electronic equipment that I had selected, I felt confident that I could accurately direct the airplane to the desired target area. Captain van Pelt, the Navigator, Staff Sergeant Ed Buckly, the Radar Operator and Commander Ashworth, the Senior Weaponeer, did not have this experience. The geographic configuration of the port and the city of Nagasaki were such that the radar presentation was clear cut and obvious. I informed the up front crew that if they told me exactly where the AP (Aim Point) was located I could direct them there."

Editor's Note: Later my father gave some of the dates that he had flown both test and combat missions. Test missions were flown on July 1,3,6,7,9 and 14. On July 19,24,26 and 27 combat missions were flown over the Japanese homeland. These dates account for ten of the 13 missions that he indicated that he had flown with only 4 missions over the Empire. Documents uncovered in his personal archive and The 509th History confirms that missions were flown on the dates Jake indicated. It also confirms that all the Captain Taylor flew on all except the July 7 mission.

According to archival documents and transcripts further validated by the *"History of the 509th Composite Group."* "The required training missions in the 313th wing were as follows: a four and a half (4t) hour Instrument Calibration and Orientation flight; an eight (8) hour flight (navigational) to Iwo Jima, returning to Rota for bombing (4-1000 lb. H.E.); a two (2) hour local night missions; two (2) four (4) hour radar and visual bombing missions on Rota (8-500 lb. H.E.); and, a shake down bombing mission on Truk (with 8-1000 lb. H.E.).

On 30 June, the first Group overseas training mission was flown: Instrument Calibration and orientation. Nine aircraft were airborne, after a briefing at 0430, with take-off at 0700, and landing at approximately 1200. The first two hours were spent in instrument calibration and the remaining three in a look at the islands composing the Mariana Group by way of Farallon de Medinilla and return.

On 1 July, training mission #2 was flown nine; (9) aircraft were scheduled and completed the mission as briefed to Iwo Jima and thence to Rota to drop two 1000 lb. H. E. from 25,000 ft. Six (6) of the bombs were dropped by radar, twelve (12) visually, with excellent results. Crews participating were Captain Wilson, Lieutenant McKnight, Lieutenant Westover, Captain Price Captain Eatherly, Captain Bock, Captain Marquardt, and Captain Taylor. Briefings for these missions, and all subsequent missions were held in the theater, with interrogations in the Intelligence Lounge.

Training mission #3 was flown on 3 July, nine (9) aircraft participating, with take-off at 1230 and ETA of 1630, was a bombing practice on Rota. Fifty-four (54) bombs were carried, forty-six (46) dropped on Rota, seven (7) salvoed, and one (1) hung up and was later pried loose. Victor #2 returned early with high oil temperature on engine #1. Results were good to excellent.

Training mission # 4 on 4 July with the same nine (9) crews flying, was a repeat bombing of Rota. Fifty-two (52) bombs were released on the target, two (2) were jettisoned because of a shackle malfunction. Results were good to excellent.

Training mission #5 was run on 5 July with nine (9) crews scheduled, five (5) scratched and four (4) flying. Completing the mission was Captain Bock, Captain Wilson, Lieutenant Westover and Lieutenant McKnight. Bomb load was six (6) 1000 lb. G.P's, briefing at 1530, takeoff at 1800, and ETA of 2400. The target was Moan (N) airfield in the Truk Islands. All four (4) aircraft bombed by radar from 25.000 feet through cloud cover ranging from 1/10th to 8/10th with unobserved results. No fighters were encountered and only three (3) bursts of A.A. were reported.

Then came a flurry of excitement, the Squadron was about to fly combat missions, which accounted for the scratching of five (5) planes on a training mission #5. The target was both runways on Marcus Island. Briefing was at 0530, take-off at 0800, and ETA at 1500, the 6th of July, bomb load was 20-500 lb. G.P., altitude was 20,000 and 20,500 feet. Captain Taylor, Captain Marquardt, and Lieutenant Devore bombed the 112° runway. Results were good to excellent, with ninety eight (98) bombs hitting Marcus, one (1) salvoed and one (1) hung up. No enemy aircraft were encountered and flak amounted to several inaccurate bursts. All crews commented on the difficulties in locating the target and the excellent navigation exhibited.

On the 7th the same mission was flown to Marcus, by Captain Wilson, Lieutenant Westover, Captain Taylor, Captain Bock and Lieutenant Devore, with good results to excellent.

On the 8th, again, Captain Eatherly, Lieutenant McKnight, Captain Marquardt, Captain Price, and Captain Bock bombed Marcus with the same results, good to excellent.

Lieutenant McKnight, Lieutenant Westover, Captain Wilson, Lieutenant Devore, and Captain Taylor bombed Marcus again on the 9th, this time with delayed action 500 lb G.P. bombs, with the usual fusing. Four (4) planes bombed by radar in this mission, with unobserved results, the fifth having excellent results visually.

Then followed a series of bombing practice missions on Rota and Guguan, interspersed with the usual orientation and training missions for the other crews who had finished ground school.

In the meantime July 21st saw Lieutenant Ray and Captain Lewis fly the Marcus mission, which was now only a training mission, much to the disgust of the crews. Both planes bombed visually from 25,000 feet, with good to excellent results, through 5/10 to 8/10 cumulus over the target.

By this time, combat strikes against the Japanese Homeland had gotten under way. Training assumed a place of secondary importance, but continued, nevertheless, throughout the Group's period of overseas operations in the form of practice bombing missions to the several unoccupied islands north of Tinian used for that purpose.

However a series of practice missions interspersed with the usual orientation and training missions for the other crews who had finished ground school in the meantime were flown on Rota and Guguan."

Jacob flew the mission of July 19, 1945 with Captain Taylor. As he recalled later the July 19 mission was especially significant: On 19 July we received orders that "313th will attack Empire Targets with 10 aircraft of the 509th Group on "D-day." Target study classes were again conducted.

Last minute special briefings were held by the staff. At the general briefing, Colonel Tibbets wished the crews well and reminded them that the eyes of the 313th Wing were upon them.

Tibbets had selected the ten crews to fly this mission. Each flew separately, against a pre-selected target. The purpose was to accustom the flight crews to combat, and the Japanese to seeing single high-flying aircraft that dropped only one bomb.

The crews had orders that if their primary targets were socked in by weather, they must under no circumstances drop their pumpkins on Hiroshima, Kyoto, Kokura, or Niigata. Otherwise, their choice of alternative targets of opportunity was unrestricted.

At 0200 (2:00 am) 20 July 1945, the first 509th aircraft were airborne en-route to the Japanese Homeland.

On the way to Japan, one of them had engine trouble and had to jettison its bomb at sea. Five managed to drop their pumpkins in or around their assigned target areas. Four, including the plane piloted by Buck Eatherly, found the weather so bad at their primary target that they were forced to seek alternative targets. Eatherly chose Tokyo and the Emperor's palace. Buck was a maverick cowboy with a "devil may care" attitude. He was completely oblivious to, or ignored, the fact that his plan was not only against the official policy of the United States but also it might strengthen the will to resist of every Japanese citizen. Only one thought concerned Eatherly. If he succeeded, he would be guaranteed a place in history. He believed he might even end the war.

Eatherly circled at thirty thousand feet just south of Tokyo while his navigator plotted a course that would allow the *Straight Flush* to drop its ten-thousand-pound high-explosive bomb directly on the emperor's palace. The navigator, Francis Thornhill, was having trouble. Tokyo, like the original target they had been assigned, was socked in with 10/10 cloud. Bombardier, Ken Wey, said he could see no gaps in the overcast. But Buck commanded him to make a radar drop. He lined up the *Straight Flush* for a radar drop and released the bomb. Eatherly, whooping with excitement, immediately threw the B-29 into a 155-degree turn. Because of the weather conditions he could not see where it hit so he returned to base.

On the afternoon of 20 July 1945 all ten aircraft returned to their home base. The Official Strike Report said: "Five had bombed their primary targets. Three visually and two by radar. Four dropped their bombs on secondary targets— targets of opportunity — by means of radar. The tenth aircraft was forced to jettison its bomb at sea en-route to the target due to an engine failure. The results of the mission were Fair to Unobserved."

The History of the 509th Composite Group also includes the following paragraph: "Another aircraft, finding its primary target completely obscured by clouds, dropping its bomb on Tokyo proper -- the only spot along the route that was open at the time. Some hours later radio Tokyo had this to say: "The tactics of the raiding enemy planes have become so complicated that they cannot be anticipated from experience or the common sense gained so far. The single B-29 that passed over the capital this morning dropped bombs on one section of the Tokyo Metropolis, taking unaware slightly the people of the city, and these are certainly so-called sneak tactics aimed at confusing the minds of the people."

On 23 July the second mission was flown over the Japanese homeland by ten 509th B-29s. Two more Pumpkin strikes over the Japanese homeland were carried out during the closing days of July. On 26 July saw ten 509th aircraft airborne. The targets were in the Nagaoka and Toyama areas.

The mission of 29 July 1945 put eight 509th Pumpkin carrying aircraft over the Japanese Homeland. Nine planes were scheduled to participate but a loading accident grounded one of the planes. The weather was somewhat more favorable for this mission. Four planes bombed their primary targets while four found breaks in the clouds over secondary target areas. All aircraft bombed visually. The results of this strike were officially catalogued as "Effective."

"This then is the summation of the combat efforts of the 509th Composite Group up to the world shaking mission of 6 August 1945."

Near the end of July the activity in the Tech Area had increased markedly with the arrival from Los Alamos of Captain Parsons who had come to Tinian to supervise the final delivery and assembly of the atomic bomb. Also lots of civilians I had met at Los Alamos and Wendover begin showing up. In addition to the American civilians we now had two Englishmen: Group Captain Leonard Cheshire and a scientist, William Penney on site. It was obvious to me that the big mission would be coming soon!

Bomb Assembly Building
Tinian Island 1945

It had been decided earlier the U-235 weapon should be delivered to Tinian by ship as it was thought to be safer than using air transport. In mid July the uranium bomb minus the U-235 target was put abroad the

Navy Captain Parsons
Tinian Island 1945

cruiser USS Indianapolis and arrived at Tinian without incident. On July 27th the U-235 target for "Little Boy" was completed back in the states and began its journey by plane to Tinian. About two days later the target arrived safely on Tinian and final preparations began for delivering the first atomic bomb.

On July 26, 1945 a list of officers who would be on the actual flight teams for the Hiroshima and Nagasaki missions was sent from Tinan to Washington.

Team 1: Captain W. S. Parsons, USN; Colonel Paul W. Tibbets, Aircraft Commander; Captain Robert A. Lewis, Co-pilot; Major Thomas W. Ferebee, Bombardier; Captain Theodore J. Van Kirk, Navigator; and, First Lieutenant Jacob (none) Beser, R.C.M. Officer (added in by hand is) Lieutenant Morris R. Jeppson Elec. OBS.

Team 2: Comdr. F. L. Ashworth, USN; Major Charles W. Sweeney, aircraft commander; First Lieutenant Charles D. Albury Co-pilot; Captain Kermit K. Beahan, Bombardier; Captain James F. Van Pelt, Jr. Navigator; and, added in hand writing, 2nd Lieutenant Phillip M. Barnes,

Elec. OBS

The following day, the names of the electronics weapons officers "weaponeers" who had been chosen for the atomic bombing mission or missions as it might be

a. Team one 2nd Lieutenant Morris R. Jeppson

b. Team two 2ns Lieutenant Leon D. Smith

Editor's Note: My father's name was on the list of officers sent to Washington for the Hiroshima mission but not on the list for Nagasaki mission. Why? It obviously was added later but maybe not sent to Washington. It is logical to assume that to have his name added to the Nagasaki mission list of officers, it probably would have to been approved by General LeMay. My father sometimes told of an incident he had with General LeMay. He quoted General LeMay as saying "Had I had known you were a "kike" I would have never let you flown the mission." Being a feisty and impulsive individuals my father said he was insulted by this ethnic comment and "punched him out." He never explained what "punched him out" meant but knowing my father as I did, I suspect it was verbal as opposed to physical. As far as I know his punishment was minimal if any - no court martial but he never received another promotion. He said he never regretted what he did.

In an interview in 1960 my father was asked why he was still a 1st Lieutenant when he got out of service. His response was: "I was pretty outspoken in some things. A spade is a spade with me, and I called a spade a spade in front of 220 reporters. The guy who was holding that spade didn't like it a bit and he was also holding the pen that could have made me a Captain. But I had no regrets about it."

"The atom bomb was no "great decision." It was merely another powerful weapon in the arsenal of righteousness. "

President Harry Truman

Truman's Controversial Decision

Editor's Note: Another subject my father was very passionate about was President Truman's decision to drop the bomb and his opinion about the decision factors, processes and objectives. These are his words extracted from a 1972 radio interview:

First and foremost, I want everyone to know that I was in complete agreement in 1945 and will be until the day I die that President Truman made the correct decision to use the atomic bombs on Japan. But it is my profound hope that atomic weapons will never again be used.

Each year during the weeks leading up to the anniversary of the first use of the bombs, articles appear in the liberal press decrying the decision to use the new weapon against Japan. More specifically, we see revisionist historians and critics from all over the map, feeding on confusion, crap, and controversy, acting like a pack of jackals attacking a prey. They seem to completely miss, or ignore, the point that we were in a declared and bloody war that had been going on for about four years. As in any war, the objective was to kill the enemy. But be killed or surrender was the option of the Japanese.

These critics, most of who were not even born in 1945, preach moral, ethical and historical reasons for their position. They "cherry pick" and take out of context isolated statements from old documents to support their claims. To paraphrase Churchill: "Never before have so many said so many things on a subject about which they know so little." They try to use hindsight as well as much publicized propaganda of expressions of guilt by the political, scientific and military personnel involved as support for their claims and condemn the wartime decisions. They usually ignore Pearl Harbor or the atrocities committed by the Japanese prior to and during the war and claim that Japan was about to surrender anyway to support their anti-war campaign.

In reality the American people wanted to see the war come to an end as soon as possible. Thousands of American servicemen were being killed or wounded each week. The war was costing the American taxpayers almost a half billion dollars each week[25]. The American people expected their leaders to be decisive and make the hard decisions that had to be made.

The Japanese did not sign or agree with the Geneva Convention rules for warfare and, in their opinion, for good reason. Based on their perspective of warfare they did not expect to take or be taken prisoner, as their code of military conduct required all soldiers to fight to the death. If faced with the prospects of capture the only honorable thing to do was to commit suicide. This code was obvious in the American Island hopping campaign. Using Okinawa as an example about 110,000 Japanese combatants were killed with only about 7000 taken prisoner.

In America, nothing is more natural in the time of war then for our leaders, which we elected to attempt to ensure victory with a minimum loss of life. For our armed forces the extravagant use of firepower was the approach to achieve the desired effect and had been employed from day one. Fire bombing raids on the Empire are good examples. Using the atomic bombs against Japan was simply the ultimate step in this approach. Some people may not want to believe it but those two bombs ended the Pacific conflict in short order.

On the other hand, the Japanese view of warfare was just the opposite of ours. Death in war was not necessarily avoided. The Shinto cult of radical self-sacrifice taught that suicide was glorious while surrender was the ultimate disgrace. Kamikaze planes, one-man suicide submarines and human torpedoes which the Japanese employed by the hundreds against the American ships are good examples of the Shinto cult mentality. When we succeeded in taking Okinawa, not only did the Japanese soldiers commit suicide but thousands of ordinary Japanese civilians did so as well to avoid being captured.

Harry Truman assumed the officer of President on April 12, 1945. Approximately one third of the war casualties in the Pacific occurred during the period of March through August with the majority occurring on President Truman's watch. In addition approximately 900 more were being incurred each week the war continued.

The majority of Americans wanted the war to be brought to a decisive end. Plans for a two-pronged invasion of the Japanese homeland

---

[25] Source: "Principal Wars in which the US Participated: US Military Personnel Serving and Casualties" prepared by Washington Headquarters Services, Directorate for Information Operations and Reports. US Department of Defense Records.

were well underway with the first invasion to occur on November 1. Based on the fierce defense the Japanese had mounted at Iwo Jima and Okinawa, the Allied casualties were estimated at a million or more and perhaps 2 to 3 times that number of Japanese for the total campaign.

I agree that one must sympathize with any legitimate movement designed to reduce or eliminate human slaughter. Nuclear warfare is indeed inhuman and ought to be banned. But, I strongly disagree with anyone who tries to rewrite history. No matter how gruesome, how horrible, or how vicious, what happened has happened! Facts are facts and cannot be changed.

The radicals and modern day pseudo-intellectual historians hold up their hands in horror every time the word atomic bomb is mentioned. Yes, the atomic bomb is a horrible thing and was a quantum leap in power over conventional bombs. Nevertheless, it is misleading to think that the political and military leaders in 1945 did not think about and seriously consider the ramifications of using them. Historical documents show that at the highest levels of government they agonized over the decision and the target selection for days before President Truman, on the advice of his closest advisors, authorized its use. But the order specifically required the bombs to be used only against targets of military significance. Those of us who carried out his orders, like most of the scientist responsible for the bomb development, had no doubt as to the legitimacy of what we were doing. I say this notwithstanding the fact that Bob Lewis, copilot of the *Enola Gay* wrote his reaction in his log as "My God, what have we done!" This statement has received worldwide attention but I'm sure those dramatic words were not spoken. What he really said at the time was "My God, look at that sonofabitch go!" I had installed a recorder at Colonel Tibbets' request on all stations to record everyone's impressions. I turned the tape over to Armed Forces Radio when we landed, and that was the last time I saw it. I know they used it, because I heard it that night.

There remains a question in many people's mind: Why did President Truman order the dropping of the atomic bombs? In my opinion a one word answer is Okinawa. It was done to stop the killing. Still some revisionists claim, without a shred of persuasive evidence, that President Truman used the atomic bombs to impress Joseph Stalin; or to prove his manhood; or the Japanese were defeated before Hiroshima and were willing to surrender; or the invasion of the Japanese homeland would have been better alternative; or, the United States was the aggressor nation and violated the Geneva Convention rules of conduct.

In the summer of 1945, President Truman confronted a death or more death situation. As commander-in-chief, he faced the reality that the war in the Pacific was an endless series of dreadful choices. War is by definition immoral. But once you are in a war, victory is achieved only by destroying the enemy. The only facts that are relevant to a discussion of Truman's decision, are those facts and numbers the president had in front of him in July 1945. The casualties at Iwo Jima and Okinawa were not projections. They were real as memorialized by rows of grave markers and hospital wards filled with broken bodies. In each case, the Japanese military had fought to the death, as they had done everywhere else in the island hoping campaign.

It was apparent to me that the fire bombings of the Japanese cities had produced little effect even though thousands of Japanese civilians had been burned to death. Of course it destroyed their cities but not their morale and will to continue fighting to the very end. The Japanese leadership repeatedly made it abundantly clear of their intentions to continue fighting until the last man, woman and child had been killed. As late as June following the horrible fire bombing of Tokyo the Japanese Cabinet issued this statement: *"With faith born of eternal loyalty as our inspiration, we shall--thanks to the advantages or our terrain and the unity of our nation--prosecute the war to the bitter end in order to uphold our national essence, protect the imperial land, and achieve our goals of conquest."* An invasion of the Japanese mainland was inevitable and President Truman had a very unpleasant decision to make.

Plans for the invasion of the Japanese homeland were in place. The plans called for a two-stage invasion. The southern island of Kyushu would be invaded on November 1, 1945, with a force of 800,000 men. In April 1946, the main island of Honshu would be invaded with a force of over one million men. The wheels of inevitability started to grind forward with a momentum that at some point would be unstoppable unless another way was found to end the war.

In anticipation of the invasion, the Japanese began to fortify the cliffs leading up from the beaches of Kyushu. The terrain would provide the perfect slaughterhouse for the American coming ashore. Those troops who survived the beaches and made it inland would face an intricate network of caves, tunnels, and bunkers. In addition, thousands of airplanes, as well as submarines, were being stockpiled for kamikaze attacks on the invasion fleet and its landing craft. Two and a half million battle-hardened troops, supported by four million able-bodied civilian military employees, were being massed on Kyushu to meet the invasion force. Thirty-two million civilians including women, children, and the elderly were being drilled in the art of resistance and guerrilla warfare.

Based upon these realities, Truman's military advisers predicted that 231,000 to 269,000 American casualties would occur just during the first thirty days of the invasion of Kyushu. Furthermore it was estimated that it would take a hundred and twenty days to secure and occupy the entire island. By the end of that four-month period, American casualties could realistically reach around 395,000. The American to Japanese casualty ratio was one to two. This would suggest 528,000 to 790,000 Japanese casualties. Over one million of our troops still awaited the second prong of the invasion which would take place in April 1946 when they would invade Honshu.

But one must keep in mind that these estimates assumed that all would go according to plan. Yet Okinawa had been expected to fall in two weeks. Instead the battle had dragged into eighty-two days, and even then it took several more weeks after that to secure the island.

As to the Japanese willingness to surrender, Truman was also faced with the reality that the relentless incendiary bombing of Japanese cities had not broken their will to fight on. Also, it had been clear from our intercepts of their secret military and diplomatic codes that a negotiated peace was acceptable to the Japanese only if it left their military in place and allowed them to keep the territory they continued to occupy. They were playing for time where they expected the massive American casualties would gain a more favorable negotiated peace.

These are the facts that President Truman knew.

Basically he had only three options available to induce the Japanese to surrender and minimize casualties on both sides:

Option 1. Continue the fire bombing and blockade.

Truman was not convinced that the B-29 bombing campaign could bring a prompt end to the war. The results of the fire bombing of the Japanese cities to date indicated that this tactic only hardened the Japanese will to fight to the end.

A naval blockade was possible but look at what they would have been up against. Japan had some small ships, submarines and airplanes as well as a million-man army in other parts of Asia still able to fight. With these forces and 5000 or more kamikaze airplanes and thousands of suicide boats and kaitens or human torpedoes on the main islands ready to attack, what would have been the final cost in American servicemen lives? The kamikazes and kaitens had proved very effective at Okinawa. The kaiten was a converted rocket-shaped torpedo about 40 ft. long and about 4 ft. in diameter with a warhead of about 3000 pounds of TNT. Properly placed underwater it had sufficient force to sink any ship we had including the largest battleships and aircraft carriers.

Option 2. Invading the Japanese Homeland.

In Truman's view, the only other alternative was an invasion. The battle for Okinawa was fresh on his mind. In the spring of 1945 the United States took about 49,000 casualties on Okinawa, where it was opposed by a Japanese force a fraction the size of the one waiting in the home islands. An invasion would cause many times that number of casualties on both sides.

Option 3. Use the atomic bomb.

The fire bombing attack on Tokyo in March killed more people than both the Hiroshima and Nagasaki bombs combined. Both American and Japanese casualties were increasing with every day that Japan refused to surrender. Had the bomb been used in March, and shocked Japan into surrender then, it would have saved nearly fifty thousand American plus an untold larger number of Japanese lives. To President Truman, the atomic bomb was his best solution to the death or more death situation that he was facing.

Truman's decision was not only justified by the circumstances at the time but also he was honor bound to use every weapon at his disposal to stop the carnage. Recognizing why the atomic bombs were dropped on Hiroshima and Nagasaki is a critical first step to understanding this important lesson of the history of the war. By examining honestly what happened in 1945, we can understand why the decisions were made. They were not made to be vindictive but to save both American and Japanese lives.

In June and July 1945, Japan attempted, without direct communications with the United States, to enlist the help of the Soviet Union to find a way to end the war. However our American leaders knew of these contacts because for a long time the United States had been intercepting and decoding Japanese diplomatic communications. From these intercepts, the United States learned that some within the Japanese government advocated outright surrender. But the United States also learned that what Tokyo might agree to would not be a surrender but a negotiated peace involving numerous conditions. These conditions would require, at a minimum, that the Japanese home islands remain unoccupied by foreign forces and Japan be allowed to retain some of its wartime conquests in East Asia. Many within the Japanese government were extremely reluctant to discuss any concessions, which would mean that a negotiated peace to them, would only amount to little more than a truce where the Allies agreed to stop attacking Japan. After over three and one-half years of war the American leaders were reluctant to accept anything less than an unconditional Japanese surrender with the one possible exception to this was the personal status of the Emperor himself.

At the Potsdam conference, President Truman and the Allies issued an ultimatum to Japan trying to encourage those in Tokyo to surrender. For those in Japan who advocated peace, the ultimatum provided assurances that Japan eventually would be allowed to form its own government. For those opposed to surrender it contained a stern warnings of "prompt and utter destruction" if Japan did not surrender immediately. Japan publicly rejected the Potsdam Declaration. On July 25, 1945, President Truman gave the order to commence atomic attacks on Japan as soon as possible.

Following the bombing of Hiroshima on August 6, 1945 and Nagasaki on August 9, 1945 the Emperor stepped forward from his normally ceremonial role and personally advocated surrender to the Allies under the terms of the Potsdam ultimatum. However the Japanese Minister of War and the heads of both the Army and the Navy held to their position that Japan should wait and see if arbitration via the Soviet Union might still produce something less than a surrender. They also hoped that if they could hold out until the ground invasion of Japan began, they would be able to inflict so many casualties on the Allies that Japan still might win some sort of negotiated settlement.

On August 10, 1945 after the Nagasaki bombing, Japan offered to surrender to the Allies, the only condition being that the Emperor be allowed to remain the nominal head of state.

On August 12, the United States announced that it would accept the Japanese surrender, making clear in its statement that the emperor could remain in a purely CEREMONIAL capacity only. Debate raged within the Japanese government over whether to accept the American terms and they continued to fight on. Meanwhile, American leaders were growing impatient, and on August 13 conventional air raids resumed on Japan with about 1000 US airplanes participating. Thousands more Japanese civilians died while their leaders delayed. The Japanese people learned of the surrender negotiations for the first time when, on August 14, B-29s showered Tokyo with thousands of leaflets containing translated copies of the American reply of August 12. Later that day, the Emperor called another meeting of his cabinet and instructed them to accept the Allied terms immediately, explaining *"I cannot endure the thought of letting my people suffer any longer"; if the war did not end "the whole nation would be reduced to ashes."*

On August 15, 1945, the Emperor's broadcast announcing Japan's surrender was heard via radio all over Japan. For most of his subjects, it was the first time that they had ever heard his voice. The Emperor explained that *"the war situation has developed not necessarily to Japan's advantage,"* and that

Signing the Japanese Surrender

"the enemy has begun to employ a new and most cruel bomb." Over the next few weeks, Japan and the United States worked out the details of the surrender, and on September 2, 1945, the formal surrender ceremony took place on the deck of the USS Missouri.

Why Were Hiroshima and Nagasaki
Selected as Targets?

Editor's Note: Based on the notes, documents and outlines discovered in my father's archives, he wanted to clarify the following factors about target selection. This chapter is our summation not his exact words.

The decision to use the atomic bombs was made at the highest levels of the government and was not made without giving careful thought to the consequences. President Truman and his advisers were well aware of the possible adverse reaction to the use of an atomic bomb and the mass destruction it would cause. They also knew that the scientists who had developed the bomb were divided on the question of whether it actually should be used. They considered and rejected a number of other alternatives that included, but not limited to, a demonstration of the weapon destructive power; a naval blockade or an invasion of the Japanese homeland; and, continuing the air war. In the end President Truman made the final decision to go ahead and use the bombs.

Once the decision was made to go ahead and use the bombs the question of target selection arose. The cities of Koyoto, Hiroshima, and Kokura in that order were first considered as primary targets for A-Bombing. Koyoto was a city of great historical significance and removed from the list and replaced by Nagasaki. Later Niigati replaced Kokuru. In order to be able to do a better bomb damage assessment these cities were spared the massive B-29 raids that had hit other military targets. Had the A-Bombs not been used, the people of Hiroshima and Nagasaki would not have been spared. They were both prime military targets and certainly would have been destroyed by air attacks using conventional high explosives or incendiary bombs.

The military importance of Hiroshima and Nagasaki were detailed in the Field Orders issued 6 and 9 August 1945 by Headquarters, 509th Composite Group on Tinian Island. Appropriate parts of these orders have been reproduced below. (See Appendix 3).

Extracted from 509th Composite Group Field Orders # 13
6 August 1945

HIROSHIMA MISSION TARGETS SELECTED FOR ATTACK
A. Primary Target: - Hiroshima Urban Industrial Area
B. Secondary Target - Kokura Arsenal and City.
C. Tertiary Target - Nagasaki Urban Area
Mitsubishi Steel and Arms Works

REASONS FOR TARGET SELECTION
Of the four cities set aside for Atomic Bomb attack, Niigata was discarded because it was so poorly laid out for this sort of an attack - the industrial concentration and the residential small factory were relatively widely separated. Of the other three Nagasaki was the poorest of the layouts, and it had a prisoner of war camp nearby so it was made tertiary. The other two - Hiroshima and Kokura were well laid out and relatively important, but Kokura had a prisoner of war camp and Hiroshima had none to our knowledge so Hiroshima was made the primary.

As for the target itself, Hiroshima was highly important as an industrial target. Prior to this attack, Hiroshima ranked as the largest city in the Japanese homeland (except Kyoto) which remained undamaged following a wave of B-29 incendiary strikes. The city had a population of 344,000 in 1940.

It is an army city - headquarters of the 5th Division and a primary port of embarkation. The entire northeastern and eastern sides of the city are military zones. Prominent in the north-central part of the city are the Army Division Headquarters marked by the Hiroshima Castle, numerous barracks, administration buildings and ordnance store houses. In addition, there are the following important military targets:

A. Army Reception Center
B. Large Military Airport
C. Army Ordnance Depot
D. Army Clothing Depot
E. Army Food Depot
F. Large Port and Dock Area
Q. Several Ship Yards and Ship Building Companies
H. Japan Steel Company
I. Railroad Marshalling Yards
J. Numerous Aircraft Component Parts Factories

The fact that Hiroshima was undamaged made it an ideal target. This was deemed necessary to assess correctly the damage which could be

100

inflicted by the Atomic Bomb. The size of Hiroshima was another important factor in the selection. According to preliminary data, it was believed that the radius of damage which could be inflicted by the Atomic Bomb was 7,500 feet. By placing the aiming point in the center of the city the circle of prospective damage covered almost the entire area of Hiroshima with the exception of the dock area to the south.

Extracted from 509th Field Orders # 17
9 August 1945

NAGASAKI MISSION

In accordance with the plans expressed in Report Number 1C, 509th Composite Group, page 34, paragraph 1, i.e. the effort would be made to launch two Atomic attacks within a short period of time for psychological as well as tactical reasons. Mission #16 was planned for 9 August 1945 - three days after the first atomic attack against Hiroshima. The planning of Mission #13 had manifested itself to be one of the most successful battle plans of this headquarter and the results of the Hiroshima mission as a strategic operation approached perfection. For this reason the Nagasaki attack was patterned after our first successful assault against Hiroshima. In fact for most phases of this second operation actual allusions were made to Field Orders #13. (See Report Number 1, 509th Composite Group, page 1, paragraph 1.)

TARGETS SELECTED FOR ATTACK
    A. Primary Target: Kokura Arsenal and City
    B. Secondary Target: Nagasaki Urban Area.
    Mitsubishi Steel and Arms Works,

REASONS FOR TARGET SELECTION
    Since the mission against Hiroshima was so successful, Kokura and Nagasaki remained as the next two logical targets for attack. Niigata could not practically be assigned as a tertiary target because it was too far removed from the other two targets. (See Report Number 8, 509th Composite Group, page 41, paragraph 3,)

    A. KOKURA ARSENAL AND CITY. Kokura is a city of 168,000

people located on northern Kyushu near the industrial center of Yawata. This target is three miles by two miles in size and has many valuable industrial targets. The aiming point is the Kokura Arsenal which is one of the largest Japanese Arsenals and probably the most important in Japan for the manufacture of light automatic weapons and the smaller type AA and AT guns. It also manufactures combat vehicles. Production rates are unknown at an arsenal with such diverse activities as this plant, but probably include several thousand machine guns of all types per month. The arsenal is known to produce 6.5 mm and 7.7 mm HMGs, 7.7 mm HMGs, 20 mm AA/AT guns and ammunition. It is reported to be equipped to mix poison gas, to load gas shells, and to store these shells underground. The most essential processes of this plant are the machining and assembly of ordnance. Forging and pressing are also essential. Damaged machine tools would be difficult to replace and would cause production loss extending over several months. Damage to the assembly facilities and work in process would be quickly felt though probably less serious in the long run than destruction of the specialized machinery of which Japan is believed to be critically short.

B. NAGASAKI URBAN AREA. Like the other two industrial cities, Hiroshima and Kokura, the selection of the city of Nagasaki as a target for the atomic bomb was threefold. Those reasons were:
1. Industrial importance.
2. Undamaged, totally virgin territory.
3. Size of the city.
Nagasaki is one of Japan's leading shipbuilding and repair centers. Nagasaki is also important for its production of naval ordnance and its function as a major military port. Outstanding among the city's objectives is the concentration of Mitsubishi Heavy Industries shipbuilding and repair facilities comprising a shipyard (Target 544), dockyard (Target 543) marine engine works (Target 829). These are located on the western side of the harbor within an area measuring about 6,500 feet NNE-SSW by 2,000 feet.

The Mitsubishi Steel and Arm "Works (Target 546) and its new rolling mill (Target 1795), located along the Urakami River in northern Nagasaki are integrated with the shipyards-producing ship plate, castings, forgings, etc., as well as naval ordnance (principally torpedoes). A wood-working plant with extensive timber and lumber storage is located just to the south of the rolling mill. It supplies lumber and wooden fittings to the shipyards.

The Kawanami Industry Company Shipyard (Target 860) located on Koyagi Island to the south of the harbor entrance, is believed to be an important producer of medium size cargo vessels. While the production of marine engines and boilers is reported at this yard, it is believed that much of these are supplied by the Hayashi Commercial Company Engine Works (Target 823), which is located at the head of Nagasaki Harbor, Koyagi Island is also the site of several groups of small beehive coke ovens. Other small ovens and a minor ship repair yard are located on the mainland, just east of Koyagi Island.

The eastern side of Nagasaki Harbor contains all the important loading and storage facilities. Its southwestern location has made this a primary embarkation and supply port for operations on the mainland, and the docks and freight yards (Target 1842) are believed to be congested with military supplies. Numerous reports refer to large-scale expansion of dock and storage facilities, and the entire waterfront is lined with storehouses. The shore to the south of the dock area is lined with small shipyards, equipped with shops, foundries, slipways and a patent slip. These yards build small wooden cargo vessels, shipping vessels, lifeboats, etc.

Several groups of fuel tanks are located at Kozeki and Megami Points (Targets 545 and 832), at the harbor entrance, While important in the aggregate, these storage's are small individually and are widely dispersed. Other small storages are reported scattered on several of the small islets near the harbor entrance and at the head of the harbor.

Three unidentified factories are located along the railway to the north of the Mitsubishi Steel and Arms Works (Target 546). Of these, the northern most appears especially significant, comprising some 8/10 shop-type buildings the largest measuring about 900 feet by 400 feet a power plant and several storage buildings. The total area occupied by buildings measures 2,000 feet by 1,500 feet. The plant's general layout and appearance suggests either a very large textile mill or a major assembly plant. In view of Japan's excess textile capacity and the fact that this plant was built after 1940, it is probably not a textile mill. Reports mention new munitions plants in this area. An aircraft engine factory at Nagasaki also has been reported and it is also possible that this plant might be an engine works supplying the Omura Naval Aircraft Factory (Target 1627), located some 15 miles to the northeast. However, no engine test stands can be identified here, although at least six are visible at Omura.

Nagasaki occupies a very limited, amphitheatre like site, extending from reclaimed land along the waterfront to the lower slopes of the surrounding hills. Small strips of built-up districts extend along the valleys to the east and along both sides of the Urakami River to the north. Other built-up areas extend down the western side of the harbor to Akunoura. In Nagasaki proper, commercial and public buildings are concentrated along the eastern and central parts of the city. Densely grouped houses crowd these buildings and extend in an almost solid mass to the hills. Four rivers and canals and a few wide streets constitute the only substantial firebreaks. It should be noted that all important industrial installations are located outside the city proper.

Another factor which entered into the selection of Nagasaki as a target was the fact that it was almost virtually untouched by previous bombings, although the Far Eastern Air Force did run one mission against the city. Little damage was inflicted on that strike. The size of the city made it ideal for an atomic bomb attack. The city is the third largest on the island of Kyushu with a population of 253,000 persons, ranking behind Fukuoka and Yawata. The city, at its broadest points, measures approximately five miles from north to south by five miles from east to west. The city is built on a horseshoe-like pattern around the prominent, Nagasaki Harbor. The aiming point was placed east of Nagasaki Harbor in the commercial district of the city. Based upon a 7,500 feet radius, it was believed that an accurate blow would destroy the bulk of the city east of the harbor and possibly carry across to the western shore.

PART 3 The Final Blow is Delivered

"War is cruelty and you cannot refine it"
William Tecumsch Sherman

"I do not want American's to die for their country, make the others die for their country."
General George Paton

Little Boy - Hiroshima Bomb

Fat Man - Nagasaki Bomb

B. 90.36 NAGASAKI URBAN AREA. Like the other two industrial cities, Hiroshima and Kokura, the selection of the city of Nagasaki as a target for the atomic bomb was threefold. Those reasons were:

1. Industrial importance.

2. Undamaged, totally virgin territory.

3. Size of the city.

Nagasaki is one of Japan's leading shipbuilding and repair centers. Nagasaki is also important for its production of naval ordnance and its function as a major military port.

Outstanding among the city's objectives is the concentration of Mitsubishi Heavy Industries shipbuilding and repair facilities comprising a shipyard (Target 544), dockyard (Target 543), marine engine works (Target 829). These are located on the western side of the harbor within an area measuring about 6,500 feet [...] by 2,000 feet.

The Mitsubishi Steel and Arms Works (Target 546) and its new rolling mill (Target 1795), located along the Urakami River in northern Nagasaki are integrated with the shipyards-producing ship plate, castings, forgings, etc., as well as naval ordnance (principally torpedoes). A wood-working plant with extensive timber and lumber storages is located just to the south of the rolling mill. It supplies lumber and wooden fittings to the shipyards.

The Kawanami Industry Company Shipyard (Target 860) located on Koyagi Island to the south of the harbor entrance, is believed to be an important producer of medium-size cargo vessels.

Page 47 from a formerly classified document that discusses the target selection process and gives the reasons why Nagasaki was selected as a target city. Other pages in the document continue to identify the numbered military and industrial complexes that were considered high priority military targets. The aim point was placed east of Nagasaki harbor in the commercial district of the city.

The Japanese Were Warned in Advance

Editor's Note: Again back to my father's words:

For the benefit of those not familiar with World War II history, I will recount some of pertinent facts, as I knew them to exist in 1945.

Almost everyone knows something, either facts or fiction, about the atomic bomb destruction of Hiroshima and Nagasaki. But few are aware that the early B-29 high altitude raids on the Empire used conventional fragmentation bombs. The damage done by these air raids was considered to be too little and our losses to were high.

In late spring and early summer of 1945 the bombing tactics changed. Instead of the planes simply carrying fragmentation bombs, they started to carry a mix of incendiaries and fragmentation bombs.

These new tactics began in March 1945 with the bombing of Tokyo. On the first raid, pathfinder planes dropped napalm bombs every 100 feet to make an "X" on the ground, a target for the rest of the planes to attack. The results as reported by the Japanese, was over 80,000 dead in the attack; over 40,000 wounded; and, a total of 15.8 square miles of the city burned to ashes with the destruction of 265,171 buildings.

The June 4, 1945 issue of Newsweek reported: "Six weeks ago Tokyo had a population of nearly 7,000,000. Last week the Japs cried that Tokyo no longer existed as a city. Using new techniques and new bombs, the largest fleets of B-29s ever to take the air and turned most of the Japanese capital into ashes in two great strikes on May 24 and 26. For 105 minutes the super fortresses filed over and dropped 700,000 incendiary bombs. Two nights later a force of more than 500 B-29s struck the Marunouchi district, the business heart of the Japanese Empire. On a target area of approximately 9 square miles the B-29s dropped 4,000 tons in one hour. The wind did the rest."

In July of 1945, in an attempt to demoralize the Japanese citizens, our bombers dropped leaflets on a number of Japanese cities warning them that they could be next. In the next few days six cities were firebombed. Despite the warnings and thousands of civilian casualties, their military leaders wanted to keep fighting.

One of the leaflets is shown here.

ENGLISH TRANSLATION OF JAPANESE ON THE LEAFLET

"In the next few days the military installations in some or all of the cities named on the photograph will be destroyed by American bombs. These cities contain military installations and workshops or factories which produce military goods. The American Air Force, which does not wish to injure innocent people, now gives you warning to evacuate the cities named and save your lives. America is not fighting the Japanese people, but is fighting the military clique which has enslaved the Japanese people. The peace, which America will bring, will free the people from the oppression of the military clique and mean the emergence of a new and better Japan. You can restore peace by demanding new and good leaders who will end the war. We cannot promise that only these cities will he among those attacked, but some or all will be. So heed this warning and evacuate these cities immediately."

After the bombing of Hiroshima, thousands of leaflets were dropped on Japanese cities. Our leaders had hoped the Japanese people would evacuate their cities as instructed. This would not only save thousands of lives but would also disrupt war production in the factories that were concentrated in cities. Furthermore they hoped that a popular citizens revolution against continuing the war would take place and force the Tokyo officials to sue for peace according to requirements of the Potsdam Declaration.

Unfortunately time was too short for it to succeed. Moreover, Japanese military authorities controlled the government, and only another nuclear bombing, that of Nagasaki, enabled the Emperor to prevail against them.

After Nagasaki was bombed additional thousands of leaflets were dropped. In 1945 I had annotated this example shown on the following page with the dates that they were dropped.

A portion of another leaflet dropped on Japan on August 7, 1945 after the first bomb was dropped on Hiroshima is shown here.

English Translation

America asks that you take immediate head of what we say on this leaflet

We are in possession of the most destructive explosive ever devised by man. A single one of our newly developed Atomic Bombs is actually equivalent in explosive power to what 2,000 of our giant B-29's can carry on a single mission. This awful fact is one for you to ponder and we solemnly assure you it is grimly accurate.

We have just begun to use this weapon against your homeland, if you have any doubt, make inquiry as to what happened to Hiroshima.

You should take steps now to cease military resistance. Otherwise we shall resolutely employ this bomb and all our superior weapons to promptly forcefully end the war.

109

THIS A WARNING TO THE JAPANESE PEOPLE!
LEAVE THIS CITY IMMEDIATELY!

The contents of this flyer are very important. The Japanese people are facing a very significant change. Your Military rulers were presented the opportunity to stop this pointless war in the Thirteen Articles of the Joint Resolution. Your Military Rulers refused. For this reason the Soviet Union has declared war on Japan. Further, the United States has invented and tested a most formidable weapon, the atomic bomb, even though it was thought impossible. This atomic bomb, alone, is as destructive as the usual bomb load of two-thousand B-29's.

You will know this is true when you have seen the devastation caused by only one atomic bomb dropped on Hiroshima. The Japanese military is causing this pointless war to continue, so we are going to destroy them with this fearsome weapon. Before the United States uses many of these atomic bombs on Japan we wish the Japanese people will accept these articles very soon, become a peace loving people and build a new Japan. The Japanese people must stop their military resistance now. If you do not stop this war the United States will be forced to use the atomic bomb and other superior military weapons.

LEAVE THIS CITY IMMEDIATELY!

Dropped @ 8/12-14/45

110

Hiroshima Mission

Editor's note: This chapter contains the most recent description of the Hiroshima mission created by my father to prepare for a Dundalk Community College Documentary film interview. This information was extracted from the film.

Hiroshima mission was perfectly planned and executed. The more important details have been thoroughly told and discussed in various books and articles by both the scientists who had participated in the development and others who had participated in the delivery mission. I will not go into a lot of detail here other than to describe what I saw, heard, and my reactions during these historical events.

As the anticipated August 3rd date for the Hiroshima mission approached, concerns developed about the ability of the *Enola Gay* to get off the ground safely. It was still not unusual for a B-29 engine to catch fire on take off and blow up on the runway. No one knew what might happen if by some circumstance the *Enola Gay* failed on take off successfully and crashed and burned on North Field. Consideration was even given to evacuating the island before the *Enola Gay* was scheduled to take off. However, some months before a two-piece breech plug for the bomb had been designed. The larger piece was an outer ring-shaped plug that screwed into the threads in the breech end of the gun tube. A smaller inner plug, containing the primers and firing leads for igniting the propellant, screwed into threads in the center of the outer plug. The inner plug, about three inches in diameter could easily be inserted by hand. This loading system provided a convenient and safe method of loading the explosive components at nearly the last moment and had been used many times in earlier tests back in the States.

The bomb itself had never been tested. Undoubtedly, if the plane crashed on take off, the conventional high explosive charges would explode and destroy the aircraft. But would there be a nuclear explosion? No one really knew. If it did, it would destroy most of the island and certainly the entire atom bomb project.

Captain Parsons was seriously concerned. He had been in charge of the bomb construction from day one. He was the "Bomb Commander" and had helped design the gun from the beginning, including the procedure for loading its high explosive charges. The time was rapidly approaching when he would have to load it for real.

111

According to the plan he had written, the bomb would be loaded into the delivery aircraft at the bomb pits. Parson's himself would load the "gun" with the high explosive packages that would propel the atomic bullet at its atomic target at sufficient speed to create the critical mass necessary to create an atomic explosion. This was to be done, of course, on the ground, under controlled conditions, before the bomb was loaded into the aircraft.

Captain Parsons had arrived on Tinian six weeks before to make sure that everything was being properly prepared. Almost daily, he read reports of B-29's that had crashed and burned on take-off or splashed into the ocean just off the edge of the reef. Between the six different runways that were used to launch B-29s against Japan, Parsons saw the wreckage of failures. Each plane meant eleven men dead.

Responsibility for the bomb had been made clear in a message by General Norstad and Captain Parsons had that responsibility. With the approval of General Farrell, Captain Parsons chose to arm the bomb after the plane was safely airborne.

This involved a major problem because the breech block as provided then was much too heavy for one person to handle in the confines of the bomb bay, thus precluding the loading of the powder charge once successfully airborne. Captain Parsons suggested the fabrication of a secondary breech block to be installed in the primary breech block of the gun[26]. This would be of minimum size to reduce its weight but still be sufficiently large to accept the powder charge.

The new breech block assembly arrived on Tinian a day or two before the Hiroshima operation. Under Parson's direction a small folding platform was installed at the rear of the *Enola Gay* bomb bay. On this platform, Parsons and Lieutenant Morris Jeppson, his weaponeer and electronics officer would load the high explosive charge into Little Boy after the *Enola Gay* was winging its way to Hiroshima. Nearly all day of

---

[26] Editor's Note: Little Boy was essentially a 5-inch gun barrel. The U-235 material was contained in two physically separated hemispheres to prevent such an inefficient "pre-detonation." To initiate a sustained chain reaction one hemisphere, the projectile, was "shot" in the gun with sufficient velocity to impact the other hemisphere, the target, and create a critical mass. A gun barrel about ten feet long was built and a powder charge developed which would provide the necessary velocity for the projectile to impact the target and "go critical". In the final design the target was also surrounded by a mass of U-238 to act as a tamper and contain the chain reaction as long as possible.

August the fifth Captain Parsons and his assistant Lieutenant Morrie Jeppson practiced loading the powder charge through the secondary breech block and making the proper connections for the detonators. Then on the day of the operation, using the detailed check off list that they had developed the day before, they would insert the powder charge after we were airborne and safely away from the air field. This was the so-called arming of the bomb that has been so frequently mentioned in connection with the Hiroshima attack operation.

Because he had the weapon responsibility, the decision to partially disassemble and reassemble bomb in flight was Parson's decision to make. Between Captain Parsons and his assistant Lieutenant Jeppson there was enough electronics savvy available so that at no time did I feel that I was out there all alone. Jeppson had been an underclassman when I graduated from Aviation Cadets, and his training followed the same path as mine - he was trained in the application, use, and maintenance of Airborne Radar.

The arming of the bomb was to take place about half an hour before the bomb was dropped. According to Morrie Jeppson: "my last job was to climb into the bomb bay and remove those three testing plugs painted green. Those plugs isolated the testing system from the bomb, so there was no chance of any voltage getting from the bomb to the testing system. I pulled those plugs and put in three red firing plugs to arm the bomb. From that point on, the bomb was running itself."

Enola Gay
Tinian Island 1945

113

For two days the *Enola Gay* sat on her hard stand, loaded and ready. A great stir of mystery surrounded the ship. Only a selected few were allowed near her. Even fewer knew her load or her mission. The crew had been given a preliminary briefing on Saturday afternoon, August 4. But even they did not know which target of three they were going to hit nor what a terrific load of destruction they were to carry. All they knew was that this mission would probably be the most talked of mission of the Pacific war if all went well and if all didn't go well - they just never thought of that. For all of them, combat was not new. Several of their number had previous tours in the European and North African theaters. The remainder (with a couple exceptions) counted their missions on the fingers of one hand. But all had confidence in their leaders and in each other. On Sunday afternoon word was received that the weather over Japan was clearing and that by Monday morning conditions would be right for a daylight visual raid. These were the conditions that were necessary to do the job and at once the wheels began to turn. Operations orders were cut, the crew was given a final briefing and all was made ready for a pre-dawn take-off. At midnight a final briefing was held and final instructions given the flight crew. Colonel Tibbets reminded us to wear the safety goggles when instructed. Then he spelled out the rules to follow - do your jobs, obey your orders and don't cut corners. This was followed by the weather officer going over the weather forecast en-route and over the target conditions. The communications officer followed with the radio frequencies to be used for various phases of the mission and gave the position of the rescue planes, ships and submarines if they were needed. Tibbets then reviewed his instructions to the navigator, bombardier, tail gunner, flight engineer, and radioman. At this point he told us that our call sign for this mission would be "Dimples 82." The chaplain offered a prayer and we were dismissed.

I briefed Dr. Doll on the results of my electronic environment searches over the Empire. I had not detected any Japanese equipment using the frequencies that we would be using for the bomb's radar proximity fuse. He informed me that he would give me the exact frequencies prior to takeoff.

From midnight until H-hour the *Enola Gay's* parking stand looked like a section of Broadway on opening night. Hugh banks of floodlights gleamed down on the *Enola Gay* and her crew as they made ready for take-off. Flash bulbs popped as the still photographers went about their job of taking pictures for posterity. Above all, there were "well-wishers" present from all the rank. Privates and Generals rubbed shoulders with each other, all crowding around the crew to wish them God Speed. Also present was a large staff of scientists who were responsible for the creation and development of the new weapon. They were just as eager to go on the mission as was the combat crew, but the *Enola Gay* could carry only so many, so all but a chosen few of their number had to remain behind. As H-hour approached the crowd began to move back. Dr. Doll handed me a piece of rice paper on which he had written the frequencies to be used and informed me to eat it if that became necessary. The crew entered the *Enola Gay* and took up their stations. All was now ready for the long flight to the Empire of Japan to begin.

H-hour, 0346 (3:46 am), Monday, August 6, 1945, had arrived. The *Enola Gay* was poised on the western edge of the runway. At precisely forty-six minutes after the hour of three in the morning her engines began to roar. As she took off into the night she had aboard a crew of confident men and left behind the well wishes of the men of the Air Force and even the entire nation.

I had not slept for 27 hours before we left Tinian for Hiroshima and it was not caused by beer boozing or carousing the night before. It was that I had a lot of hard work that had to be done before we left.

When I had finished my work I had fully intended to get some sleep before we left. But just before leaving for my bunk I was called to report to Colonel Tibbits' office immediately. There he introduced me to Bill Laurence senior science editor for the New York Times. He told me that Bill had been loaned to the War Department to do all the press releases for our project. He also felt that Bill and I had a lot in common and that I would be a good companion for him for the next several hours. I interpreted this to mean, "please keep him occupied and out of my hair."

So much for getting any sleep before the mission. Instead I learned a lot. Bill spoke in a very heavy Russian Jewish accent and had a mind that could comprehend the most complicated scientific theory and reduce it to simple layman's language. I assumed that Bill must have known what was going on and I think he assumed the same about me otherwise Colonel Tibbets would not have selected me to accompany him. He had questions but I hid behind the veil of security and didn't provide him anything specific that I couldn't have done anyway. I simply told him that I could listen but could neither confirm nor deny! I did provide him with some

115

unclassified information. As it turned out my descriptions and words were used in his description of the Manhattan Project that won him a Pulitzer Prize for his work.

We had just gotten the wheels off the ground when I went up forward to talk to Parsons. When I got back I used my parachute as a pillow and went to sleep and was awakened when we neared Iwo Jima.

Just after dawn tiny Iwo Jima appeared right on course. All was well on board. The weather up until then had been somewhat better than the briefing officer had said it would be. That was promising. Everyone now waited to hear the radio operator notify the pilot that they had contact with the weather reconnaissance planes that had preceded us by one hour. Then the decision would be made as to which target would be hit. The weather report was scheduled for nine fifteen. It came through right on time. Primary target was open. Hiroshima was it. The course was altered to fly to Hiroshima.

We started the climb to bombing altitude and I fired up my search receivers looking for enemy radar signals. Around 300 miles off the coast I begin to pick up early warning radar signals. I soon determined that they were tracking us and I started listening to their radio command channels. I could not understand the language but I could tell the difference between airborne and ground channels and if they were sending fighters up after us. No fighters came up and we approached the target area unopposed.

The weather over central Honshu was beautiful that fateful morning, as if especially ordered so as not to interfere with our mission plan. There was a minimum of conversation over the interphone once we left Iwo Jima for the selected target area; an occasional steering correction from the navigator to the pilot, or a response from the flight engineer to a question from the pilot. Once in a while the pilot would ask the tail gunner if the two B-29s going with us with instrumentation and cameras were still in sight.

As we neared the target area Colonel Tibbets advised the crew that the moment of truth would soon be upon us. We were about to enter the critical phase of our mission. We were about to deploy our first "Gimmick," as the bomb was know to us. He reminded me that I was to record the interphone conversation and that this recording would become a "historical document, so keep it clean, fellows!"

Editor's Note: *This recording was made but was lost in 1945 and was recently found (2006).*

The *Enola Gay* was now on the bomb run. The navigation had been perfect. When the bombardier sighted the target he had to give one minor course correction. All was tense. No one spoke except the bombardier to the pilot. His reply was a terse "Roger."

The navigator informed the bombardier as we approached and arrived at the Initial Point of the bomb run. As the briefed aiming point was acquired in the bombsight's tracking telescope the bomb-bay doors were opened. A tone signal was initiated on the command radio informing the escort aircraft that the bomb drop was about to occur.

Hiroshima August 6, 1945 After Bomb Exploded

The *Enola Gay* lurched as on an up draft as it lightened when the bomb was released. The air operated bomb-bay doors were slammed shut and the violent escape maneuver was initiated - turn hard to the right for 155 degrees; lose about 3000 feet in altitude; and, put as much distance between us and the explosion as was possible before it happened.

In what seemed an eternity, although it was less than a minute, a brilliant flash of light appeared. The flash was followed after a noticeable interval by the shock wave and reflected shock wave of the explosion down below. The airplane lurched as if it had come into contact with a cumulus cloud.

117

The interphone was momentarily quiet, then the New Jersey accented voice of Captain Robert Louis was heard to shout, "My God! look at that sonofabitch go"! The story is often told that Bob entered in his diary "My God what have we done." I'm sure those dramatic words were not spoken but what I heard him say over the interphone is what he really said. But there were many things happening at the time including guys running around to the windows to watch for fighters so we'll let history speak for itself. When the interphone recording is found we'll really know what he said!

The airplane was now circling the target area giving one and all aboard a chance to observe what had happened. Colonel Tibbets then informed the crew that they had seen history's first Atomic Bomb in action. As I recorded the conversation with a specially designed disk lathe, he queried each and every man aboard for his reaction. The reactions ranged from astonishment to disbelief. When I was able to get to the window to see out, I never saw the city of Hiroshima. I saw the mushroom cloud that had climbed above our flight level and beneath it was a churning, boiling mass of flame and debris that only minutes before had been a thriving city, vital to Japan's plans for resisting the invasion that they knew had to come. The scene was so bizarre that it defied belief. It was difficult to comprehend that one airplane and one bomb had created all of the havoc that was so apparent. We had truly opened the door to a new era of man's inhumanity to his fellow man. We were able to continuously see the mushroom cloud for over two hundred miles as we withdrew from the target area to return to our base on Tinian, in the Marianas Islands.

No event has so stirred the human mind nor aroused such a diversity of opinion as this one single event in human history. To even the most casual observer, the death and destruction at Hiroshima had to be enormous and beyond comparison to any other single aircraft assault in the whole of World War II. For myself, my frame of reference was very limited. I had been over Japan on single aircraft sorties on numerous occasions where we had dropped a bomb shaped like the Nagasaki bomb but loaded with 6-7000 pounds of high explosive. The explosions of these blockbuster bombs were massive and would destroy an entire smelter or chemical plant or even a local neighborhood.

When the flash of light had disappeared, all hands rushed to the windows to observe what had happened. What their eyes beheld was almost unbelievable. There below, where just a few minutes before had lain the seemingly quiet and peaceful town of Hiroshima, was now a mass of furiously boiling smoke and flame the likes of which none of them had ever seen. And climbing much higher than our flight level was a huge

118

mushroom of white smoke filled with fire and explosions. At the same time all on board realized that they had witnessed the unveiling of a new and terrible weapon which might very easily end the war.

I must admit that I was a little slow in getting up from my operating position. When we were over the target we all had flak suits on. It was heavy and hard to move around in. I had it draped around and was sitting on part of it. By the time I got it cleared off and I got to the window the cloud was already up to our altitude and the city was a mass of flames. The cloud to me looked something like being at the seashore and stirring up sand in shallow water to see it billow up. I was not mentally prepared for the sight below. Besides the mushroom cloud, I could see more fires breaking out all around the periphery. It was of such a magnitude that it could have easily caused one to "go over the edge." But, I am a member of a survivor group of people that throughout the millennia of history had been subjected to every extreme form or mental torture and physical cruelty. It was my Judaic ancestry and knowledge of Jewish history that had given me the survivor's inner strength to accept what I saw below. It was immediately obvious that we humans now had within our grasp the power to self-destruct and be removed completely from the face of the earth. We must now accept a new reality that must change the way we cope with one another. Ultimately the human race must make warfare, as an instrument of government, as obsolete as the ancient sling-shot and battering ram.

Just as we were leaving the coast of Japan a couple of Japanese fighters were spotted. I was up front talking with Parsons and Jeppson when we got the fighter alert and I was stuck up there without a parachute. Tibbets said, "stay here" and he would not let me go crawling back to my station. In about two minutes the fighters broke away and did not bother us.

As we returned to Tinian, Tibbets put the *Enola Gay* in cruise control to minimize fuel consumption and we were in a long powered glide all the way back to Tinian. During this time I thought back to the briefing that we received prior to take-off for Hiroshima. Captain Parsons, who briefed us on the results of what is now known as the Trinity Test conducted at Alamogordo, New Mexico, spoke in terms of twenty kiloton (20,000 ton) TNT equivalent yield. The very words were enough to boggle one's mind. My only prior experience with TNT was the results of one pound blocks that we used in training as Aviation Cadets and later in pre-overseas readiness training. It was absolutely impossible to mentally extrapolate from the 1 pound to 20,000-ton equivalencies. Besides, my limited combat experience had not been gathered as part of any large, multi-aircraft

119

operations. I just didn't have the mental tools to make a realistic estimate of what it would be like.

The single item giving emphasis to the above was the fact that we did all of this with a single airplane and a single bomb. Just imagine what could happen in the future when many of these bombs could rain from the skies from many aircraft simultaneously all over and adversary nation. An entire nation of people could be instantly obliterated. What I saw at Hiroshima, and then again at Nagasaki, began a process within my mind that has ultimately led me from what initially started out as a hope to the present where hope is no longer the operative but has been replaced with an axiomatic truth. If mankind is to survive, we must never again allow ourselves to use nuclear weapons.

As one would expect, there was quite a bit of elation on board the *Enola Gay* on the way home. After all, the mission had been technically correct; the weapon worked as advertised; and, it was obvious that what we had just seen could likely happen again. This wonderful new weapon could bring the war to a speedy conclusion! But I knew that there were a total of four bombs available; the war was not yet over; and, I knew that I would be going on any more missions if there were any more.

Upon our return to our base we were greeted as conquering heroes. As Colonel Tibbets stepped from the airplane, he was called to attention, and a Distinguished Service Medal was pinned to the breast of his flying suit by none other than the Commanding General of the Strategic Air Forces in the Pacific, General Carl Spaatz. As with any crew returning from a mission we were debriefed. In our case we were interrogated by the Generals and Admirals including Generals Spaatz and Nathan Twining. Before the post strike interrogation session began Tom Classen took me over for a personal meeting with General Spaatz. He was a hell of a nice guy and we talked for about 15 minutes before the others arrived. After the interrogation sessions were over the whole 509th Group was treated to a beer bust and barbecue.

But questions did not stop with the official post strike interrogation session. Our comrades and others began asking questions not at all unlike the questions that are still being asked some forty-four years later.

Nagasaki Mission - The Complete Story

Editor's Note: And now we come to the chapters containing information taken directly from the most personal, secret and well documented section of my fathers archive. This chapter written by my father was started years ago to respond to another book's incorrect version of the story but became yet another radio interview instead of a publication. Correcting revisionist portrayals of history was the motivation for my father to initiate his book project "Quote The Raven Nevermore. It was his lifetime quest and post retirement mission that he was unable to complete. This is my attempt using my father's notes to finish the job that he started with this publication. These are my father's words as best as I can recount them.

While the more important details of the Hiroshima story are well documented in the literature, the Nagasaki story has never been fully told. This may be a result of the rush of events leading to Japan's complete surrender. Then, too, it may be because this mission was plagued with preflight problems and en-route emergencies and nearly ended in disaster. But our mission problems did not stop once we landed at Okinawa as I will mention later in this chapter.

For me, my exposure to this wonderful new weapon was not yet over. Three days later, on another B-29 called *Bock's Car*, I participated in the second atomic bombing of Japan, over the city of Nagasaki, which has to date been the last time this weapon has been used in warfare.

As I made ready to leave for the second mission, I remember telling William Laurence of the New York Times who was to go along with Fred Bock on the *Great Artiste* "Bill, if you miss this one, there isn't going to be anymore. He asked me then, "Jake, are you saying that because you think we have made the point with the Japs, or is it because you don't want to see anymore?"

I answered both!

Upon returning from the mission Bill Laurence, wrote the following *"Eyewitness Account of the Nagasaki Mission."* This article became the historical documentation widely accepted as the whole story. However Bill was not on the *Bock's Car* and not personally aware of what happened on the strike aircraft. Also the security policies in place at the time did not permit him to report many of the other things that happened.

In this chapter I will try to fill in a number of the blanks in the untold story of the Nagasaki mission as well as correct some of the myths that have been propagated over the last 45 years.

By Bill Laurence for the New York Times
WITH THE ATOMIC BOMB MISSION TO JAPAN, AUGUST 9 1945
(DELAYED)

"We are on our way to bomb the mainland of Japan. Our flying contingent consists of three specially designed B-29 Superforts, and two of these carry no bombs. But our lead plane is on its way with another atomic bomb, the second in three days, concentrating its active substance, and explosive energy equivalent to 20,000, and under favorable conditions, 40,000 tons of TNT.

We have several chosen targets. One of these is the great industrial and shipping center of Nagasaki, on the western shore of Kyushu, one of the main islands of the Japanese homeland.

I watched the assembly of this man-made meteor during the past two days, and was among the small group of scientists and Army and Navy representatives privileged to be present at the ritual of its loading in the Superfort last night, against a background of threatening black skies torn open at intervals by great lightning flashes.

It is a thing of beauty to behold, this "gadget." In its design went millions of man-hours of what is without a doubt the most concentrated intellectual effort in history. Never before had so much brain power been focused on a single problem.

This atomic bomb is different from the bomb used three days ago with such devastating results on Hiroshima.

I saw the atomic substance before it was placed inside the bomb. By itself it is not at all dangerous to handle. It is only under certain conditions, produced in the bomb assembly, that it can be made to yield up its energy, and even then it gives up only a small fraction of its total contents, a fraction, however, large enough to produce the greatest explosion on earth.

The briefing at midnight revealed the extreme care and the tremendous amount of preparation that had been made to take care of every detail of the mission, in order to make certain that the atomic bomb fully served the purpose for which it was intended. Each target in turn was shown in detailed maps and in aerial photographs. Every detail of the course was rehearsed, navigation, altitude, weather, where to land in emergencies. It came out that the Navy had submarines and rescue craft, known as "Dumbos" and "Super Dumbos," stationed at various strategic points in the vicinity of the targets, ready to rescue the fliers in case they were forced to bail out.

The briefing period ended with a moving prayer by the Chaplain. We then proceeded to the mess hall for the traditional early morning breakfast before departure on a bombing mission.

A convoy of trucks took us to the supply building for the special equipment carried on combat missions. This included the "Mae West," a parachute, a lifeboat, an oxygen mask, a flak suit and a survival vest. We still had a few hours before take-off time but we all went to the flying field and stood around in little groups or sat in jeeps talking rather casually about our mission to the Empire, as the Japanese home islands are known hereabouts.

Bock's Car Flight Crew
Standing l to r: Capt. Beahan, Capt. van Pelt, Jr., 1st Lieutenant Albury, 2nd Lieutenant Olivi, and Major Sweeney.
Kneeling: S/Sgt. Buckley, M/Sgt. Kuharek, Sgt. Gallagher, Staff Sgt. DeHart, and Sgt. Spitzer.

In command of our mission is Major Charles W. Sweeney, 25, of North Quincy, Massachusetts. His flagship, carrying the atomic bomb, is

123

named "The *Great Artiste*," but the name does not appear on the body of the great silver ship, with its unusually long, four-bladed, orange-tipped propellers. Instead it carried the number "77," and someone remarks that it is "Red" Grange's winning number on the Gridiron.

Major Sweeney's co-pilot is First Lieutenant Charles D. Albury, 24, of Miami, Florida. The bombardier upon whose shoulders rests the responsibility of depositing the atomic bomb square on its target, is Captain Kermit K. Beahan, of Houston, Texas, who is celebrating his twenty-seventh birthday today.

Captain Beahan has been awarded the Distinguished Flying Cross, the Air Medal, and one Silver Oak Leaf Cluster, the Purple Heart, the Western Hemisphere Ribbon, the European Theater ribbon and two battle stars. He participated in the first heavy bombardment mission against Germany from England on August 17, 1942, and was on the plane that transported General Eisenhower from Gibraltar to Oran at the beginning of the North African invasion. He has had a number of hair-raising escapes in combat.

The Navigator on "The *Great Artiste*" is Captain James F. Van Pelt, Jr., 27, of Oak Hill, West Virginia. The flight engineer is Master Sergeant John D. Kuharek, 32, of Columbus, Nebraska. Staff Sergeant Albert T. DeHart of Plainview, Texas, who celebrated his thirtieth birthday yesterday, is the tail gunner. The radar operator is Staff Sergeant Edward K. Buckley, 32, of Lisbon, Ohio. The radio operator is Sergeant Abe M. Spitzer, 33, of North Bronx, New York. Sergeant Raymond Gallagher, 23, of Chicago, Illinois, is assistant flight engineer.

The lead ship is also carrying a group of scientific personnel, headed by Commander Frederick L. Ashworth, U.S.N., one of the leaders in the development of the bomb. The group includes Lieutenant Jacob Beser, 24, of Baltimore, Maryland, an expert on airborne radar.

The other two Superforts in our formation are instrument planes, carrying special apparatus to measure the power of the bomb at the time of explosion, high speed cameras and other photographic equipment.

Our Superfort is the second in line. Its Commander is Captain Frederick C. Bock, 27, of Greenville, Michigan. Its other officers are Second Lieutenant Hugh C. Ferguson, 21, of Highland Park, Michigan, pilot; Second Lieutenant Leonard A. Godfrey, 24, of Greenfield, Massachusetts, navigator; and, First Lieutenant Charles Levy, 26, of Philadelphia, Pennsylvania, bombardier.

The enlisted personnel of this Superfort are the following: Technical Sergeant Roderick F. Arnold, 28, of Rochester, Michigan, flight engineer; Sergeant Ralph D. Curry, 20, of Hoopeston, Illinois, radio operator; Sergeant William C. Barney, 22, of Columbia City, Indiana, radar operator; Corporal Robert J. Stock, 21, of Fort Wayne, Indiana, assistant flight engineer; and Corporal Ralph D. Belanger, 19, of Thendara, New York, tail gunner.

The scientific personnel of our Superfort includes: Staff Sergeant Walter Goodman, 22, of Brooklyn, New York, and Lawrence Johnson, graduate student at the University of California, whose home is at Hollywood, California.

The third Superfort is commanded by Major James Hopkins of Palestine, Texas. His officers are Second Lieutenant John E. Cantlon, Tacoma, Washington, pilot; Second Lieutenant Stanley C. Steinke, West Chester, Pennsylvania, navigator; and, Second Lieutenant Myron Faryna, Rochester, New York, bombardier.

The crew are Technical Sergeant George L. Brabenec, Evergreen, Illinois; Sergeant Francis X. Dolan, 30-Elmhurst, New York; Corporal Richard F. Cannon, Buffalo, New York; Corporal Martin G. Murray, Detroit, Michigan, and Corporal Sidney J. Bellamy, Trenton, New Jersey.

On this Superfort are also two distinguished observers from Great Britain, whose scientists played an important role in the development of the Atomic Bomb. One of these is Group Captain G. Leonard Cheshire, famous RAF pilot, who is now a member of the British Military Mission to the United States. The other is Dr. William G. Penney, Professor of Applied Mathematics London University, one of the group of eminent British scientists which has been working at the "Y-Site" near Santa Fe, New Mexico, on the enormous problems involved in taming the atom.

Group Captain Cheshire, whose rank is the equivalent of that of Colonel in the AAF, was designated as an observer of the Atomic Bomb in action by Winston Churchill when he was still Prime Minister. He is now the official representative of Prime Minister Attlee.

We took off at 3:50 this morning and headed northwest on a straight line for the Empire. The night was cloudy and threatening, with only a few stars here and there breaking through the overcast. The weather report had predicted storms ahead for part of the way but clear sailing for the final and climactic stages of our odyssey.

We were about an hour away from our base when the storm

broke. Our great ship took some heavy dips through the abysmal darkness around us, but it took these dips much more gracefully than a large commercial airliner, producing a sensation more in the nature of a glide than a "bump" like a great ocean liner riding the waves. Except that in this case the airwaves were much higher and the rhythmic tempo of the glide much faster.

I noticed a strange eerie light coming through the window high above in the Navigator's cabin and as I peered through the dark all around us I saw a startling phenomenon. The whirling giant propellers had somehow become great luminous discs of blue flame. The same luminous blue flame appeared on the plexiglass windows in the nose of the ship, and on the tips of the giant wings it looked as though we were riding the whirlwind through space on a chariot of blue fire.

It was, I surmised, a surcharge of static electricity that had accumulated on the tips of the propellers and on the dielectric material in the plastic windows. One's thoughts dwelt anxiously on the precious cargo in the invisible ship ahead of us. Was there any likelihood of danger that this heavy electric tension in the atmosphere all about us may set it off?

I express my fears to Captain Bock, who seems nonchalant and unperturbed at the controls. He quickly reassures me: "It is a familiar phenomenon seen often on ships. I have seen it many times on bombing missions. It is known as St. Elmo's Fire."

On we went through the night. We soon rode out the storm and our ship was once again sailing on a smooth course straight ahead, on a direct line to the Empire. Our altimeter showed that we were traveling through space at a height of 17,000 feet. The thermometer registered an outside temperature of 33 degrees below zero centigrade (about 30 below Fahrenheit). Inside our pressurized cabin the temperature was that of a comfortable air-conditioned room, and a pressure corresponding to an altitude of 8,000 feet. Captain Bock cautioned me, however, to keep my oxygen mask handy in case of emergency. This, he explained, may mean either something going wrong with the pressure equipment inside the ship or a hole through the cabin by flak.

The first signs of dawn came shortly after 5:00 o'clock. Sergeant Curry, who had been listening steadily on his earphones for radio reports while maintaining a strict radio silence himself, greeted it by rising to his feet and gazing out the window. "It's good to see the day," he told me. "I get a feeling of claustrophobia hemmed-in in this cabin at night."

He is a typical American youth, looking even younger than his 20 years. It takes no mind reader to read his thoughts.

"It's a long way from Hoopeston, Illinois," I find myself remarking.

"Yep," he replies, as he busies himself decoding a message from outer space.

"Think this atomic bomb will end the war?" he asks hopefully.

"There is a very good chance that this one may do the trick," I assure him, "but if not then the next one or two surely will. Its power is such that no nation can stand up against it very long."

This was not my own view. I had heard it expressed all around a few hours earlier before we took off. To anyone who had seen this man-made fireball in action, as I had less than a month ago in the desert of New Mexico, this view did not sound over-optimistic.

By 5:50 it was real light outside. We had lost our lead ship but Lieutenant Godfrey, our Navigator, informs me that we had arranged for that contingency. We have an assembly point in the sky above the little island of Yakoshima, southeast of Kyushu, at 9:10. We are to circle there and wait for the rest of our formation.

Our genial Bombardier, Lieutenant Levy, comes over to invite me to take his front row seat in the transparent nose of the ship and I accept eagerly. From that vantage point in space, 17,000 feet above the Pacific, one gets a view of hundreds of miles on all sides, horizontally and vertically. At that height the vast ocean below and the sky above seem to merge into one great sphere. I was on the inside of that firmament, riding above the giant mountains of white cumulous clouds, letting myself be suspended in infinite space. One hears the whirl of the motors behind one, but soon becomes insignificant against the immensity all around and is before long swallowed by it. There comes a point where space also swallows time, and one lives through eternal moments filled with an oppressive loneliness, as though all life had suddenly vanished from the earth and you are only one left, a lone survivor traveling endlessly through interplanetary space.

My mind soon returns to the mission I am on. Somewhere beyond these vast mountains of white clouds ahead of me there lies Japan, the land of our enemy. In about four hours from now one of its cities, making weapons of war for use against us will be wiped off the map by the greatest weapon ever made by man. In one-tenth of a millionth of a

127

second, a fraction of time immeasurable by any clock, a whirlwind from the skies will pulverize thousands of its buildings and tens of thousands of its inhabitants.

Our weather planes ahead of us are on their way to find out where the wind blows. Half an hour before target time we will know what the winds have decided.

Does one feel any pity or compassion for the poor devils about to die? Not when one thinks of Pearl Harbor and of the death march on Bataan.

Captain Bock informs me that we are about to start our climb to bombing altitude. He manipulates a few knobs on his control panel to the right of him and I alternately watch the white clouds and ocean below me and the altimeter on the Bombardier's panel. We reached our altitude at 9:00 o'clock. We were then over Japanese waters, close to their mainland. Lieutenant Godfrey motioned to me to look through his radar scope. Before me was the outline of our assembly point. We shall soon meet our lead ship and proceed to the final stage of our journey.

We reached Yakoshima at 9:12 and there, about 4,000 feet ahead of us, was "The *Great Artiste*" with its precious load. I saw Lieutenant Godfrey and Sergeant Curry strap on their parachutes and I decided to do likewise.

We started circling. We saw little towns on the coastline, heedless of our presence. We kept on circling, waiting for the third ship in our formation.

It was 9:00 when we began heading for the coastline. Our weather scouts had sent us code messages, deciphered by Sergeant Curry, informing us that both the primary target as well as the secondary were clearly visible.

The winds of destiny seemed to favor certain Japanese cities that must remain nameless. We circled about them again and again and found no opening in the thick umbrella of clouds that covered them. Destiny chose Nagasaki as the ultimate target.

We had been circling for some time when we noticed black puffs of smoke coming through the white clouds directly at us. There were 15 bursts of flak in rapid succession, all too low. Captain Bock changed his course. There soon followed eight more bursts of flak, right up to our altitude, but by this time we were too far to the left.

We flew southward down the channel and at 11:33 crossed the

coastline and headed straight for Nagasaki about a hundred miles to the west. Here again we circled until we found an opening in the clouds. It was 12:01 and the goal of our mission had arrived.

We heard the pre-arranged signal on our radio, put on our ARC welder's glasses and watched tensely the maneuverings of the strike ship about half a mile in front of us.

"There she goes!" someone said. Out of the belly of the *Artiste*[27] what looked like a black object came downward.

Captain Bock swung around to get out of range, but even though we were turning away in the opposite direction, and despite the fact that it was broad daylight in our cabin, all of us became aware of a giant flash that broke through the dark barrier of our Arc-welder's lenses and flooded our cabin with an intense light.

We removed our glasses after the first flash but the light still lingered on, a bluish-green

Nagasaki Mushroom Cloud

light that illuminated the entire sky all around. A tremendous blast wave struck our ship and made it tremble from nose to tail. This was followed by four more blasts in rapid succession, each resounding like the boom of cannon fire hitting our plane from all directions.

Observers in the tail of our ship saw a giant ball of fire rise as though from the bowels of the earth, belching forth enormous white smoke rings. Next they saw a giant pillar of purple fire, 10,000 feet high, shooting skyward with enormous speed.

---

[27] Editor's Note: The initial War Department release identified the Nagasaki strike aircraft as the "Great Artiste". The "Great Artiste" had flown on the Hiroshima mission as the instrumentation aircraft. Since the instrumentation for the Nagasaki mission would be the same as the Hiroshima mission, "Bock's Car" was used as the strike aircraft on the Nagasaki mission.

By the time our ship had made another turn in the direction of the atomic explosion the pillar of purple fire had reached the level of our altitude. Only about 45 seconds had passed. Awe-struck, we watched it shoot upward like a meteor coming from the earth instead of from outer space, becoming ever more alive as it climbed skyward through the white clouds. It was no longer smoke, or dust, or even a cloud of fire. It was a living thing, a new species of being, born right before our incredulous eyes.

At one stage of its evolution, covering missions of years in terms of seconds, the entity assumed the form of a giant square totem pole, with its base about three miles long, tapering off to about a mile at the top. Its bottom was brown, its center was amber, its top white. But it was a living totem pole, carved with many grotesque masks grimacing at the earth.

Then, just when it appeared as though the thing has settled down into a state of permanence, there came shooting out of the top a giant mushroom that increased the height of the pillar to a total of 45,000 feet. The mushroom top was even more alive than the pillar, seething and boiling in a white fury of creamy foam, sizzling upwards and then descending earthward, a thousand old faithful geysers rolled into one.

It kept struggling in an elemental fury, like a creature in the act of breaking the bonds that held it down. In a few seconds it had freed itself from its gigantic stem and floated upward with tremendous speed, its momentum carrying into the stratosphere to a height of about 60,000 feet.

But no sooner did this happen when another mushroom,

Nagasaki August 9, 1945

smaller in size than the first one, began emerging out of the pillar. It was as though the decapitated monster was growing a new head.

As the first mushroom floated off into the blue it changed its

130

shape into a flower-like form, its giant petal curving downward, creamy white outside, rose-colored inside. It still retained that shape when we last gazed at it from a distance of about 200 miles."

Editor's Note: My father then continued by saying: Now I will fill in some of the details that Bill Laurence was not aware of and/or not permitted to include in his article.

On the way home from Nagasaki I am sure that we all hoped this would be the last Atomic Bomb ever to be dropped. As of now, the fall of 1989, this still appears to be the good possibility.

The primary target for the second mission was to be Kokura with Nagasaki as the secondary target. The decision was made to go ahead immediately after dropping the bomb on Hiroshima since it was important to convince the Japanese that the United States had multiple atomic bombs and was willing to use them. The objective was to persuade the Japanese leaders to immediately surrender on our terms and avoid a third atomic bombing.

Orders were cut and pre-mission briefing held on August 8. Colonel Tibbets the 509th Composite Group commander, who had piloted the *Enola Gay* on the Hiroshima mission, assigned the mission command to Major Charles W. Sweeney. Chuck was now our Squadron Commander and as such had the option of selecting any of the squadron crews for his job. However instead of the regular *Bock's Car* crew he selected Don Albury and Fred Olivi's crew since he had most of his experience with them and they had accompanied us to Hiroshima. This crew had also had several "pumpkin" missions[28] behind them. Except for Ralph Taylor and Claude Eatherly, who led the squadron in missions flown, they were right up there with the best.

Some of us felt that Chuck had been selected as mission commander by Colonel Tibbets because of his friendship and experience with him on the B-29 test program and not because of previous combat experience. Although we all liked Chuck and had confidence in his B-29 flying ability, there were some of us in the original 393rd cadre that thought Tom Classen, our original 393rd squadron commander, would have been the

---

[28] Editor's Note: The bulbous shape of the plutonium bomb Fat Man dropped on Nagasaki was made necessary by its complicated firing mechanism. Because of this shape the inert practice bombs used by the 509th became known as "pumpkins". Eventually a few were filled with explosives and used on selected Japanese targets.

more logical choice based on capabilities, combat experience and demonstrated valor. But this was not to be because Tom was now on his way back to the states on a very "strange mission" for Colonel Tibbets. It was rumored that he was being sent back to pick up the next weapon. This was indeed very strange since airplane commanders had delivered previous weapons. Another rumor, although I seriously doubt it, said that he was being sent to Alaska for a security violation for having improperly used the Silverplate priority code. I never knew the real answer.

This would be Chuck's first combat mission as the commander. He was fully aware that Colonel Tibbets and his crew had flawlessly executed the Hiroshima mission to plan and he was confident that he and his crew could do the same for the second mission. But, as I will discuss further this was not to be!

The military tactics to be followed for the second mission were to be the same as the first. The strike formation would consist of three B-29s. One would carry the bomb. A second would carry photographic equipment and scientific personnel along with an official British representative. A third would carry instrumentation to document the mission scientifically. Also following the same scenario as the Hiroshima mission, two weather planes would be dispatched about an hour ahead of the strike formation to report the weather conditions over both targets but the bomb would not be armed en-route as the previous one had been. Radio silence en-route between the bombers was to be absolute. If any of the planes had to ditch, rescue ships and submarines were in position; also, aircraft had been alerted to be available to locate a downed plane or its crew. If Japan had surrendered before the drop was made, a signal would be sent from Tinian to scrub the mission.

Major Charles Sweeney

The strike aircraft originally scheduled to make the second flight was the *Great Artiste*. However, it had been used three days earlier as the instrumentation aircraft on the Hiroshima Raid. Rather than removing this special set-up it was decided to use the airplane assigned to Captain Fred Bock, known as *Bock's Car* to carry the bomb. Major Chuck Sweeney and his crew would fly the *Bock's Car* and Captain Bock would fly the instrumentation load in the *Great Artiste*. It would also be carrying William L. Laurence, a reporter for The New York Times. Major James I. Hopkins, Jr., group operations officer, was assigned to fly the *Full House*, which would carry photographic equipment and scientific personnel. On board would be Group Captain Leonard Cheshire, Winston Churchill's official representative. A fourth aircraft was to proceed to Iwo Jima and stand by in case of an early abort by the strike aircraft.

Such switching around of the aircraft and crews was not an uncommon procedure. In this instance, however, this crew switch was to play a significant role in a mission that almost came to disaster. Major Sweeney and this crew's unfamiliarity with some of the idiosyncrasies of this particular airplane contributed in no small measure to this situation as did Major Sweeney's unwillingness to listen to the advice of his flight engineer.

Wednesday, August 8 was to be a day of "worries." The mission was scheduled to depart at 0330 (3:30 am) the next morning. The weather over Japan had deteriorated in the past 48 hours and the forecast for the next 24 hour interval was somewhat "iffy." There had never been a full blown test drop of the "Fat Man" configuration. This would be the first time one of these would be dropped in full operational configuration - except for the nuclear load - including upgrades to the proximity fusing mechanism. The test would be conducted over the ocean, just a few miles away from the island. This would allow for better observation, rather than taking it to some remote site with inadequate instrumentation. The data was needed NOW, and there was no time to construct a new test site.

The test flight was to be flown as soon as a clear window could be obtained; that is minimal flying in the immediate area of the island. After the test, the airplane would have to be taxied to the special loading area to receive the weapon that would be delivered that night. If any malfunctions develop during the test flight, a standby airplane had to be made ready if needed, so the ground crew must be on constant alert until the mission is ready to go. The test drop was made just prior to noon, during a lull in the local flying. Those of us on the ground were startled to hear what sounded like a speeding freight train heading right for the field. This apparition suddenly ceased only to be followed by a loud "crump" as the bomb impacted the ocean several miles out. The results of the test were known immediately and they were good. Another major milestone had been passed. Now it was just a well airplane and acceptable weather were all that were needed to clear the way for the mission.

The Nagasaki bomb was jinxed from the start. I think Costello flew it out from the states. He had a hair-raising experience. Immediately after take-off the life raft door blew off and the raft fouled his elevator. As a result they had an emergency go-around and landing with a load of gas, twelve guys and the bomb onboard. It was at March Field, that this happened.

Costello was a real interesting person. He very seldom showed any excitement when things were happening. But, to hear him tell about it later was a real comedy. That guy came close to having "it" right then and there. But he was a skilled pilot. He knew his B-29 and he knew what he could do with it. So he managed to stay airborne long enough. They kept him up there a couple of hours to lighten his load and then he maneuvered it in using mostly trim tabs because he had a fouled elevator.

On Tinian I went into the assembly area as the bomb was being readied for loading on the airplane. In a few hours it was to be loaded but there were two holes that did not align properly. A technician was busy with a rat-tail file enlarging one of the holes. I never knew whether this was a design, a dimension or a workmanship problem. Was there ever a fit-check made back in the states? But in any case the problem was corrected on site.

This airplane had been pre-flighted by the assigned ground crew and was signed off as flight worthy by the Ground Crew Chief S/Sgt Fred Clayton. There were two minor discrepancies that "red lined" the airplane, but Lieutenant Don Albury the assigned Co-Pilot signed off on them and the airplane was released for the mission.

The crew got onboard the plane and got the engines running but instead of taxing out they shut the engines down. Additional pre-flight checks on the engines were run by the flight engineer, Sgt. John Kuharek who expressed some concern about the spare fuel transfer system. There were approximately 600 gallons stored in the aft bomb bay in two three hundred gallon tanks. There was a fuel transfer pump that would move this fuel from the reserve tanks to the main fuel tanks that appeared to be inoperative. When the flight was over, Kuharek wrote in the Form 1A Flight Report, "check bomb bay tank hook-up-lower tank works erradict (sic). It appears that booster is at fault."

The crew deplaned to await instructions on what to do next. I recall hearing Chuck telling Colonel Tibbets "we cannot transfer the 600 gallons of reserve fuel we have in the bomb bay tanks and it will take too long to change the pumps." Colonel Tibbets was obviously displeased and told him, "You don't need that gas, so there's no reason to delay this." He further reminded Chuck that he was the pilot and in command of the mission and had a decision to make. The 600 gallons of fuel was there mainly for balance reasons and not needed for a nominal mission. They moved away out of ear shot range where a conference ensued. I was not invited since I obviously could not contribute. Major Sweeney and his navigator Captain van Pelt, and the third pilot, Lieutenant Olivi re-figured the flight for the lesser amount of fuel that might be available and determined that with the availability of an alternate return base, there was no special risk in not having the reserve fuel available. Colonel Tibbets reviewed their findings. After his review and approval, he who reminded them that they were off to a late start and timing was crucial to a successful drop. Major Sweeney made the decision to go ahead immediately with the mission. A primary consideration was that bad weather was moving in over Japan which could delay the mission for a week or more and it was felt extremely important to convince the Japanese that the United States had multiple atomic bombs and would use them. If a fuel shortage developed, the *Bock's Car* would simply refuel at Okinawa before returning to Tinian.

I will describe the execution of the mission as I recall it, and as I do, I will point out a few of the many and more obvious blunders that were committed.

The flight departed Tinian Island sometime after four o'clock in the morning of August 9th even though by this time the local weather had deteriorated. We were seeing scattered thunderstorms with heavy lightning all around the air field. If everything had gone according to plan and the weather forecast en-route and at the target had held up, this flight could have still been completed in an uneventful manner. But such was not to be the case.

Our take-off was late but routine and uneventful. In less than three minutes after the wheels were up I was on the floor and sound asleep. I did not even hear the tower clear Fred Bock or Jimmy Hopkins, the two commanders of the escort airplanes that would accompany us on this mission.

135

Today we would attribute the pre-flight and en-route anomalies that occurred on this flight to Murphy's Law, wherein it says that if something is going to go wrong, it will. In 1945 this law had yet to be propounded, but Kilroy and Gremlins usually bore the blame. When you get right down to cases, it was usually poor exercise of human judgment or just plain old-fashioned incompetence that usually got you into trouble. In the case of *Bock's Car* on the Nagasaki mission it was both of these, with the addition of a little plain old bad luck.

There were two possible targets for this mission; Kokura on the Northeast comer of Kyushu, or Nagasaki on the Southwestern comer of Kyushu. Kokura was briefed as the Primary Target. The weather reports from neither one of these two cities was very good, but Kokura seemed to be somewhat better than Nagasaki. Kokura was an arsenal city and at that time was concentrating on making vehicles for use in resisting the anticipated invasion of Japan. It was decided to go to Kokura.

The flight route to Kokura was planned to proceed via Iwo Jima, but stormy weather en-route forced a change in the route to the rendezvous point at Yakushima Island. The strike formation of three B-29's did not fly in a tight formation to avoid the possibility of a midair collision as they headed over the Pacific under radio silence and without running lights. The weather was rough at the planned altitude of 8,000 to 10,000 feet. Sweeney didn't want to subject the bomb to any more shock or vibration caused by rough air than he had to. So he flew at 17,000 feet and burned more fuel.

When the *Bock's Car* arrived at the rendezvous point, only the photographic plane was there. Due to poor visibility, the instrumentation aircraft had lost visible contact with the other planes.

In the pre-mission briefing, It had been agreed that they would not linger more than 15 minutes over the rendezvous point. Major Sweeney was the Mission Commander but there seemed to be some "discussions" between Sweeney and Ashworth, who outranked him, as to who should decide how long to wait for the missing plane. Ashworth felt that the instrumentation plane was necessary and "convinced" Sweeney, against his orders, to circled for at least 45 minutes looking for the other airplane. Fred wanted the mission to be a complete and documented success. Even though Colonel Tibbets did not consider photography and instrumentation a mandatory requirement both Fred and Chuck felt it would be difficult to call it a total success if the explosion were not properly photographed and documented by data from the instrumentation planes.

These aircraft piloted by Captain Fred Bock and Major James Hopkins had left shortly after Sweeney in *Bock's Car*. Upon arriving at the designated rendezvous point, thirty-one thousand feet over the island of Yakushima off the South Coast of Kyushu Sweeney begin to circle. Two to three minutes later Fred Bock in the *Great Artiste* caught up with him. We continued to loiter for an additional forty-five minutes and there still was no sign of Hopkins. Major Sweeney continued this additional loitering knowing full well that there was a touch and go fuel transfer situation on their hands.

To this day no one has advanced a rational reason for this delay other than poor judgment on the part of the Mission Commander. However another possible explanation is contained in a note written by Richard F. Cannon, the Radar Operator on Hopkins' airplane. In his note he wrote *"When we rendezvoused at Yakushima, the other two planes were not there. We stayed for our agreed forty minutes, then went on to the primary, Kokura. At this point our pilot, Major James Hopkins told everyone on board to get near any blister seat*

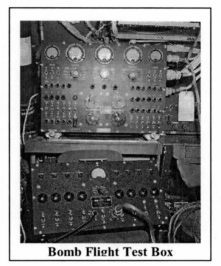

Bomb Flight Test Box

to watch for the other two planes. My normal position after radar was to take the left scanner seat where I hoped to see the other two aircraft. Due to cloud formations, we realized no one could have bombed it."

Through the years I have attempted to determine a reason for Hopkins' missed rendezvous. Quite fortuitously on the night of November 3, 1989, Sweeney called me on another matter. During the course of the conversation, the name Hopkins came up. I brought it up referring to a recent lecture I had given at the Johns Hopkins University. Sweeney became quite agitated when he heard the name and thought that I was referring to Major James Hopkins, pilot of the aircraft that missed the rendezvous over the Island of Yakushima. He told me of a conversation he had in London with Group Captain G. Leonard Cheshire of the RAF, a very experienced aviator, who was aboard Hopkins aircraft as the personal representative of Prime Minister Clement Atlee of Great Britain. Cheshire told Sweeney that he could not understand why Hopkins "was flying at thirty-nine thousand feet, when he had been briefed to fly at thirty-two thousand." This could account in some way for the missed rendezvous but in no way accounts for the extended loitering time in the face of a suspected fuel shortage.

Major Hopkins, the *Full House Pilot*, was not what I would call a close friend of Major Sweeney. Finally Hopkins broke radio silence and asked Tinian: "Has Sweeney aborted?" The message came through as "Sweeney aborted." I was told that this created a lot of confusion on the ground at Tinian.

Finally Sweeney dipped his wings and headed to Kokura, the mission's primary target. Captain Bock followed.

As soon as we were clear of the island of Tinian Lieutenant Phil Barnes, the Asst. Weaponeer, performed an internal test on the bomb using a black box provided in the aircraft. At some point during the testing something appeared to have gone wrong with the bomb. The test box contained electrical switches and a red light. As long as the light slowly blinked at a regular rate, it meant that the bomb was healthy. If it blinked fast and irregular, something was malfunctioning. At one point during the tests Lieutenant Barnes noticed that the red light was flashing fast and erratic. He quickly traced the problem to a switch wiring problem which he promptly fixed. Had he not noticed the problem and promptly corrected it, there was the possibility, although very remote, that the bomb could have prematurely detonated in the airplane bomb bay.

Don Farrell in his abstract of "The Tinian Atomic Bomb Files" records this event as follows: "*After reaching the low altitude cruising level, U.S. Navy Commander Frederick L. Ashworth opened the round, pressurized door that led into the forward bomb bay, braced himself, reached down to the bomb and removed the green safety plugs from the Fat Man casing and replaced them with the red safety plugs. Air Force Lieutenant Philip Barnes, Ashworth's assistant weaponeer on this flight, checked the electrical circuits as they appeared on flight test box. They proved satisfactory and he so advised Ashworth. Thirty minutes after take off, the Bock's Car advised Tinian that the bombs electrical circuits showed the Fat Man was active and ready to drop.*

Barnes repeated this test every two hours on the ride to Japan. During one of these tests, a small white light appeared on the board, which indicated that the bomb was completely hot. That could mean that even an accidental signal from the fusing circuit could initiate the detonation process. Although Ashworth and Barnes were quite sure it was a faulty indicator, they felt obliged to inform Major Sweeney. This message got through the plane and caused some concern among the crew.

Barnes pulled out the wiring diagram, opened the box, traced the circuits, found a switch that was incorrectly set, re-set it, and the little white light went out. All breathed a sigh of relief. This was why Ashworth and Barnes were aboard as weaponeers."

When the testing was complete the bomb was ready to be placed in a full firing condition by removing the green safety plugs which shorted out the arming system and replacing them with red plugs to complete the arming circuits and the bomb was ready. When these plugs were changed all that was needed to cause the bomb to detonate was a signal from the fusing mechanism. In contrast to the insertion of the powder charge through the secondary breech block and making the proper connections for the detonators on the Hiroshima bomb, these operations were the only "arming" requirements for this weapon.

Our orders from Washington did not permit us, under any circumstances, to drop the bomb using radar unless in the judgment of the Senior Weaponeer an emergency developed that required deviation from the tactical plan." Washington wanted us to be absolutely sure that we were bombing the assigned target. Upon arriving in the vicinity of Kokura it became immediately obvious to Beahan, the bombardier, that he was going to have trouble making a visual drop, that is visually selecting his aiming point with the tracking telescope of his Norden bombsight. The first run was made in accordance with their preflight briefing. One useful bit of information had been omitted from the preflight briefing. Kokura was situated East of Yawata, the Pittsburgh of Japan, which had been firebombed by other groups of the 20th Air Force just two nights previously and the city was still burning. To make matters worse, Kokura lay downwind of Yawata and was being obscured by the smoke and debris of that burning city. Because of this, Beahan was unable to get a good sighting on his first run. The people up front decided to circle the city and select a different approach angle, which would perhaps give him a better view.

We circled the area to try the second run. The second run was as fruitless as the first. This time we not only didn't drop, but we were now receiving anti-aircraft fire. Couple this with a serious fuel problem and the situation became tenser. While milling around over Kokura, the throttles were "bent to the wall" and the airplane was consuming fuel at the rate of 900 gallons per hour. Almost an hour had passed since arriving over the city.

At this point there was considerable "discussion" on the flight deck concerning fuel remaining and alternate flight plans. It seemed to me that Chuck and his flight engineer had a serious difference of opinions as to what the alternatives should be. They quickly decided we couldn't take the bomb back to Tinian, so Sweeney said that we have to drop it by radar or drop it in the ocean—and we sure as heck didn't want to drop it in the ocean. But a cool head prevailed. Ashworth walked off somewhere in the plane and came back a few minutes later. I distinctly remember him saying "if we absolutely have to drop it by radar, then we can. So that's what we were going to do. We do not have enough fuel to haul a 10,000 bomb back home."

There was no time for a lengthy debate. We were burning precious fuel just boring useless holes in the sky. We should make one more pass at Kokura and if we don't drop then head for Nagasaki where if the weather had not cleared, we would drop by radar. Commander Ashworth, as General Groves' deputy on this flight and the senior project representative aboard, would take the responsibility. After bombing Nagasaki, we would head down the coast of lower Kyushu for an emergency landing at Okinawa. As I learned later the assumption by Fred that his instructions from General Groves superseded the Field Orders was a real controversial point with Colonel Tibbets[29].

---

[29] Editor's Note: Responsibility for the bomb had been made clear in a message sent to General LeMay by General Norstad, Chief of Staff US Army Air Force, on May 29, 1945 addressing command responsibility in case an emergency arose. It read: "In actual delivery it is desired that the B-29 airplane which carries the bomb also carry two military officer specialists. The senior officer specialist will be qualified by familiarity with the design, development and tactical features of the bomb, to render final judgment in the event that an emergency requires deviation from the tactical plan." This order was critical during the Nagasaki mission.

We began a third pass over Kokura at still another approach angle. About that time I began to detect activity on the Japanese fighter control radio frequencies. It was obvious that they were now getting interested in this crazy B-29 milling around overhead. I alerted the cockpit and advised the scanners[30] and tail gunner to be looking out for ascending fighters. The characteristics of the airborne channel signals were constantly changing. This indicated to me that the aircraft emitting the signals were coming closer all of the time.

Editor's Note: When they broke away from their bombing pattern, they turned toward the mountains and began to receive flak. Under pressure to bomb their primary target by visual sighting and under fire, it was once again decision time. Should they skip the target and go directly to Nagasaki, or make another run? Ashworth writes, "Early on I had become aware that General Groves had expressed his policy that every attempt should be made to insure that the two bombs that we had be dropped as closely together as practicable in order that there would be no possibility that the Japanese might assume we had only one bomb, and that there probably would be more to come. Kokura was our primary target and we should make every attempt to drop the bomb there on this mission. Since the Aircraft Commander did not seem to have in mind how we should continue the mission, I proposed that we make another bomb run from a different direction, hoping that visibility of the target might be adequate for the Bombardier to make a successful visual attack." The result was the same, "No drop."

"In hindsight," Ashworth later wrote, "my proposal to try different directions was quite stupid. Whatever direction we approached the target from would not change what was happening on the ground. The smoke and haze were still there obscuring the target."

The results of this third bomb run were no better than the previous two, except that now we had flak[31] and had burned more precious fuel,

---

This argument is further reinforced by the message General Farrell sent to General Groves shortly after takeoff for Hiroshima which read as follows: "Little Boy mission left Tinian at 05 1645Z with Parsons and Tibbets in charge. Everything normal.

[30] Editor's Note: Some crewmembers of the B-29 were assigned to the windows with the additional responsibility of scanning sky visible from the window for enemy aircraft.

[31] Editor's Note: Flak was the term used for antiaircraft gun fire.

making even our return to Okinawa doubtful. We broke off from any further effort in the vicinity of Kokura and the city was spared.[32]

We headed across the Shimonosaki Straits and followed the coastline down and then across to Nagasaki. As we left the Kokura area, after about one hour and several power cycles of turning on and off the weapon in our bomb bay, our tail gunner announced that he could see fighter aircraft breaking through the clouds below. None of this gave any of us an easy feeling. As luck would have it, the Japanese fighters must have had a different target in mind, because they never came after us.

On the way to Nagasaki a revised estimate of our fuel cast more doubt upon our ability to make it all the way to Okinawa. It was decided that for sure we would make only one bomb run on Nagasaki and use radar if needed. After the drop we would head for the open water and point the airplane in the direction of Okinawa. By taking advantage of a lighter airplane, and going into a shallow glide we still had a prayer of making it to Yontan airstrip and not have to ditch in the East China Sea.

It should also be noted that after the "discussion" with Sweeney while still over Kokura, Kuharek was ordered to stop trying to transfer the reserve fuel. This discussion seemed to concentrate on who had responsibility for flying the airplane and making the safety decisions. We felt that Kuharek came out on the short end of that "discussion." It has been indicated to me on several occasions since, by both Captain Bock and Sgt. Clayton that if Sgt. Kuharek had been allowed to activate the transfer system and just leave it on, the desired fuel transfer would have taken place. However unknown to Sweeney and against Sweeney's orders Kuharek was babying along the faulty fuel pump and feeding fuel from the auxiliary tanks into the main tank. There was an undiagnosed gremlin in this airplane that caused the system to operate this way. A review of the

---

[32] Editor's Note: From my perspective, as a Monday morning quarterback, the recent fire bombing of Yawata and its physical location with respect to Kokura and the known prevailing wind direction should have been given serious consideration when Kokura was selected as the primary target. General LeMay knew, or should have known, the details of the second mission and the probability would be very high that smoke and haze from firebombing of Yawata would obscure Kokura. He should have taken that into consideration and either foregone the fire bombing of Yawata or else designated Nagasaki as the primary target. It would appear that Sweeney and his crew "went the extra mile" to carry out orders under foreseeable and impossible conditions. In my opinion at least part of the blame for the missions problems must be shared by General LeMay.

Form 1 of the airplane, now on file at the United States Air Force Museum at Dayton, Ohio, reveals this to indeed be the case.

One other serious blunder happened while preparing to leave the Kokura area. As Sweeney was about to make his turn away from the city, he pushed what he thought was his interphone button. He asked, "Where is Bock" In an instant, to everyone's surprise, a voice was heard to say "Chuck, where the hell are you?"

Sweeney had accidentally pushed his radio call button, and Hopkins, who had missed the rendezvous, was still milling around the wrong island somewhere southeast of Kyushu. Sweeney realized that he had mistakenly broken radio silence thus endangering the mission and chose to ignore the call.

Things settled down for the remainder of the journey to the new target area. The original flight plan called for us to skirt the island of Kyushu if we were going to attack Nagasaki. But by now the fuel was critical and the most direct route was taken to conserve the rapidly dwindling fuel supply. This route traversed an area full of Japanese fighter bases. For this reason, everyone assigned a window was expected to keep a sharp lookout for interceptors, and I kept a close watch on the fighter control radio frequencies. Kuharek recalculated his diminishing fuel reserves and informed Sweeney that there was insufficient fuel to make it back to Iwo Jima. This last bit of information narrowed the options considerably. One pass at Nagasaki, head for Okinawa and pray. This would require that Sweeney fall back on every last bit of his skill in the art of "Cruise Control," a discipline practiced many times before leaving Wendover, the base at which we had trained in the States.

As luck would have it, as we neared Nagasaki the weather had deteriorated even more from what the weather observation aircraft had reported several hours earlier. The undercast beneath the *Bock's Car* was now essentially solid with an occasional hole here and there.

By now, Sweeney knew, the plane did not have enough fuel to make it back to Tinian or to the backup base at Iwo Jima. He also knew that he had only enough fuel for one bomb run on Nagasaki and still possibly have enough fuel to make it to Okinawa.

I had been on about 13 other flights over the Empire testing and re-testing my electronic equipment. I had more trips than anybody in the Group because every day the 509th flew, I moved all my electronic equipment onto another airplane because I wanted to be able to do my job right when the time came. And I wanted to get familiar with the electronic environment over Japan as well as the radar signatures of ground features. That's what I was there for. I had compared the radar images of the ground features with maps and visual observations. With this experience and my confidence in the advanced electronic equipment that I had selected, I felt confident that I could accurately direct the airplane to the desired target area. Captain van Pelt, the Navigator, Staff Sergeant Ed Buckly, the Radar Operator and Commander Ashworth, the Senior Weaponeer, did not have this experience. The geographic configuration of the port and the city of Nagasaki were such that the radar presentation was clear-cut and obvious. I informed the up-front crew that if they told me exactly where the AP {Air Point} was located I could direct them there. My inputs played an important role in getting us to and confirming that we were attacking the assigned target.

Ashworth was convinced that a radar drop was the only viable alternative available to us so and he made the decision to do just that. He also recognized that his field orders specifically required a visual drop but he felt his instructions from higher authorities superseded the field orders. More specifically General Norstad, Chief of Staff, twentieth Air Force, had written to General LeMay: "*In actual delivery it is desired that the B-29 airplane which carries the bomb also carry two military officer specialists. The senior officer specialist will be qualified by familiarity with the design, development and tactical features of the bomb, to render final judgment in the event that an emergency requires deviation from the tactical plan.*"

Disobeying the field orders the bomb run was initiated by radar. Ashworth wanted to be sure that the city we were approaching was indeed Nagasaki. He kept looking at the Navigator's radar scope until he was convinced that we were headed for the correct city. The Navigator was giving the bombardier steering directions, substituting what the radar was seeing for what the bombardier would normally be seeing through the bombsight telescope. About ten to fifteen seconds before we reached the aiming point and the bomb would have been dropped automatically, we heard Beahan say, "I have a hole, I see it." He quickly synchronized his bombsight as the aim point approached. The bomb bay doors opened, making the plane wobble because of the drag. When the bomb was released, the plane abruptly jumped as it lost 10,000 pounds.

Apparently, Beahan which he later confirmed to me in a private correspondence had spotted an opening in the clouds only seconds before releasing the bomb. But in my opinion the only trouble was he had a hole about one-millionth the size he really needed to tell what he was bombing. He had something in the cross hairs of his sight that he thought was his briefed aiming point. Well he didn't. We bombed the other end of the city about three miles to the northwest right smack in the middle of this industrial valley where the Mitsubishi plant and other heavy industry was located instead of near the

Capt. Beahan

center of the city. I think the same God that was protecting us was also protecting many innocent Japanese on the ground. If we had hit the briefed aiming point, the casualty rate would have been higher.

"Our only choice was to drop it," Ashworth said later. "I didn't know whether we could make it back to Okinawa hauling around a 10,000-pound bomb. But Beahan was the flight's hero. He held his cool. He had only one shot at the target. He reacted and he did his job." Olivi, the third pilot, commented "Beahan saved our necks, we would have been in whole lot trouble for disobeying the not to use radar order."

Sweeney immediately went into a steep bank and headed 155 degrees in the opposite direction to outrun the impending radioactive blast cloud. As I recall, even with our dwindling fuel supply, he circled the mushroom cloud once and headed for Okinawa. When the bomb went off, the scanner on the down wing side of the turning airplane saw the mushroom cloud rising, with a compression wave of air ahead of it. Due to the diffraction as a result of this compression wave. It appeared to him that the mushroom cloud was headed straight for his window. With all the other problems and mishaps that had already taken place that morning, this was enough to unnerve him to the extent that he cried out, "we're in the way, we're going to be hit by the cloud!" This was enough to cause all on-board to have a few anxious moments, until the cloud passed us on the way up, and we were at least six to eight miles from it.

When I got to the window, unlike the scene at Hiroshima, I was able to see parts of the city that appeared relatively unharmed. The cloud

145

cover that we had going in had now disappeared, but in the immediate area where the bomb had gone off it was much the same as three days earlier at Hiroshima. When we felt three distinct shock waves this caused some wonderment. We had only expected two. Ashworth and the Navigator reasoned that we must have hit in the Urakami Valley, some three miles from where we were supposed to bomb. This bothered the cockpit crew no end, until after we got back to Tinian where Admiral Purnell recognized this as a fortuitous happening. We had hit the center of the industrial area of the city, and not the densely populated residential area. Nagasaki had been selected to convince the Japanese that we could rain destruction on them almost daily if need be; so they had better convince their government to sue for peace. We had accomplished the mission objective but were unable to loiter long in the target area. The airplane was pointed towards Okinawa and we gradually began to lose altitude and pick up speed. Along the way, we could see numerous friendly aircraft, mainly B-24s and P-47s below us bombing their targets.

As van Pelt set the *Bock's Car* on a heading for Okinawa, the radio operator informed the submarines of our position and destination.

Ashworth immediately sent a preliminary strike report to Tinian.

As we approached Yontan Airstrip on Okinawa we saw a large group of B-24's in the landing pattern. Sweeney attempted to contact the Control Tower by radio. I do not know if he had made reference to the Signal Operating Instructions that had been given him prior to take-off, but for some reason the tower never acknowledged his call. He then sent the voice "May-Day" signal, the International Distress Signal. Still no answer. He then instructed the Navigator to fire the Flare Pistol. No one on the ground seemed to pay any attention. Sweeney yelled, "Get out of my way I'm coming straight in." I have never been able to ascertain whether he followed the code of the day or just opted for attention. The rear end of the airplane where I was working suddenly filled up with smoke. Since I saw it coming up from under the floor boards, I immediately went for the area under the floor where I had special electrical equipment. I was sure that the way things were going that we now had an onboard fire.

Just as I was about to tear out the floor board, one of the fellows back there with me tugged at my arm and told me that they had fired all the flares up front. Whatever he did the Navigator got the attention of one of the crews in the landing pattern. Someone surmised that the big bird was in trouble and he peeled off. Those behind him followed suit and they created a gap in the pattern that allowed Sweeney to land.

It is often said that an airplane landing is nothing more than a controlled crash. That's about the only way to describe Sweeney's landing that day. I had been with him on previous occasions when he did much better. He came in hot {fast} and long, about a third of the way down the runway. As he flared to land, with the nose up to touch down, his two inboard engines coughed and died. Whatever fuel remaining in the tanks could no longer be made to flow. As he neared the end of the runway he was faced with a decision - make the 90-degree right turn, regardless of remaining speed, or go over the cliff to the bay down below. Naturally, Sweeney opted for the turn. There was no warning to those of us in the rear of the plane, and at the speed he was going, the centrifugal force resulting from the turn was almost enough to put us through the side of the airplane. You can't come any closer to disaster than we had on that landing, and live to tell about it!

By the time that the FOLLOW ME Jeep had led us to a parking hard stand those of us in the rear of the airplane could rationally face our leader and congratulate him for getting us on the ground safely, rather than cast aspersion upon his ancestry.

As I mentioned earlier our problems did not stop upon landing at Okinawa. Our welcome at Yontan Field on the ground was about the same as it had been in the air. After all we were just another B-29 among the hundreds of other aircraft parked along the apron. Of course there was no transportation available just to accommodate us.

In accordance with our orders we were obligated to send by radio a strike report to our home base at Tinian immediately after the drop. Unfortunately our pre-arranged code had been designed for all the "possible situations" that we could anticipate but nothing adequately covered what really happened on this mission. The message, long over due on Tinian simply meant "We need a conference before any news releases are made!" It was now absolutely necessary that we make a complete report using the communication facilities on Okinawa as soon as possible.

A passing Jeep driven by a GI was the answer to our transportation problem. At first he was reluctant to go out of his way to accommodate us after all we were just another B-29 crew wanting a ride. But after a few words from Commander Ashworth and a little encouragement from his .45 caliber automatic service weapon, the driver become most accommodating. He happily provided the transportation we needed and took Major Sweeney and Commander Ashworth to the communications center of the Eighth Air Force Headquarters.

In a private correspondence Ashworth wrote *"The Army Air Corps Colonel in charge of the communications center turned out to be no more interested in me and my communication problem than had been the control tower at the air field in our need for landing instructions. I doubted that the same technique used on the driver of the Jeep would*

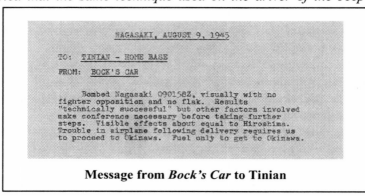

Message from *Bock's Car* to Tinian

work with a bird Colonel, particularly coming from a disreputable looking individual dressed in a sweaty flight suit without rank marks of any kind claiming to be a Commander, U.S. Navy. However, at my request, he did direct me to the Headquarters tent of General Jimmy Doolittle commanding the Eighth Air Force, with the comment that it probably would do me no good either. The General's tent consisted of two pyramidal tents joined together, the half at the entrance being occupied by his Chief of Staff, General Partridge. I knocked on the door, walked in, introduced myself, stated that we had just dropped the second atomic bomb on Japan and that I needed some help with his uncooperative Communications Officer to permit me to send my detailed after-strike report to my Headquarters on Tinian. General Partridge grinned and said that he could help but that I had better tell General Doolittle all about it first. Whereupon he escorted me into the inner sanctum, introduced me to the General and left us alone.

I told General Doolittle that we had taken off from Tinian at 3:30 AM that morning, it now being some twelve hours later, that we

148

had flown directly to the Empire to rendezvous with the two other B-29s in the operation, one with observers aboard and the other carrying blast gages to be dropped and suspended by small parachutes to attempt to telemeter information back to the aircraft to obtain an approximate measure of the yield of the bomb. I told him of our 45 minute delay at the rendezvous awaiting the third plane which apparently had become lost, and our concern over the delay because we were carrying 800 gallons of fuel in the after bomb bay which was unusable because of a faulty fuel transfer pump. We proceeded to our first priority target Kokura where we used another fifty five minutes trying to make a visual bomb run without success because of smoke and haze in the area due to B-29 raid the previous night on the city of Yawata close by. Being unsuccessful there I recounted our flight direct to Nagasaki with anti-aircraft fire and Japanese fighters being directed toward us, and how the flight engineer calculated that we probably had not enough fuel aboard to get the bomb safely back to Okinawa. I described the radar approach to Nagasaki contra to our orders and the drop of the bomb at the last minute under visual control by the Bombardier. With aid of my target maps I pointed out to the General that we had apparently missed the city by a mile and a half and actually dropped the bomb over the Urakami River valley, and that this estimate had been fairly well confirmed by the other B-29 with us which stayed in the target area to verify where the bomb actually exploded. We noted from the target maps that the apparent ground zero was directly on the Mitsubishi arms works and that the blast must have been focused up and down the valley and that probably there had been only minor damage if any at all in the city of Nagasaki.

At this point General Doolittle stood up, put his arm around my shoulder as he led me to the door and said "Don't worry, son, about the miss of the target. I am sure that General Spaatz will be very happy that the city of Nagasaki was spared and the destruction mostly restricted to military targets in the river valley. Now go back to my communications center and I will see to it that you get the attention that you should have had before". At the communications center one might have thought that I was at least the Vice Chief of Naval Operations sending my message back to our base."

Upon landing, we were informed that the Russians had now entered the war against Japan (Whoopee!) and that Nagasaki had been A-

Bombed. You should have seen the expressions on the faces of our informants when we told them we had just come from Nagasaki and had been the very aircraft that delivered the blow to Nagasaki.

Shortly behind us came Bock in the *Great Artiste*. Not too far behind Bock was Hopkins. He was about to call us again when on the horizon he saw the mushroom cloud rise over Nagasaki. He headed for the city and took pictures. He described the havoc we had created and confirmed that we had bombed Urakami. I really no longer remember his excuse for missing the rendezvous in any case but he had sufficient fuel to hang around a while and see what was to develop.

After the messages were sent to Tinian and the airplanes were refueled we were told we had to be out of there by 5 PM as that was when the daily kamikaze raid came in. Since we still had a long flight ahead of us, we left as soon as possible.

All the way back to Tinian, about a five hour flight, not much was said on board the airplane. There was none of the euphoria that was evident after the drop at Hiroshima. So far we had experienced fourteen long and trying hours, and although it was now all down hill, it wasn't over yet. I am sure that each person on board had pretty much the same ideas. I already knew for a fact that if there were to be another drop, I would go again. I kept thinking over and over "Japan how soon before you spare your people more of this agony." But I must confess that at that time, compassion was hard to come by after Pearl Harbor and the Death March of Bataan. Our arrival back on Tinian was late at night. There were no crowds to greet these crews, no medal pinning ceremony, only those who would be concerned with our interrogation were there. We were taken to the intelligence Quonset to await our inquisitors. Before the interrogation crew arrived, Admiral Purnell, in discussing our "miss" with Fred Ashworth pointed out that this was perhaps a most fortunate happening for if we had hit the city the loss of life would have been far greater. He also described for us the concern of General Farrell when we were overdue. The poor, old man "tossed his cookies." Now that was real concern, not feigned concern, and we all liked him and appreciated his feelings for us.

In 1985 Commander Ashworth (Now Admiral Ashworth) wrote the following in a private correspondence:

"Three bombing approaches to the target were unsuccessful because of our requirement to use only the Norden bombsight to control

150

the drop of the bomb. Smoke and haze obscured the target during the approach. And it was frustrating to find each time that when directly over the target it was clearly visible but by then too late to make an accurate visual bombing run. Fifty-five more minutes of precious fuel had been expended and we made the decision to proceed to the secondary target, Nagasaki. This decision was punctuated with anti-aircraft fire and Japanese fighters being vectored to our altitude. And so the job was done. We had made a successful attack albeit not exactly in accordance with the operation plan because we had missed the city center, the assigned target aiming point. Undoubtedly, as General Doolittle had observed, the ground zero we actually achieved was more advantageous to our country from a historical point of view than would have been a ground zero directly in the city. Certainly, compared to Hiroshima, the casualties were significantly less and the real damage turned out to .be important in the destruction of the war making capability of the Japanese. Fortune had aided our bold approach and luck was on our side. Now we were cruising serenely at 30,000 feet headed for our home base on Tinian Island."

Ashworth went on to say: *"As the years of World War II recede into memory and one contemplates the trend toward the concentration of war management into the Pentagon and the White House, it is difficult to escape asking a question and finding in its answer a disturbing conclusion. Consider for a moment the problems and decisions that confronted Major Sweeney and me at Nagasaki. We had been given specific instructions as to how the mission should be accomplished, and these came from the highest levels of government in Washington. Circumstances beyond our control precluded strict conformance with these instructions and we exercised our on the scene judgment and made the appropriate decisions that permitted us to press home an aggressive and a successful attack. I believe that this represents the essence of great leadership*

Our seniors gave us the guidance, they saw to it that those responsible for the execution were fully aware of the principles upon which those instructions were based, and that we were professionally qualified to do the job assigned. Two important conditions emerge from the exercise of that kind of leadership. The on scene tactical commander is afforded the courage to make his own decisions as the circumstances require, and the top-side leaders have our confidence that there is very good reason to expect that those decisions will be sound. It is impossible to avoid comparing this leadership environment with that which is seen today. As has been shown throughout the Cuban missile crisis, the Viet Nam war and the Mayaguez incident it is the policy of leadership now, a policy certainly established by Secretary of Defense McNamara, that detailed management of practically all combat situations will be carried out from the office of the Secretary of Defense and the White House.

If one contemplates the possibility of managing the operational situation experienced at Nagasaki in this centralized fashion, one can only conclude that failure would have been the inevitable result. Time simply would not have permitted referring the problems to Washington for guidance. One can only hope that next time when war comes, and indeed it will, there will be time to recognize the bankruptcy of the current policies and permit the leadership of combat operations to return to the tactical commander on the scene where it must reside if we expect our combat leaders to carry a war through to victory. We lost one war through this bankrupt policy, let us not lose the next one that may well be the one that civilization can not endure."

My father continued. After having our pictures taken in front of the *Bock's Car,* the crewmembers were debriefed, ate a late dinner, and, shared a few drinks. We had completed our mission, glitches and all, and now waited to see the response of the Japanese government. It was obvious that everyone, including our superior officers, were glad to see us, but not particularly well pleased with the performance of our mission. At about 0400 (4:00 am) of the 10th, I was finally able to get to bed.

But time has a way of healing hurts. I am sure it hurt our superiors that we performed, shall we say, not quite up to expectations, but yet we had made our drop and the rest was up to the Japanese to decide - take more or give up. Five days later their answer would be forthcoming.

While on the ground at Okinawa I heard that one cook - not knowing to whom he was talking - tell Olivi all about the bombing, claiming a P-38 fighter from Okinawa was involved and the bomb was the size of a golf ball.

I was just glad it was over," Olivi said. "*Just before we dropped the bomb, it flashed through my mind that we would kill a lot of children, elderly and other people. But that was the nature of the beast, and I put it out of my mind quickly.*"

152

All of the crewmembers have thought about it since. Some have visited Nagasaki. But none express any regrets. *"At the time, I didn't think about it,"* Gallagher said. *"Now I think about the people on the ground and how horrible it must have been. But you know, if someone is beating you up with an iron bar and you have a gun - what would you do?"*

My father went on to say. In retrospect Chuck Sweeney was a good B-29 pilot. He got us home safely in spite of bad weather, technical problems, en-route emergencies, onboard personnel problems, "arguments" and personal screw-ups. The mission was a success even though he took off late with a known fuel transfer problem, ignored the advice of his experienced flight engineer and violated the cardinal rule -- "if you no-drop on the first bomb run, don't try a second for the enemy will get you." Three bombing approaches on Kokura were unsuccessful. Smoke and haze obscured the target during each of these approaches. It was impossible to satisfy our requirement to use only the Norden bombsight to control the drop of the bomb. In the process we used a lot of fuel. By necessity Ashworth and Sweeney made the gutsy decision to proceed to Nagasaki in the spite of anti-aircraft fire and Japanese fighters being vectored to our altitude.

At Nagasaki with my assistance, we made a radar approach in defiance of very specific field orders not to do this. We had a successful drop but missed the city center. But the ground zero we actually achieved was more advantageous to our country from a historical point of view than would have been a ground zero directly in the city. Certainly, compared to Hiroshima the civilian casualties were significantly less. Important military targets were still destroyed and this was the most important criterion.

Jacob Beser poses with the Enola Gay upon their return from the Hiroshima mission August 6, 1945. This is the most publicized photo of my father ever taken.

Were the Bombs Necessary?

Editor's Note: In this chapter and those that follow we have tried to summarize various conversations, public lectures, interviews and TV appearances given by my father over a 40 year period.

Japanese leaders throughout the summer of 1945, expecting an invasion, told their people to "form a wall of human flesh and when the invasion begins, to push the invaders back into the sea." They all seemed to share a mystical faith that their country could never be invaded successfully. And they again would be saved by the "kamikaze (*shimpu*) or divine wind" as had happened in the year 1281 A.D., when two large Chinese fleets set sail for the Empire of Japan. Their purpose was to launch a massive invasion on the Japanese home islands and to conquer Japan in the name of the Great Mongol Emperor Kublai Kahn. The Mongol invasion force was a modern army, and its arsenal of weapons was far superior to that of the Japanese. All over Japan elaborate Shinto ceremonies were performed at shrines. A million Japanese voices called upward for divine intervention. Miraculously, as if in answer to their prayers, from out of the south a savage typhoon (kamikaze or divine wind) sprang up and the Mongol fleet was devastated and ended the invasion.

I was aware in the summer of 1945 that an invasion of the Japanese mainland was planned for November under the code name Operation Downfall. Operation Downfall itself was divided into two parts - Operation Olympic and Operation Coronet. We all knew that the Japanese would fanatically defend their homeland and the American casualties would be high. The will to fight to the death had been shown by the kamikazes and human torpedoes during the Okinawa and Iwo Jima campaigns. Similar resistance would certainly be encountered in an invasion.

Operation Olympic would be a diversionary landing on southern Kyushu. It was fully expected that the Japanese would be able to repel the first landing with the help of suicide tactics. Hundreds of ships and planes and as many as 300,000 American troops would be "written off" for the invasion.

Operation Coronet, the main invasion force, would land on Honshu about two months later. Again fierce resistance was expected.

155

All told the American casualties for Operation Downfall were expected to be a million or more lives lost with considerably more on the Japanese side. I believe Harry Truman made an excellent decision to use the atomic bombs. In my opinion the bombs not only saved many American and Japanese lives but it may have also saved the nation {of Japan}. If their homeland had been invaded there would have been fanatical resistance from both the military and civilians. I believe we would have been compelled to destroy everything in sight as a potential military threat.

We cannot redo the strategy of World War II, nor can we deny the facts as they existed at that time. The events of August 6 and 9, 1945 cannot be changed. We can only judge the results of our actions and the impact that they have had on subsequent events. The fact is, that the Japanese, who were digging in to resist the impending invasion that they knew had to come, were persuaded to alter their plans to resist and accept the terms of surrender that were evolving. In essence, the horrible effects of the atomic bombs that were dropped on Hiroshima and Nagasaki were sufficiently persuasive to change their minds. When the announcement of the successful use of the atomic bombs on Hiroshima and Nagasaki and the surrender of Japan was made, the American people almost unanimously approved. The war with Japan had been going on for almost four years and the world wanted to get it over with as soon as possible. In some families a generation of American boys had been killed. These bombs had ended the war and would bring back home thousands of boys and that was what counted.

During my trip to Japan for the 40th anniversary of the bombings in 1985 I had the opportunity to talk with many Japanese citizens. One Hiroshima survivor by the name of Yoshiteru Kosakai, commented: *"Following the attack on Pearl Harbor on December 7, 1941, World War II had steadily intensified to a desperate fight to the death. Japan with irresistible drive had swept over Malay and the Philippines, then Java and finally Burma, conquering Southeast Asia in about a half a year. However, the tide turned at a naval battle in June 1942, and Japan began to retreat. Air attacks on the homeland increased in number and severity. Hiroshima, like all of Japan, had determined to fight to the finish...with the same heart as our soldiers on the battlefield, we push fearlessly along the road to victory "*

To me it was obvious that the fire bombing raids on their major cities did not demoralize the Japanese but stiffened their will to resist and defend

156

the Emperor. It is my opinion that bombardment of the Japanese cites from the air alone would not have ended the war and an invasion would have been necessary. On several occasions I have spoken with former Japanese soldiers and civilians both men and women who shared the same beliefs.

In these conversations, Japanese soldiers and civilians told me, again by both men and women, that the Japanese leaders and their people were not ready to surrender but were preparing to fight to protect their homeland until the last person was dead. The words "unconditional surrender" were not in their vocabulary. By their choice, when an invasion occurred, there would be no prisoners taken on either side. They had, and were accumulating, a stockpile of weapons and explosives and civilians including men, women and children were being trained on their use. Several thousand kamikaze airplanes and pilots as well as human torpedoes were available. Any invasion would be a "blood bath" for both sides.

As for other eyewitness accounts, I worked with scientist, engineers and technicians involved with the bomb development as well as World War II veterans who were in the American task force being assembled for the invasion of the Japanese homeland and shared their eyewitness experiences with me. These included sailors who were on destroyers performing picket duty in the waters off Okinawa; sailors on ships delivering men and material for the planned invasion of the Empire; sailors who were on ships preparing to "soften up" the landing sites with naval gunfire; and, soldiers and marines on Iwo Jima and Okinawa who had already been briefed on their assignments.

One scientist had worked on the Manhattan Project in Oak Ridge, Tennessee for almost four years developing processes to extract and purify bomb grade uranium. Another was an engineer who helped develop high vacuum pumps and another was a production technician. They all worked around the clock doing their job to perfect the weapons. The Manhattan Project was a super secret program. Only the scientist knew (or suspected) that the final outcome of his labor was to be a super weapon of war. After the bombs were used each of these individuals were proud that they had contributed in some small way to ending the war and had no regrets.

I talked with a sailor who was on one of the over 100 US destroyers performing picket duty protecting Okinawa and Iwo Jima from air attacks by the Japanese. He told me that over 80 percent of the destroyers were damaged or destroyed by Japanese kamikazes resulting in a significant loss of life.

Another former sailor told me of his experiences during submarine attacks while delivering supplies to the islands. Still another sailor who was on a battleship preparing for shore bombardment, he commented that the atomic bombs probably saved his life.

It was said that when the announcement was made that the Hiroshima bombing was successful, the troops assembled for the invasion went wild with excitement and frantic joy. "We did it! We gave it to Hiroshima." Another sailor who was also on picket duty, and I am sure he spoke for many, said that the day he heard news of the atomic bombing of Hiroshima was the happiest day of his life.

A former marine and a veteran of the island hopping campaigns said that he was not interested in another big fight. He recounted the briefings he had received pertaining to his unit's objectives if an invasion took place. He said that they were told that their objective was well protected and to expect at least 90% casualties. He said after the surrender he visited their planned objective and looked over the defenses that were not visible from the air. His comment was the 90% casualty number was low and in his opinion the number would have been closer to 100%.

And some revisionist historians say that a naval blockade of the Japanese islands would have been a better alternative than an invasion or the use of the atomic bombs. Yes, the United States Navy could have blockaded the Japanese homeland. But look at what they would have been up against. Japan still had some small ships, submarines and airplanes as well as a million-man army in other parts of Asia still able to fight. With these forces and 5000 or more kamikaze airplanes and thousands of suicide boats and kaitens or human torpedoes on the main islands ready to attack, what would have been the final cost in American servicemen lives? The kaiten was a converted rocket-shaped torpedo about 40 ft. long and about 4 ft. in diameter with a warhead of about 3000 pounds of TNT. Properly placed underwater it had sufficient force to sink any ship we had including the largest battleships and aircraft carriers. The kamikazes and kaitens had proved very effective at Okinawa. I recall talking with a clerk on Okinawa on our way from Nagasaki to Tinian after the second drop. He told me that if I looked down right after take off I would be able to see almost six hundred ships lying on the bottom of Buckner Bay, all victims

158

of kamikazes. It was my opinion that after we invaded the Empire there probably be hundred if not thousands more ships and their crews suffering the same fate.

Furthermore even after the atomic bombings and total destruction of two cities not all the Japanese military leaders were ready to surrender. It took more B-29 raids and threats of another nuclear attack that made them give up. In their mind, surrender was the ultimate disgrace.

"With faith born of eternal loyalty as our inspiration, we shall--thanks to the advantages of our terrain and the unity of our nation--prosecute the war to the bitter end in order to uphold our national essence, protect the imperial land, and achieve our goals of conquest."

**Japanese Cabinet Response
to
President Truman's Surrender Ultimatum
June 1945**

Japan Surrenders

Yesterday we were at war. I had spent sixteen hours and fifteen minutes aboard the B-29 called *Bock's Car.* This was how long it took to go from Tinian to Kokura to Nagasaki to Okinawa to Tinian. For the second time in three days we had unleashed on Japan the most devastating explosion yet devised by man. On the day after we were speaking in terms of being prepared to go again in ten days. This was August 10, 1945. General Leslie Groves reported to the War Department that the next bomb, another plutonium weapon, would be ready for delivery on the first suitable weather after 17 or 18 August. A B-29 with a replacement crew and the essentials for the next bomb sat poised on the runway at Wendover Army Air Field, Utah, expecting to leave on August 13th for Tinian. This flight never took off. It was canceled on August 11 after President Truman on the 10th ordered a halt to further A-Bombing except upon his explicit orders.

For me, I had sensed on the day after our raid on Nagasaki that this was the beginning of the end and the "Rising Sun" would soon set. Furthermore I had witnessed from a front row seat the dawn of a new age--The Age of Atomic Energy--for I had personally observed the tremendous forces that had been unlocked for the first time in history. This feeling was not confined to me or to my colleagues in the 509th Composite Group, but all over the Island of Tinian one could sense a feeling of relaxation as the enormity of the destruction at both Hiroshima and Nagasaki became better known.

Armed Forces Radio, our primary news media, began almost immediately to expand the coverage of the "Atomic Bomb Story." Several of our Group made the trip to Guam for personal interviews with Armed Forces Radio. While there, the newsreel cameras caught up with them. Colonel Tibbets, our Group Commander and the Hiroshima Pilot; his Navigator Captain Theodore van Kirk; and, his Bombardier, Major Thomas Ferebee were all permitted to make brief non-sensible statements as no one had yet decided what could or should be said. The early newsreels portrayed these three as a mutual admiration society, telling the world that without each other none of this could have happened. In all fairness to these men, they were victimized by a medium with an insatiable appetite that was unwilling to wait for a thought out approach to exactly how this story could be covered and yet not violate the cloak of security under which they were still operating.

On Saturday morning, August 11, 1945, the 509th hosted the World Press Pool that was flown up from Guam to Tinian to interview the strike crews and meet some of the Project and other 509th personnel that were on the island. As I recall there must have been over 200 press people in attendance. By this time a plan had been formulated that allowed a reasonably free exchange between the press and the crew. The general conference was chaired by Brigadier General Thomas Farrell, General Grove's deputy on site, assisted by Colonel Hazen Payette, the 509th Group Intelligence Officer. Every big name correspondent in the area appeared at this conference.

It was interesting to watch and listen to these men (and two women) as they worked. Aside from their intelligence, one had to be impressed by their perception. They gave us the feeling that the war, for all intents and purposes, was already over. The fact that people on both sides were still being killed and would continue until the terms of a cease-fire were reached seemed to be part of a way of life to which they were well adjusted. While doing their jobs with us, they continually expressed concern over the ways and means available to them "to get to Japan to witness the surrender."

The Hiroshima mission crew was interviewed first. When this crew stepped down from the platform and the Nagasaki crew stepped up, I stayed put. One reporter, Dick Tregaskis, zeroed in on this and really wanted to delve into my role in the missions. This was still classified information. He was only told that I had special instrumentation associated with me and with the weapon. However, Dick was an avid fact finder and really wanted to know. Not getting all the answers that he was looking for, he figured it out real fast what I probably was doing on both missions. This became a touchy subject and General Farrell cautioned him that this discussion was off the record.

I became a special object of curiosity because of my role on both strike crews. For this reason, Captain Joseph Buscher, the Group Security Officer, was assigned to monitor each and every one-on-one interview that I had. There were quite a few. The one thing that still stands out in my mind after all these years is none of the reporters ever asked me if I thought we should do it again. I may have disarmed them in a way when I told them that I would accompany however many more of these bombs we would drop. Two other questions significant by their absence were - "Was this the right thing to do? Or should we do it again?"

The question most often asked was "When will the next one be used?"

162

Obviously, they all felt that we were now in a position for the 509th Group to deliver to Japan the Coupe-de-Grace!

I have always felt that in World War II as we came to know it, the ultimate weapon was the thing to use. Although on the way home from Nagasaki I strongly hoped that we would not have to go again, I never once thought that I would not go if it was decided to drop a third bomb.

This immediate post-Nagasaki drop period was an agonizing time for the Japanese people and their government.

Cabinet Ministers in Tokyo could not instantaneously turn off the war, which had started fourteen years earlier by Field Army Commanders in Manchuria. Too much had happened and too much blood had been shed, and Japan was in ruins. Not only were her cities smashed, her economy devastated, but the flower of her manhood had been lost in battles far from home and on the seas in between.

Old men who controlled the Army and Navy could not or would not accept the realities of her present circumstance. Some even thought that the war could still be won. Most thought that the Allies could be made to pay dearly in the Final Battle where even women and children were being prepared to die in an all out resistance to the invasion that they knew was coming.

One concern existed that was common to all; the National Polity must be preserved. The Emperor and all that he stood for is the only focal point around which the Japanese people can rally and revolution avoided. Despite the fact that within the Palace a revolt was already in progress the struggle had not yet reached the streets. The Emperor had decided that he would go to the people via the National Radio and announce Japan's acceptance of the inevitability of surrender to avoid further shedding of blood.

History tells us that Emperor Hirohito up until now had only been a helpless bystander in the war effort, seen but never heard by the Japanese People. This Man-God had decided to cast aside his Deity and to display his humanity by going over the heads of his Generals and Cabinet Ministers and announce that all was lost and the war was being brought to an end. He appealed to the citizens of Japan, the kamikazes poised to defend the homeland, and the armies in the field to give in. He believed what Harry Truman had said and felt that the United States was prepared to deliver the same fate to the other surviving cities in Japan that we had done to Hiroshima and Nagasaki. At noon, August 15, 1945, the following recorded message from the Emperor of Japan to his subjects was broadcast over Radio NHK. This message brought the war to an end in accordance with the terms and conditions that had been agreed to by the Allies at the Potsdam conference and thereby saved millions of lives. In my opinion, this was a direct result of what

163

we did at Hiroshima and Nagasaki!

"To Our good and loyal subjects: After pondering deeply the general trends of the world and the actual conditions obtaining to Our Empire today, We have decided to effect a settlement of the present situation by resorting to an extraordinary measure.

We have ordered Our Government to communicate to the Governments of the United States, Great Britain, China and the Soviet Union that Our Empire accepts the provisions of their Joint Declaration.

To strive for the common prosperity and happiness of all nations as well as the security and well-being of Our Subjects is the solemn obligation which has been handed down by Our Imperial Ancestors, and which we lay close to heart. Indeed, We declared war on America and Britain out of Our sincere desire to ensure Japan's self-preservation and the stabilization of East Asia, it being far from Our thought either to infringe upon the sovereignty of other nations or to embark upon territorial aggrandisement. But now the war has lasted for nearly four years. Despite the best that has been done by everyone -- the gallant fighting of the military and naval forces, the diligence and assiduity of Our servants of the State and the devoted service of Our one hundred million people, the war situation has developed not necessarily to Japan's advantage, while the general trends of the world have all turned against her interest. Moreover, the enemy has begun to employ a new and most cruel bomb, the power of which to damage is indeed incalculable, taking the toll of many innocent lives. Should We continue to fight, it would not only result in an ultimate collapse and obliteration of the Japanese nation, but also it would lead to the total extinction of human civilization. Such being the case, how are We to save the millions of Our subjects; or to atone Ourselves before the hallowed spirits of Our Imperial Ancestors? This is the reason why We have ordered the Acceptance of the provisions of the Joint Declaration of the Powers.

We cannot but express the deepest sense of regret to our Allied nations of East Asia, who have consistently co-operated with the Empire towards the emancipation of East Asia. The thought of those officers and men as well as others who have fallen in the fields of battle, those

164

who died at their posts of duty, or those who met with untimely death and all their bereaved families, pains Our heart day and night. The welfare of the wounded and the war sufferers, and of those who have lost their homes and livelihood, are the objects of Our profound solicitude. The hardships and sufferings to which Our nation is to be subjected hereafter will certainly be great. We are keenly aware of the inmost feelings of all ye, Our subjects. However, it is according to the dictate of time and fate that We have resolved to pave the way for a grand peace for all the generations to come by enduring the unendurable and suffering what is insufferable.

Having been able to safeguard and maintain the structure of the Imperial State, We are always with ye, Our good and loyal subjects, relying upon your sincerity and integrity. Beware most strictly of any outbursts of emotion which may engender needless complications, or any fraternal contention and strife which may create confusion, lead ye astray and cause ye to lose the confidence of the world. Let the entire nation continue as one family from generation to generation, ever firm in its faith of the imperishableness of its divine land, and mindful of its heavy responsibilities, and the long road before it. Unite your total strength to be devoted to the construction for the future. Cultivate the ways of rectitude; foster nobility of spirit; and work with resolution so as ye may enhance the innate glory of the Imperial State and keep pace with the progress of the world.

14th day of the 8th month of the 20th year of Showa."

PROCLAMATION DEFINING TERMS FOR JAPANESE SURRENDER
(The Department of State Bulletin, Vol. XIII, No. 318, July 29, 1945)

(1) We - the President of the United States, the President of the National Government of the Republic of China, and the Prime Minister of Great Britain, representing the hundreds of millions of our countrymen, have conferred and agree that Japan shall be given an opportunity to end this war.

(2) The prodigious land, sea and air forces of the United States, the British Empire and of China, many times reinforced by their armies and air fleets from the west, are poised to strike the final blows upon Japan.

This military power is sustained and inspired by the determination of all the Allied Nations to prosecute the war against Japan until she ceases to resist.

(3) The result of the futile and senseless German resistance to the might of the aroused free peoples of the world stands forth in awful clarity as an example to the people of Japan. The might that now converges on Japan is immeasurably greater than that which, when applied to the resisting Nazis, necessarily laid waste to the lands, the industry and the method of life of the whole German people. The full application of our military power, backed by our resolve, WILL mean the inevitable and complete destruction of the Japanese armed forces and just as inevitably the utter destruction of the Japanese homeland.

(4) The time has come for Japan to decide whether she will continue to be controlled by those self-willed militaristic advisers whose unintelligent calculations have brought the Empire of Japan to the threshold of annihilation, or whether she will follow the path of reason.

(5) Following are our terms. We will not deviate from them. There are no alternatives. We shall brook no delay.

(6) There must be eliminated for all time the authority and influence of those who have deceived and misled the people of Japan into embarking on world conquest, for we insist that a new order of peace, security and justice will be impossible until irresponsible militarism is driven from the world.

(7) Until such a new order is established AND until there is convincing proof that Japan's war-making power is destroyed, points in Japanese territory to be designated by the Allies shall be occupied to secure the achievement of the basic objectives we are here setting forth.

(8) The terms of the Cairo Declaration shall be carried out and Japanese sovereignty shall be limited to the islands of Honshu, Hokkaido, Kyushu, Shikoku, and such minor islands as we determine.

(9) The Japanese military forces, after being completely disarmed, shall be permitted to return to their homes with the opportunity to lead peaceful and productive lives.

(10) We don not intend that the Japanese shall be enslaved as a race or destroyed as a nation, but stern justice shall be meted out to all war criminals, including those who have visited cruelties upon our prisoners. The Japanese Government shall remove all obstacles to the revival and strengthening of democratic tendencies among the Japanese people.

166

Freedom of speech, of religion and of thought, as well as respect for the fundamental human rights, shall be established.

(11) Japan shall be permitted to maintain such industries as will sustain her economy and permit the exaction of just reparations in kind, but not those which would enable her to rearm for war. To this end, access to, as distinguished from control of, raw materials shall be permitted. Eventual Japanese participation in world trade relations shall be permitted.

(12) The occupying forces of the Allies shall be withdrawn from Japan as soon as these objectives have been accomplished and there has been established, in accordance with the freely expressed will of the Japanese people, a peacefully inclined and responsible Government.

(13) We call upon the Government of Japan to proclaim now the unconditional surrender of all Japanese armed forces, and to provide proper and adequate assurances of their good faith in such action. The alternative for Japan is prompt and utter destruction.

JAPANESE ACCEPTANCE

September 12, 1945

By the Grace of Heaven, Emperor of Japan, seated on the Throne occupied by the same Dynasty changeless through ages eternal,

To all who these Presents shall come, Greeting!

We do hereby authorize Mamoru Shigemitsu, Zyosanmi, First Class of the Imperial Order of the Rising Sun to attach his signature by command and in behalf of Ourselves and Our Government unto the Instrument of Surrender which is required by the Supreme Commander for the Allied Powers to be signed.

In witness whereof, We have hereunto set our signature and caused the Great Seal of the Empire to be affixed.

Given at Our Palace in Tokyo, this first day of the ninth month of the twentieth year of Syowa, being the two thousand six hundred and fifth year from the Accession of the Emperor Zinmu.

> Seal of the Empire
> Signed: H I R O H I T O
> Countersigned: Naruhiko-o
> Prime Minister

By the Grace of Heaven, Emperor of Japan, seated on the Throne occupied by the same Dynasty changeless through ages eternal,

To all who these Presents shall come, Greeting!

We do hereby authorize Yoshijiro Umezu, Zyosanmi, First Class of the Imperial Order of the Rising Sun to attach his signature by command and in behalf of Ourselves and Our Government unto the Instrument of Surrender which is required by the Supreme Commander for the Allied Powers to be signed.

In witness whereof, We have hereunto set our signature and caused the Great Seal of the Empire to be affixed.

Given at Our Palace in Tokyo, this first day of the ninth month of the twentieth year of Syowa, being the two thousand six hundred and fifth year from the Accession of the Emperor Zinmu.

> Seal of the Empire
> Signed: H I R O H I T O
> Countersigned:
> Yoshijiro Umezu, Chief of the General Staff of the Imperial
>   Japanese Army
> Soemu Toyoda, Chief of the General Staff of the Imperial
>   Japanese Army

INSTRUMENT OF SURRENDER

We, acting by command of and in behalf of the Emperor of Japan, the Japanese Government and the Japanese Imperial General Headquarters, hereby accept the provisions set forth in the declaration issued by the heads of the Governments of the United States, China, and Great Britain on 26 July 1945 at Potsdam, and subsequently adhered to by the Union of Soviet Socialist Republics, which four powers are hereafter referred to as the Allied Powers.

We hereby proclaim the unconditional surrender to the Allied Powers of the Japanese Imperial General Headquarters and of all Japanese armed forces and all armed forces under the Japanese control wherever situated.

We hereby command all Japanese forces wherever situated and the Japanese people to cease hostilities forthwith, to preserve and save from damage all ships, aircraft, and military and civil property and to comply with all requirements which may be imposed by the Supreme Commander for the Allied Powers or by agencies of the Japanese Government at his direction.

We hereby command the Japanese Imperial Headquarters to issue at once orders to the Commanders of all Japanese forces and all forces under Japanese control wherever situated to surrender unconditionally themselves and all forces under their control.

We hereby command all civil, military and naval officials to obey and enforce all proclamations, and orders and directives deemed by the Supreme Commander for the Allied Powers to be proper to effectuate this surrender and issued by him or under his authority and we direct all such officials to remain at their posts and to continue to perform their non-combatant duties unless specifically relieved by him or under his authority.

We hereby undertake for the Emperor, the Japanese Government and their successors to carry out the provisions of the Potsdam Declaration in good faith, and to issue whatever orders and take whatever actions may be required by the Supreme Commander for the Allied Powers or by any other designated representative of the Allied Powers for the purpose of giving effect to that Declaration.

We hereby command the Japanese Imperial Government and the Japanese Imperial General Headquarters at once to liberate all allied prisoners of war and civilian internees now under Japanese control and to provide for their protection, care, maintenance and immediate transportation to places as directed.

The authority of the Emperor and the Japanese Government to rule the state shall be subject to the Supreme Commander for the Allied Powers who will take such steps as he deems proper to effectuate these terms of surrender.

Signed at TOKYO BAY, JAPAN at 0904 on the SECOND day of SEPTEMBER, 1945.

MAMORU SHIGMITSU
By Command and in behalf of the Emperor of Japan and the Japanese Government
YOSHIJIRO UMEZU
By Command and in behalf of the Japanese Imperial General Headquarters

Accepted at TOKYO BAY, JAPAN at 0903 I on the SECOND day of SEPTEMBER 1945, for the United States, Republic of China, United

169

Kingdom and the Union of Soviet Socialist Republics, and in the interests of the other United Nations at war with Japan.

DOUGLAS MACARTHUR, Supreme Commander for the Allied Powers
C.W. NIMITZ, United States Representative
HSU YUNG-CH'ANG, Republic of China Representative
BRUCE FRASER, United Kingdom Representative
KUZMA DEREVYANKO Union of Soviet Socialist Republics Representative
THOMAS BLAMEY Commonwealth of Australia Representative
L. MOORE COSGRAVE, Dominion of Canada Representative
JACQUES LE CLERC, Provisional Government of the French Republic Representative
C.E.L. HELFRICH, Kingdom of the Netherlands Representative
LEONARD M. ISITT, Dominion of New Zealand Representative

Japanese Envoy Signs Surrender Documents September 2, 1945

History has recorded August 15, 1945 as VJ Day and the beginning of a new era for Japan but the Japanese did not actually sign the surrender document, aboard the battleship USS Missouri, until the 2 September 1945. As I recall, there was suspicion in some quarters that the surrender was a trick and our Marines may have waited a week or so before actually landing. I am not 100% sure this actually happened but when they landed and saw the devastation that bombing had caused they came to the realization that the war was finally over.

But there are still revisionist who repeat their claims that Japan had fought a "war of liberation" to free Asians from the influence of Western cultures and rule. They avoid any discussion that the Empire of Japan launched a war of aggression against the Americans at Pearl Harbor that killed both American military and civilians personnel. Never do you hear anything about the Japanese brutal war of conquest against China in which hundreds of thousands of civilians were mercilessly tortured and killed. It was the same fanatical group of military leaders that wanted to fight the United States down to the last man. Never do you hear anything about the Japanese Imperial Army's complete control over the Government and their vicious decisions in the 1930s and 1940s. Even today they refuse to teach in their schools the lessons of their country's dreadful past.

Historians and others have documented the transition in Japan from a defeated nation for the first time in her history to her present state. It is not my intention to repeat that here. Suffice it to say that during my visit to Japan in the summer of 1985 I saw little left of the ashes of the War. What I did see was a strong, modern, industrial nation that openly reflects little of the old Imperial Japan. A nation that now leads much of the Industrial World in a strong and dominant way, free of the burden of completely providing for her own defense. This was a burden that we forced her to legislate out of existence and have accepted on her behalf. A provision of her post-war constitution limits Japan's army and weapons to those required for self-defense and the expenditures therefore to the neighborhood of one percent of her gross national products, thus leaving huge amounts of capital available to develop her industrial base and to pursue world trade.

July 25 1945

We met at 11 A.M. today. That is Stalin, Churchill and the U.S. President. But I had a most important session with Lord Mountbatten & General Marshall before that. We have discovered the most terrible bomb in the history of the world. It may be the fire distruction prophesied in the Euphrates Valley Era, after Noah and his fabulous Ark.

Anyway we think we have found the way to cause a disintegration of the atom. An experiment in the New Mexico desert was startling - to put it mildly. Thirteen pounds of the explosive caused the complete disintegration of a steel tower 60 feet high, created a crater 6 feet deep and 1200 feet in diameter, knocked over a steel tower 1/2 mile away and knocked men down 10,000 yards away. The explosion was visible for more than 200 miles and audible for 40 miles and more.

This weapon is to be used against Japan between now and August 10th. I have told the Sec. of War, Mr. Stimson, to use it so that military objectives and soldiers and sailors are the target and not women and children. Even if the Japs are savages, ruthless, merciless and fanatic, we as the leader of the world for the common welfare cannot drop this terrible bomb on the old Capitol or the new.

He & I are in accord. The target will be a purely military one and we will issue a warning statement asking the Japs to surrender and save lives. I'm sure they will not do that but we will have given them the chance. It is certainly a good thing for the world that Hitler's crowd or Stalin's did not discover this atomic bomb. It seems to be the most terrible thing

Page one of seven pages from President Truman's diary at the Postdam conference in which writes that he told the Secretary of War to use the bomb but placed restriction that it not be used on the old or new capital and that military targets were to be the objective, not women and children. He also says that he will give the Japs a chance to surrender before any atomic weapons are used.

The War is Over

The day after V-J Day we all began to count our "points," those credits that each soldier received for length of service, combat duty, etc. This would determine how soon we could expect to be demobilized or separated from the service. I had sufficient points to expect early demobilization but the future of the 509th Composite Group was uncertain because of the nature of our special mission and capability. I was initially told that I could not expect early demobilization because of the extreme sensitivity of the information that had been imparted to me. This had considerable influence on what I was to do over the next several months.

It seems that the immediate plans for the 509th was to: (1) Get the men back to the states (2) Put them in a place where they could be watched more closely (3). Allow those eligible to go home on leave, and (3) Supply replacements as rapidly as possible so that the unit could be retrained and refurbished in order to implement any future tests that everyone knew had to be conducted. It was now a known fact that these weapons were too good to let die on the vine and too little was known about them. Besides there were the Soviets in Europe and Asia now flexing their muscles in an openly hostile manner.

It was decided to ship the unit back stateside as soon as possible. As it turned out, an additional officer was required to accompany our troops on the transport ship going home. This choice tid-bit of information was made available to me by an informant in the orderly room. I went to the Colonel and asked for and received permission to fill this billet. In this way, I found a twenty-six day ocean voyage wherein I would have ample time to come up with some kind of a plan for my future. I felt that this would be much better alternative to three days and twenty-six hours flying back home. Once back home I would be caught up in the many details of moving the unit from Wendover Army Air Field, Utah, our former home, to Roswell Army Air Field in northern New Mexico.

Let there be no mistake, this was not to be a luxury cruise. Our departure was scheduled for early October near the end of the typhoon season. The vessel would be the APA-160, USS Deuel, an assault transport that was used to carry troops for the invasion of Iwo Jima the preceding April. Immediately after launching her assault boats, she began service as a hospital ship thirty minutes later. The men from the Deuel were in the twenty-sixth wave and still classified as assault, not reinforcements.

I no longer remember the date that the Deuel sailed from Tinian Harbor, nor can I find any mention of it in my personal files. Since most of my records were lost in the fire at the Veteran's Record Center in St. Louis several years ago there is little chance that I will recover that date. It is not really important, but what is important is that within twenty-four hours of sailing from Guam, where we stopped to have the ship fueled, we began to feel the effects of Typhoon Louise.[33]

It was never clear to me if we were skirting the storm or riding right into it. For once in my life I was undergoing a new experience towards which I was not looking forward. The extent of my maritime experience consisted of many excursions on the Chesapeake Bay

USS Deuel San Francisco, CA 1945

aboard the *Emma Giles* and her sister ships going from Baltimore Harbor to Tolchester Beach, about twenty miles away on Maryland's Eastern Shore, or up the Bay to the Sassafras River and Betterton Beach. None of this could have been considered adequate indoctrination for what we were soon to encounter.

Up to this time I had accumulated a goodly number of flying hours in a variety of aircraft all over the continental US and in the Caribbean and the Central Pacific Ocean areas. At no time did I encounter motion sickness. On several occasions when others near me began getting sick, their power of suggestion almost did me in. Somehow, I managed to survive, and as time went on I even developed immunity to "suggestion."

As the storm built in intensity, the troops, who were now confined in cargo holds became violently seasick. Also the accompanying officers, although not confined to the holds, were confined to the wardroom or their dormitory quarters in the center of the ship. It was absolutely impossible to get a breath of fresh air. It

---

[33] Records show that the USS Deuel (APA-160) left Tinian on October 18, 1945 and made port at Oakland, CA on November 4, 1945.

wasn't long before one became immune to the sickly aroma that permeated the ship.

Illness was not confined to the passengers, it also overtook some members of the ship's crew. Early on after we boarded the ship I introduced myself to the ship's radar officer and was given a tour of his facilities. Little did I realize then that in about thirty-six hours this same man would seek me out to help his radar crew during the storm. It seems that three of his six operators/watch keepers were totally wiped out and unable to function.

I was assigned to a radar display console in the wheelhouse, where for the next three and one half days I stood watch sharing the duty with one of the ship's regulars. Throughout the storm, we never left the wheelhouse except to take care of "nature calls" and to get periodic four-hour naps. There was no time to get sick and they were able to maintain a steady flow of fresh air in the working area. More important, I learned the validity of the old mariner's advice - keep a full stomach and you won't get seasick.

Although the USS Deuel was a 20,000-ton ship, she bobbed like a cork on the waves. It was all that the helmsman could do to "keep her headed and lying to." We made very little forward progress and lots of leeway. The waves were breaking above the height of the masts; the bow would go down; and, the propeller would come out of the water. You would hear the shaft rev up as the bow went down. The ship would shudder when this happened and then there was the solid slap as the stern came back down. It made us think that at any moment the ship would break apart.

As night turned to day the only thing that changed was the ambient light. Visibility hardly improved. At the height of the rain, one could hardly see the bow of the boat from the wheelhouse. It was perhaps the eeriest situation I had ever been in. It is often said that ignorance is bliss, and I am sure that in this situation the bliss borne of ignorance was what kept me from being so frightened that I would have been unable to function.

Enough could not be said for the ship's crew. Her captain was a Merchant Marine Skipper, Naval Reserve Officer on duty for the duration. He was admired and respected by the crew. His facial features and ruddy complexion reflected a life at sea. The concern that he showed for his men could not help but make one comfortable in what to me were trying circumstances. My notoriety as a member of both strike crews at both Hiroshima and Nagasaki had reached him. He was thankful for what we had done. As he put it to me one night, "I was not looking forward to being part of the invasion of Japan. It could only have been another Iwo Jima, but on a larger scale."

175

When the storm abated, the ocean became like a sheet of glass. Not a wave or a ripple as far as the eye could see. This happened on the fifth day of our voyage, and from that time forward I had time to contemplate and plan for the beginning of the rest of my life.

For the next twenty-one days the weather was beautiful. It soon became apparent, without looking at the daily position chart that was being maintained in the wardroom, that we were heading north. One began to feel a touch of fall in the air. We were no longer seeing porpoises or flying fish. The men had a continuous dice game going on a blanket on the fore deck. In the wardroom, contrary to the Captains wishes, along with Cribbage, Casino, Bridge, and Pinochle we had a continuous Poker Game being played.

About mid-November we arrived in Oakland, California, on a Sunday morning. We were greeted by "Welcome Home Ships." The 509th went right from the ship to a troop train that was waiting for us on the dock, and twenty-four hours later we were in Roswell, New Mexico, which would be the Group's home base for the next several years.

At Roswell, the Army Professionals[34] were all jockeying for position to take over the 509th. They saw only the headlines and not the need for an orderly transition to a peacetime program wherein the new skills required could be developed. To these people it was axiomatic that wartime reserve officers and enlisted men had to go. I thought that since I was only a reserve officer and not a professional that they would be glad to let me go. I felt this for several reasons: the professionals were already moving in and the dislike of reserve officers that existed all through the war was rapidly becoming hate. Instead of being allowed to pursue specialties, we were being assigned duties such as supply officers, mess officers, etc. Those of us that had special technical knowledge, were allowed to continue to serve in our specialty with a professional shadow, hoping that within a few weeks or months the shadow would be as smart as we were and then we could be let go. This was proof enough to me that I did not want to remain in the Army. But instead of letting me go as I requested, I was told in so many words that I was indefinitely frozen by command of General Arnold. His reason was that I knew too much about the new weapon, and until a decision was made on the handling of the whole situation, I wasn't going anywhere.

I immediately made an appointment with the new chief of the Fusing and Firing Lab at Los Alamos and met him in Albuquerque the next day. Colonel

---

[34] Editor's Note: The term "professional" is used here to describe West Point and Naval Academy graduates and other officers who intended to make the military a career as opposed to "reserve" officers.

Tibbets was kind enough to get me an AT-6 and a pilot for the trip. After an interview of several hours, the good Doctor made me an offer I could hardly refuse contingent to my obtaining my release from the service. Within three days I had this offer in writing.

The same person that told me that I was not going anywhere until a decision was made told me in the next breath that I was entitled to thirty days rehabilitation leave. I did not object to this, as my home was in Baltimore, Maryland, just 40 miles from Washington. On the 16th of November 1945, I was granted 45 days of rehabilitation leave effective 21 November. 1 knew exactly what I was going to do, and I did it. While on rehab leave I went to Washington to see the senior senator from my state, the late Millard Tydings, who was also the Chairman of the Senate Armed Forces Committee.

I told the Senator who I was, where I had been, and what it was I would like to do. I also showed him my letter offer from Los Alamos. Within five minutes he told me to go home and enjoy my leave, and by the time I get back to Roswell, there will be orders there separating me from active duty.

I did exactly as he told me and returned to Roswell Army Airfield, New Mexico, on the 5th of January 1946 1 reported back to my unit, the 393rd Bomb Squadron. I thought it best that I not say anything about my having seen Senator Tydings, except that I did share it with my very good friend Charlie Perry.

As promised, within a week a telegram came in from Washington authorizing my release from active duty on the 14th of January and ordering me to report to Mitchell Field on Long Island not later than January 19.

I passed this word to Charlie and found out that he too was ordered back to the East Coast for separation. We both cleared the base as fast as we could. In the interim I purchased a car from another colleague in the squadron, and on the 15th of January, Charlie and I headed South out of Roswell in order to get out of a severe snowstorm that had developed over night.

We ran out of the snow at Hobbs, New Mexico, where we now headed east. Three days later we arrived Baltimore, where I put Charlie on the train to Boston while I spent the night with my parents. Needless to say, I made it to Mitchell Field on time the next day.

In a period of two months I had devised a plan for obtaining my release from the service, implemented the plan, and was only awaiting what I thought was an automatic final step to transfer my prior security clearance to my next work location. My basic security clearance had been granted on Certificate of Eligibility Number 5-42244, dated March 16, 1943, and was issued by command of Lieutenant General Arnold and authenticated by A.W. Brock, Jr., Colonel, G.S.C.,

Director of Intelligence Service, War Department, Headquarters Army Air Forces, Washington. Prior to that time, I have no idea on what basis I had been granted access to classified information. I did know that during my initial weeks at radar school, operatives of US Army Intelligence Services visited all of my references. A complete background investigation was done and the certificate of eligibility that I received on March 16, 1943 was issued. There were no further endorsements entered on the certificate as late as the day I was separated from the service.

The automatic transfer of clearance that I was awaiting would not be forthcoming. It seems that the moment one left the service one automatically became a security risk. To be re-cleared required a completely new and extensive background investigation. The fact that I was to be employed as a civilian in essentially the same capacity as I had served as a soldier on the day before carried no weight. In addition, an entirely new set of rules would be evolving, and the new "Q" Clearance would be created for employees or others that would be working on the new Atomic Weapons. It took an additional two months before I was re-qualified and cleared.

Until my clearance came in, I was banned from the facilities where I would be working. However, on the day my clearance arrived, I was called from Los Alamos and told to report to their new facility at Sandia Base, just to the east of Albuquerque, New Mexico. The Z-Division, which had hired me, was being moved to this location. These were the people charged with the responsibility of developing new and improved fusing and firing mechanisms for existing and as yet to be developed newer versions of the a-bomb. The University of California was still to be operating the laboratories, but the Corps of Engineers would be the housekeepers. This made for some sticky situations. The Lab was university turf, but the storerooms from which we drew needed material, was Corps of Engineers turf. To this day I still remember quite vividly the bureaucratic squabbles that took place.

I worked with some of the people that I had met back in September of 1944, when I was first taken to Los Alamos, and many others that knew me, even though we had never been formally introduced. The group that I worked in was known as the Informer Group and we were supervised by William B. Caldes who had come to Los Alamos as one of the early volunteers from the Campus of Princeton University. We were charged with the continuing development of the FM/FM Telemetry System used to monitor the performance of various test models of the bomb and its subassemblies; hence the name Informer Group. We developed everything from the transducers used to interface with the items under test to new test equipment, recorders, and receivers and antennas. The hardware that we didn't actually build in house was subcontracted to certain approved vendors. This was an excellent environment in which to prepare myself for the future in the new and exciting electronics industry.

Albuquerque was only four hours drive from El Paso, Texas, where on an occasional weekend I would meet up with some of my former colleagues that were still serving in the 509th Composite Group at Roswell, New Mexico. When I would meet with these friends and hear about post-war jockeying for position that was taking place in the old outfit. I never for one moment regretted leaving the army. Had I stayed I would have been in continual hot water and probably would have been invited to leave. I could take all kinds of stress very well, but pettiness and chauvinism were not one that I was ever amenable to, and I was usually sounding off whenever I encountered these two torments.

I made some very good friends at Sandia, but one with whom I am still in contact was Francis Critchlow of Los Angeles, California. Now a retired radiologist living in La Canada, California, Fran and I have kept tabs on each other periodically over the ensuing years. We were roommates at Sandia in the bachelor quarters, and shared our mutual uncertainties about the future. I think he was more concerned than I was, or at least a little more determined than I was at the time. Although he had a degree in Chemical Engineering and had served in the Navy during the War, he was not very content in his job with us at Sandia. He made up his mind that he was going to go to Medical School. He applied to the University of California and was given a conditional acceptance, provided that he complete some required course work during the summer of 1947. He left Sandia early in 1947 to complete the requirements for acceptance into the Medical School.

Watching my friend carry through the way he did provided me with the little added incentive that I needed to keep my own educational plans moving. In early January 1947 I contacted Dr. William B. Kouenhoven, Dean of the Engineering School at the John Hopkins University, and arranged for my return to the campus in February. My intention was to return to school and complete my final semester needed for my degree, and then return to Sandia and continue working on the developments as required for more advanced weaponry.

I was able to arrange a leave of absence from the facility and in mid-January I traveled east, to resume my studies at Hopkins.

Upon arrival on campus, I was informed that I was too late to qualify for my degree under the requirements of my pre-war curriculum, but I would have to spend another year in school and would be graduated in June of 1948. I was a little upset at this turn of events, but I was told that I should have returned in

September of 1946 to qualify under the old rules. I immediately went to my pre-war advisor, Dr. Ferdinand Hamburger

After he reviewed the schooling that I had in the Army, and my actual work experience, I was qualified for completion in 1947 if I could get into the one course that he felt I really needed. Unfortunately, this course would not be offered again until the spring of 1948. He did work out an interesting syllabus for me and also offered me a job working for him on a Navy Project in his Systems Laboratory. Everything worked out very well, except that my plans to return to Sandia over the summer were thwarted by an administrative directive that no one thought to tell me about. Instead of having my clearance put on HOLD while I was back in school, it was terminated. Because of this termination, it would require an entirely new background investigation, which could not be completed in time for me to return to Sandia by late May 1947. Since Dr. Hamburger now gainfully employed me, it was agreed that I would stay there until I graduated and then return to Sandia.

It was during this same time period that I began to accept invitation to speak to various audiences around the city of Baltimore and elsewhere.

People from all walks of life began to express curiosity about my experiences during the war. I discovered that contrary to my own feelings, there were some others who felt that what we did was not called for while some even regarded it as a heinous act. One thing became immediately obvious. The closer a person had been to the war, the more he was likely to have approval for Truman's decision to use the bomb. There were even those who felt that once Germany was defeated all work on the bomb should have stopped.

From February 1947, until June of the following year, there was very little play and one hell of a lot of hard work. It was not an easy transition back to the somewhat regimented life of a schoolboy. When I was not in class or doing home assignments, I was working in the Systems Research Lab, helping to build a Radar Simulator for the Navy. My income from the job, and the stipend that I received from my benevolent Uncle Sam for being a WW II veteran and college student allowed me to live comfortably and periodically take a date to a show or sporting event.

My social calendar was replaced by the many requests I was receiving to speak to various men's and women's clubs and "societies" around town. I also was asked to speak on the radio on behalf of different causes that ranged from Universal Military Service to various types of Loyalty Act Proposals. It should be obvious that at this period I was not held in very high esteem by many of my friends who were of liberal persuasion.

My most rewarding moments came when a fellow student or a member of my lecture audience would come to me and say, "if it were not for you and your colleagues I probably would not be here today. The atomic bomb saved my life." One classmate had been in a Japanese Prisoner of War Camp right in Nagasaki harbor, more dead than alive as a result of starvation and maltreatment. When he picked up his morning paper one day and read an article reviewing my talk from the night before, he suddenly realized that I was the fellow sitting two seats away from him in Power Plant Design class. He was waiting at the door for me to come in. He embraced me and cried like a baby as he told me his story. Not only that, before the morning session was over, he told his story to the entire class.

The "you saved my life" commentary is still quite strongly felt forty-five years later. It has come from survivors of Japanese Concentration Camps in the vicinity of Shanghai, China, from veterans who were en-route from Europe to the Pacific where they would have taken part in the invasion of Japan, to people that were already in the staging area for the invasion.

As the end of the school year 1948 was approaching, I began to have some misgiving about running right back to New Mexico. My collegiate advisors were pressing me to apply for graduate school. I was ambivalent about this step. I felt that I was still pretty up tight from the war, I needed to relax, and I had a plan in the back of my mind that included going back into the service.

I had applied for a regular army commission when I was still overseas. While at Sandia I had gone before a preliminary screening board at Ft. Bliss in El Paso, Texas. I evidently scored very well there. I was told that I would be recalled for further evaluation in the next few months. When I returned to school, I notified the Board at Ft. Bliss of the impending move. In early May 1948, 1 was called before the Final Officer Evaluation Board that was sitting at Ft. Meade, Maryland. This was a three-day session.

My appearance before this board was no earth shattering experience. In fact it appeared to me to be a rather benign review of my career and experiences at Hiroshima and Nagasaki. My responses to each and every question were terse and to the point. I had been advised early on by the Adjutant that I was there because serious consideration was being given to offer me a regular army appointment. The Army was becoming aware of the fact that their future would be highly dependent upon the Technical Officer, especially in the Air Corps.

The entire interview lasted approximately forty-five minutes. There was one member of this board that was known by me. He had been a student, as a Lieutenant Colonel, in one of my classes at the Army Air Corps School of Applied

Tactics in Orlando, Florida. At the time I was a Second Lieutenant. The Lieutenant Colonel was a key member of a B-24 cadre that was going through the Heavy Bombardment Course prior to going to Operational Training. My class was devoted to Communication Procedures in the UK. This is where the American Bombers were being based in Europe. Since the British Communications Systems and Procedures were entirely different than ours, the course was considered a "must." My class was at seven in the morning.

I have to admit that at this un-Godly hour, I too, if I had my rathers, would have been somewhere else. The Lieutenant Colonel obviously felt this way because after the first class, I never saw him again until the end of the month when he managed to show for the last class. It also happened that this was the day for the Final Test, and as I have noted, this was a "must."

The questions were multiple choice, and of such a nature that by chance the odds were good that it could be passed, even if one had slept through all of the lectures and visuals, and demonstrations. But this fellow was consistently wrong 100% of the way.

The result of this was that he could not be certified as having successfully completed the course. To his embarrassment he was "held over" and his orders were delayed. To his way of thinking, it was my fault because I did not "come after him." He knew that this was so much baloney, since I had sent message to him each day through his cadre message center. Anyway, I was the villain in his eyes.

As the Chairman was dismissing me, the above noted Lieutenant Colonel came up with one more question for me. It touched upon a subject about which I had been very vocal - civilian control of the Atomic Energy Program. I was a staunch advocate of this in 1947 and I am still of the same mind in 1990.

The issue was the confirmation of the first chairman of the Atomic Energy Commission: One David Lilienthal who had been nominated by President Truman.

David Lilienthal was a skilled administrator with an excellent record of Government Service. When the Tennessee Valley Authority had been established, Lilienthal had been named and confirmed as its first administrator, and had established an excellent reputation. It was a difficult situation where the Federal Government had stepped into a role that traditionally had gone to private industry. However in this instance, the natural resources of the region were to be exploited to generate low cost hydro-electric power to help modernize and impoverished region of the agricultural south.

A bitter court fight had been waged and the Commonwealth and Southern

Utility Company, after carrying its case all the way to the Supreme Court, lost the case. This was a bitter blow to the conservative Southern Democratic congressional delegation, some of whom were members of the losing law firms.

As a result of the seniority practices in the United States Senate, and further as a result of the political solidarity of the South, most of the major committees of the Senate were chaired by the Southern Conservatives. The Senior Senator from Tennessee chaired the Senate Atomic Energy Committee that had to pass on the nomination of David Lilienthal.

For weeks they lined up witnesses that were against the nomination. They might have won, had they not carried on an overt and scurrilous Anti-Semitic campaign against the nominee. Besides being Jewish, David Lilienthal was born in Austria and later became naturalized when his parents moved the family to the United States. They used the dodge, that they regarded this appointment to be of the same caliber as the President and the Constitution requires that the President be a "Natural Born American." How could anyone entrust this "Alien" (Read Jew) with the awesome responsibility inherent in this job?

The country still had fresh in its mind the Hitler experience and the Holocaust, and few men of reason were buying this attack. The nominee was confirmed almost unanimously.

As I have said, I and many of my colleagues from Los Alamos Manhattan Project, and from Sandia Base were pulled into the counter-attack to provide testimony for the record in favor of the nominee and the system of civilian control.

When the Lieutenant Colonel chose to re-plow this ground with me, I made a decision then and there. The United States Army Air Force was not big enough to hold both he and I at the same time, and since he had more years of service than I did, he could have it all to himself. I got up and ask that any consideration the Board might be ready to show me be respectfully be withdrawn. Then I marched myself right out of the room.

The Adjutant followed close on my heels. He wanted to be sure that I meant what I said and that I just wasn't having a temper tantrum. I assured him that I knew precisely what I was doing and that I had no intention of serving in the United States Army Air Force unless another war placed me under such an obligation. There were many more far rewarding ways that I could serve my country and not have to put up with that kind of B— - S—.

I was now wholly committed to being a civilian and selecting a career path to follow for at least the next several years.

"As with all accounts that are based upon human recollection the passage of time has a way of modulating the recollection so that the details become melded into the whole, and what comes out is a composite of what the individual can best recall and human rationalization of the remainder. In other words, unless one is debriefed immediately after an event or within a short interval of time thereafter, what he relates is what he thinks he recalls as the detailed description of the event. But there are exceptions to this. When the event that has occurred is of such uniqueness or of such a bizarre nature that it has been indelibly installed into the human memory system, and thus can be recalled forever exactly as it happened. Events that fall into this category are usually those that have some profound effect on the life or times of the viewer. The atomic bombings fall in this category."

Jacob Beser

PART 4
Interviews With the Men Who Flew the Hiroshima Mission

Over the years Jacob Beser, as well as some of the other crew members of the *Enola Gay*, participated in many discussion groups and interviews where they were asked thousands of questions about the atomic bombing missions. Jacob saved copies of his interview transcripts and tapes as well as a good collection of similar material for other members of the *Enola Gay* crew. Many of the questions from the public, historians, psychologists and book authors dealt with items of a controversial nature. Jacob's archived information provides for the first time real, and unedited answers to these questions without a third party's interpretation. These rare documents will be available to researchers.

Standing: Major John Porter (ground maintenance officer), Capt. Theodore J. Van Kirk, Major Thomas W. Ferebee , Colonel Paul Tibbets, Capt. Robert Lewis, and Lieutenant Jacob Beser.
Kneeling: Sgt. Joseph S. Stiborik S/Sergeant George R. Caron, PFC Richard H. Nelson, Sgt. Robert H. Shumard and S/Sgt. Wyatt E. Duzenbury

These questions and answers have been selected from thousands, which are available in the various interview transcripts and voice tapes that were generated over a 40-year period. In most cases these are the exact words spoken. However in some cases the answer to a question may have been sanitized to remove some of the "four letter adjectives." But in any case the meaning of what was said has not been changed.

Interview with the Enola Gay Pilot
Colonel Paul W. Tibbets Jr.

Question: Do you remember anything in particular that happened? Maybe the night before the mission? During the mission? Did anyone carry a rabbit's foot with him?

Answer: No, I don't think so. Because the initial selection of these people which took place over a period of months, we tried to get people that were emotionally stable, that were technically capable or professionally qualified depending on what their particular job was. We tried to select the best. By this I mean we got people that were very well qualified, but on the other hand we didn't have anybody that we were the least bit suspicious about as being particularly emotional one way or the other. And from this point of view we didn't have anybody who was filled with superstitions or anything like that.

Question: How do you feel about that particular A-bomb?

Answer: Well, you're asking me a question I find real hard to answer. I don't have any particular feelings about the subject. I presume the thing that you're hinting at is that the type of question whether I think it ought to be used or not. And I could say under the circumstances that we used the weapon, yes it should have been used. I state this for the simple reason that I believe this weapon prevented the United States and the Allied Forces from invading Japan as such. And because of the prevention of such an invasion, I'm sure that we saved many, many lives. I couldn't hazard a guess as to how many, but I think it brought about a quick end to the war. As such it was a lifesaving thing from that point of view. The lives lost as a result of the explosion were war casualties. These are the things that you have to expect in a war.

Question: How do you feel about the use of atomic bombs?

Answer: You're asking me a very difficult and possibly a very controversial type of question to answer. If wars are going to be fought, I believe the objective is to win the war. You're going to win it with all resources at your disposal. And if you're fortunate enough to possess powerful weapons or weapons more powerful than those of your enemy, there's only one thing to do and that is to use them..

Question: Do you ever have any feelings of personal guilt or was this just a military order you carried out?

Answer: I have been ask that question before. I can assure you I have absolutely no feeling of guilt quite to the contrary to some of the material that has been written about my being in an insane asylum or an institution because of remorse over the thing. I have no remorse whatsoever. It was an assignment, a military assignment in the time of war and I don't believe that anybody should necessarily attach anything personal to their war activities in relation to entering combat as we did in this instance. No, this was a straight out and out military mission. I was directed to do it. If I were directed to do such a thing, or anything similar to this today, I've learned in all those years of military service to follow orders, so I'd follow them without question.

Interview with the Enola Gay Bombardier
Major Thomas W. Ferebee

Question: Was the bomb actually dropped on a military installation?

Answer: Actually it was dropped on the Headquarters for the whole defense of the Japanese Empire which had moved to Hiroshima.

Question: Did you have any thoughts about the people on the target or were they just enemies?

Answer: No I don't think I considered them any different from any other targets I've ever bombed, because you never know where you're going to kill one person or thousands of people. It is just a job to be done. I didn't consider that at all.

Question: Is there anything on this mission, anything that happened that mad you feel something might go wrong. Any incidents in the aircraft or in preparing the bomb?

Answer: No. I had flown 63 missions before in Europe and this was the easiest mission I ever flew.

Interview with the Enola Gay Navigator
Captain Theodore J. van Kirk

Question: Before dropping the bomb, did you give any thought to the people on the target or were they just the enemy?

Answer: Well, I think this is true for any bombing mission. You always give some thought to the to the people on the target. We were, I believe, in fact I am sure, that we were bombing military targets. We were not bombing people. And this is an important thing to remember. I felt that we were always bombing military targets. Now it is quite unfortunate that in many cases in modern day warfare you can't separate people from military targets. This happened to be the case with Hiroshima.

Question: How many missions had you flown prior to this?

Answer: I had 54 missions over Europe and Africa.

Question: What were your thoughts when the bomb was dropped?

Answer: I have thought about it for some time and I think that this is the question that I'm answering by looking back on things. I really believed that my biggest thought was "what a relief": Here we gotten the thing there, and we're done the mission we started. So I think the first feeling, of course, after that we get more of an opportunity to think about what happened.

Interview with the Enola Gay Co-Pilot
Captain Robert A. Lewis

Captain Robert A. Lewis was the Co-pilot on the *Enola Gay's* historic mission that dropped the first atomic bomb used in warfare on Hiroshima, Japan August 6, 1945. The extent of his participation and his comments made over Hiroshima minutes after the bomb exploded remain the subject of controversy and to interpretation to this day. He felt strongly that his post-war feelings as well as his comments and feelings expressed over Hiroshima are often grossly misrepresented. In this interview he addressed these topics head-on and attempted to put to bed some of the myths that have shadowed him for many years. At the time of this interview he, understandably, did not remember the exact words that he may have said over the intercom during the excitement after the bomb detonated. But in this interview he clearly expressed what he meant about his written comment "My God, What have we done?" He also requested that his written words never be interpreted in any other way. The following are his words from the interview transcript.

Question: During the actual time of dropping the bomb, what were your thoughts? Did you think anything that may have been happening at home, or did you devote your thoughts exclusively to what may have been happening down below, to the people below, to the military targets? Did you think at that time when you saw this cloud coming up that this was it. This was the end of the war?

Answer: I'm sure that there was very little would have entered my mind that day other than this bomb and the delivering of it; the dropping of it; and, the getting away safe. Because dropping an atomic bomb was still untried from an airplane and our biggest thought naturally was our own survival. To get out of there and be able to get back {home} safely.

Question:When the bomb exploded, do you remember saying anything, or the crewmembers saying anything, like Holy Moses, or WOW?

Answer: I wrote down in my book, and this was a minute or two afterwards. Just a little letter I prepared, and whether {or not} I said it out loud or what I wrote down that I said "My God, What have we done?" Meaning what has mankind done in designing and developing a bomb like this to destroy mankind. THAT IS WHAT I MEANT BY THAT {STATEMENT}. If you should quote "My God, What have we done?" explain and qualify the statement.

Question: I will do that. In other words, the unwritten part {in your log} is what you have explained to me?

Answer: That's right. I should have written it out, you know. I have quoted it a couple of times and people get the wrong meaning that we immediately felt sorrow. This was NOT the intent {of what I said}. The intent was that it {the explosion} was so enormous that I thought of human beings developing something {a bomb} to destroy human beings to the point of a whole city at a time was utterly incomprehensible.

Question: Let's go to some specifics. What do you recall most about the atomic bomb mission? Can you describe your most vivid thoughts?

Answer: I thought that from the knowledge of some of these questions, some other aspects will come up. But I think that the most vivid recollection that I will ever have of this bomb is the point that when we immediately turned around and looked at the results. This is within about three minutes of detonation. You see, we turned around and got out of the area as soon as we could. But we were still within sight or ten miles of the city and from 32,000 feet it was quite visible. The effect of it, or the effects and lasting impression that I, and most of the crew should have, was where there had been a city with trolley cars and boats in little channels - the tributaries that run down through the city--this was all obliterated. The fire and debris was covering about 95% of the city by the time we looked at it. This was the lasting impression that was in my mind of this thing. I also recall very vividly the smoke and the fire that was climbing the mountainside adjacent to the city. This was something that was not easy to comprehend - to see a city disappear in front of your eyes,

Question: In relationship to the fires, were there huge blasts of red lights or what?

Answer: It was, well, from that altitude you couldn't tell individual blasts. There were many, many fires visible. And then of course, they would be covered by such dense smoke that you couldn't pick anything, or any particular spot that was more on fire than any other. It was just a huge mass of clouds, debris, smoke and fire all mixed together.

Question: Do you ever have any feelings of guilt or was this strictly a military order that you carried out?

Answer: I had no feeling of guilt. This was a mission.

Question: If everything was at it was in 1945, and you had the chance to volunteer again for this mission, would you volunteer? If there were a war and you know what were happening and the strength of the A-Bomb, would you offer your services again in this situation?

Answer: There would be no hesitancy on my part to defend my country. None whatsoever! If it meant that the dropping of an atomic bomb, or a hydrogen bomb, this would be something that I would readily do. But, first of all I would have expected that our country, prior to requesting {such} a mission, would have {exercised} the greatest wisdom in deciding this {was necessary}. In other words, I have some very clear ideas on the use of a weapon like this. If the conditions exist, I expect that the judgment of the Air Force and the leaders of our country would also have similar feelings and {would have considered these feelings before} they would decide the action of dropping the bomb {was necessary}. Such as, ... I think I have to be specific of some of these factors.... I think that we should drop it on a military target and then only as a last resort. In other words, there are so many innocent people that are gobbled up by and Atomic Bomb that there should be {specific} conditions existing before the use of a weapon like this, if it were ever permitted again.

Question: How did you happen to be on this flight, or how did you happen to become involved with the 393rd Bomb Group initially? From the United States? Was there any particular story?

Answer: Well, I had been a test pilot for the Air Corps, first at Eglin Field, Florida and later on at Alamagardo testing B-29's against our own fighters. The day that Tibbets was given the job he was on the field with me. I came down from a high altitude mission and I was talking with him. He got a phone call from Second Air Corps about this mission. He didn't know too much about it at the time but they indicated over the phone that this may be a very big project. He enlisted me right away. He spoke to me because I had done all his test flying for him. He was liaison between Washington and the test section at Eglin Field, the Second Air Corps and so forth. I did the flying and he did the deskwork as it were.

Question: So, you were requested by Tibbets to join his group?

Answer: That's right. As a test pilot more than anything else, but then of course, I wanted to see some overseas service. I figure that I had a good deal more time than most other pilots in this B-29 and test work. As far as I am concerned that might have been the reason for his choice.

Question: So, through the virtue of experience alone?

Answer: That's right.

Question: Does the name *Enola Gay* have any special meaning. Can you tell me how this ship got the name *Enola Gay*?

Answer: Well, I know that it was Tibbets' mother's name. Now how it was named I really don't know. He put the name on this ship, although the ship was assigned to me as the airplane commander. He went unbeknownst to myself and had it put on. It was just that he cared to put it on.

Question: Wasn't it sort of a custom that crew, together, would get together and decide upon a name? Wasn't this then a little out of the ordinary that one person should take it upon himself to...

Answer: Well, it was the airplane commander, it was within his own authority to name his own plane. He would do this in any number of ways. But in this case, I was not spoken to about it. It was put on unbeknownst to myself.

191

Question: During the mission, on the flight, what were you doing on the flight. I understand that Tibbets was actually piloting the plane. What was your function?

Answer: Well, on any long mission such as this was, lasting 12 to 15 hours, you generally have two or three pilots because no one man sits at the controls {for that length of time}. Tibbets had a snooze. I at times would get up out of the seat. Actually our automatic pilot flew the entire mission for us. But someone has to be there to put into the automatic pilot any direction or altitude changes that may occur through the equipment or due to the elapses of time.

Interview With the Enola Gay Radio Operator
Cpl. Richard N. Nelson

Question: Do you have any special recollections when the bomb was dropped such as "Oh my God, How big it is?" Did you feel sorrow that it was done.? If you felt that it was going to end the war, did that make you feel better?

Answer: I think that the best description {of how felt} was the magnitude of the bomb. I don't think of what it did down there but just the size you visualized from above. For this reason we were elated.

Question: Did you give any thought to the people down below?

Answer: No, nope. I purposefully never think of what was happening down below a bombing mission. This is conditioning. You are conditioned to believe this is the way you fly combat. I am sure that all the people, anyone in the service no matter what their job is has been conditioned this way.

Interview with the Enola Gay Flight Engineer
T/Sgt. Wyatt Duzenbury

Question: Do you have any feelings of guilt that the bomb shouldn't have been dropped?

Answer: No, I don't. That was something we had no control over. It was decided by the President of the United States that the bomb be dropped and who am I to say to the Commander in Chief he isn't right?

Question: Did you ever have any feelings of guilt?

Answer: This was strictly an order. When a military man gets an order he carries it out to the best of his ability.

Question: Did you ever think of it afterwards, the consequences and perhaps lose some sleep?

Answer: Negative

Interview With the Enola Gay Assistant Flight Engineer
Sgt. Robert Shumard

Question: What were your thoughts when the bomb was dropped:

Answer: Well, there's the vicious rumor going around that someone said: "My God." I don't know who said it. That was a very much publicized explanation shortly after the war was over.

Question: Of course, I imagine you were saying it in jest but in sincerity you meant it?

Answer: Well, if you get deep down into the thing, I believe you are right. Nobody actually wants to cause the destruction we caused. But, it was through a necessity rather than a wanton type destruction. It was something that had to be done. As much as a man has gangrene in his leg and they had to cut it off. It's something that has to be done. It was a cancer in the world situation that had to be removed - that's all. That's how I felt about it.

Interview with the Enola Gay Tail Gunner
Sgt. George R. Caron

Question: If everything was as it was in 1945 and you had a chance to volunteer for this mission, Would you volunteer?

Answer: I believe I would. I think everybody would do what they have been doing and would do it again given the opportunity. If I had known then what I know now, would I volunteer? I think I would. I remember back to the colonel, and I think he was one of the best C.O.'s in the air force and I would volunteer to go with him. He asked me if I would like to go overseas and I said I would. I thought I would like to go overseas and see a little bit of this scrap. So, knowing what I know now, I think I

193

would volunteer. It is just another job. As far as I'm concerned, it was just another mission for us. It might have been an important one and I guess it might have been a little bit of a worry on the colonel's part knowing the full scope of the mission as to whether we would get back or not since nobody had ever fired anything that big from an airplane before. So I guess there was an element of doubt there. So we made it and made it back fine. I feel that I may be contradicted on this but I feel that this helped shorten the war considerably. I believe that if it wasn't for something as big as the atom bomb, the Japanese would have kept on fighting for quite a long time. And an invasion of the Japanese Empire, the islands themselves, would have been a very costly operation on both sides. We not only saved a lot of American lives, but I also believe we saved a lot of additional Japanese lives, compared to the number of casualties made at Hiroshima and Nagasaki.

Question: How did you feel when you saw the first A-bomb being dropped?

Answer: I guess I was too busy then to feel much. But, I really did think to myself once, "Oh those poor devils down there." But again, thinking about it later, sure one bomb wiped one a city. I believe the casualties proved to be about 100,000 but I am not sure of the exact figure. But, how much worse is that than a blanket raid of hundreds of airplanes on a target dropping small bombs? I think it's the same thing. I think of the poor devils down there that were killed or maimed but I didn't think it was worse than an ordinary mission or a fire bomb raid. The Japanese Naval Forces, I'm sure, didn't think of the poor devils when they started in at Pearl Harbor. I'll always be glad to keep that in mind.

Question: Did you believe that this mission would help end the war, or all wars?

Answer: I believe it might, and I hope it definitely will. We had only two nuclear bombs that have been dropped, let's say in anger, and the rest have been tests. We know that with those two relatively small bombs what had been done - wiped out two cities. So, you can imagine what some of our newest ones can do! They must be terrific. Let's hope they are frightening enough, looking at the results of these two bombs, frightening enough so that people will remember it and nobody will ever drop one on anybody else in anger. The thought is it may be a deterrent and I hope so.

Question: Before dropping the bomb, did you give any thought to the

194

people on the target, or were they just the enemy?

Answer: I believe they were just the enemy.   You don't want to think about things like that.   We had bombed Japanese targets before.   We had missions before over the Empire and we had some after the bomb.   We feel that we hit industrial targets.   But, with those big 10,000-pound pumpkins we were dropping we might have done other damage and hit civilian.   But, it was still enemy country and I like to think that justified what we did.

Interview with the Enola Gay Radar Operator
Sgt. Joseph A. Stiborik

Question: If everything was it was in 1945, would you volunteer again for this mission?

Answer: If it were like it was in 1945, I think I would.

Question: Do you feel that the mission saved a lot of lives, American lives?

Answer: From what I have been able to find out, well, the invasion was supposed to take place sometime in November, and I'm sure that it would have cost a lot of American lives to try and invade Japan.

Question: What were your thoughts, first what was your duty on the aircraft?

Answer: I was radar operator.

Question: What were your impressions when you let it go?

Answer: We didn't know how strong, or how big it would be.   When the thing did go off we felt two concussions in the airplane and we thought we were flying through flak.

Question: Colonel Tibbets told me that immediately after dropping the bomb they went into a 150 degree bank and weren't able to see anything. Were you near a window hat you could see?

Answer: Well, I was instructed to watch my radar scope and see if there was any reaction on the scope.   But in the turn the radar set went out. There was no reaction on the radarscope at all.

Question: Did you give any thought to the casualties?

Answer: Not until, of course, we didn't know how many we killed; maimed; or, crippled.   After we found out what we had done, it did make

195

me feel kind of bad to kill that many people.

Interview with the Enola Gay ECM Officer
1st Lieutenant Jacob Beser

Question: Exactly what did you do on the two A-bomb bombing missions and what equipment did you use?

Answer: You ask EXACTLY what I did on the atomic bomb missions. I will recap for you what it was that I was doing as closely as I can.

One thing that that has been plaguing me for several years - what was the exact line-up of "black boxes" I used on the two missions to Hiroshima and Nagasaki.

I have been able to recall all but the designation of the special disk recording lathe that I carried and made the long lost recordings.

Just prior to take-off for each mission, Dr. Edward Doll who is now a retired V.P. of TRW, Inc. and living- if still alive- in Santa Barbara, CA, gave me a slip of rice paper with four frequencies written on it. These frequencies were the measured operating frequencies of the modified APS-13's that were being used as proximity devices on the weapon. They were, in both cases, in the region of 400-420 mHz.

What I was supposed to do, in the target area, was to monitor for approximately 390 - 430 mHz. This I did with a AN/APR-4 Receiver with the appropriate tuning unit installed. It had a controlled auto-scan function, which I had set to the desired range. The receiver had attached to it one AN/APA-5 Panoramic Adapter that I set to the proper bandwidth scan. It allowed me to examine incoming signals and their adjacent side bands. This allowed me to differentiate various types of signals, i.e. pulse radar, CW, etc. Also attached to the receiver was an AN/APA-23 Thermal Paper Tape Recorder which allowed me to make a permanent visual record of any incoming signals. I also had an AN/AP-42 (Home built prototype which I got at Harvard RRL), a direction finding device which automatically allowed me to locate the direction from which incoming signal was coming. If time would allow, I could triangulate and locate the source of the signal.

These devices allowed me to do my thing in the target area. To keep an eye out for fighters I had an AN/ARR-5 communications receiver. This was the airborne version of the popular Hallicrafter SX-40 Ham Receiver which I used to scan the Japanese fighter control frequencies. I could selectively listen to this set or the APR-4.

My headset I had modified to a 2-channel device not unlike today's stereo-headsets, and I had built a special junction box which allowed me to select two receivers or one receiver and the airplane interphone channel.

On the way to the target areas I used the APR-4 to scan the active Japanese radar frequencies and kept track of radars that might be tracking us. I carried with me all of the latest intelligence info on Jap sites. This was distributed from 20th AF RCM Office weekly.

In the event it would become necessary, I carried two jamming devices, AN/APT-1 and AN/APT-4. I did not have a chaff dispenser on either aircraft nor did we carry any hand dispensable chaff packages.

At no time did I see any need to take these kinds of measures. You see, once a radar locked on us, I monitored the Fighter Control Voice channels to try to determine if any interceptors had been launched.

En-route from Kokura to Nagasaki we traversed an area full of interceptor bases. Most of them were constructed to assist in the defense against the invasion. This kept me busy all the way and really kept my mind off the problems of the airplane.

Now Jack you have information that I have only told to one other person.

Question: As I indicated to you before, the paper I am doing, and that is my primary interest in you, is how the military people, leadership and otherwise, saw the ethics and morality of dropping the bomb. And I think I pointed out that my co-paper presenter is doing Tokyo raids and from what I understand, a number of people or many people believe that the Atomic bomb was far more moral, if you will, than firebombing.

Answer: Well, to begin with, I have noticed over the years and more markedly in the last couple, two, three years, (*Editor's Note: 1985 time period*) a distinct change in attitude towards the bombing. And I have noticed very markedly this past summer a lot of revising of history by historians who know better, As a perfect example, this Dr. McWiggins here at Towson State University--think it was eight, nine, ten years ago, used to run a mini-mester seminar called Hiroshima, and he invited me as a guest panelist. This was a select group of students that intensively studied all of the issues and the ramifications of the Hiroshima bombing.

197

And I was invited for about, I think, a two-hour session. And I appeared on time and I started my presentation on time and I got out of there—on time was 8:30 in the morning, and I got out of there about four o'clock that afternoon. The kids just wouldn't let go. And he wouldn't let go. And it appeared to me at that time that the point he was trying to make with this class was that while there are a lot of questions on the periphery of this thing, the basic issues, whether it justified a raid was "Yes." Now, he presents it as an overreaction, as a totally unnecessary thing, and so forth. Now, there is a lot of {archived} data become available in recent years which wasn't available eight, ten years ago. And these people look at that and I don't think they always look at the dateline. And sometimes the date line is ten years after the event, and it is somebody else's interpretation, or somebody else's creation after having read fundamental documents. And a man would say, "I am of the opinion that..." Now, what are his credentials? Who is he? And what? The only thing I can say and I have said consistently for forty years is, to the best that we knew, and I have to reserve that "we" to the guys in the pits now, not at the decision making level, the best we knew, there was an invasion coining. We saw them training for it on our island. We saw kid marines every day going ashore off landing craft. We saw huge supplies of ammunition and guns being accumulated there in support of these people. We had no indication that the Japanese were trying to surrender, that Tokyo had gone to Russia, or that approaches were being made in Geneva. We had no indication of any of that. We were out there to carry out a mission that was defined to us the first very day we met as the 509th Group in September, 1944. We were going to deliver a special weapon that, if it would successful, could bring about a rapid conclusion too the war. That's all they ever told us about it as a group. We were ready to do our job. Now, I think this whole subject of morality is a joke. War, by its very nature, is immoral. There is no question in my mind that this is true. Now, if you have a choice of weapons, one that will allow the war to run its course, the other that will bring it to an abrupt halt, I think it is more immoral not to use that modern sophisticated weapon than it is to let the thing run its course. And this is a doctrine that I have been preaching for forty years, and I have seen nothing, archival or otherwise, than can change my opinion.

The second point that I would make is that you have to look at these things in the context of the time and place in which they happened. Hindsight is beautiful. We all have 20-20 hindsight. But you must evaluate the event in terms of what data did they have on which they based their decision to use the weapon? Was there support for that decision? And was it a popular decision at the time because this was obviously a political decision. We know it was political and it was—we know it was tempered by the politicians. The generals could not unilaterally made the decision to use this weapon. But at the highest levels of government committees were formed, reporting directly to the President and advising the President. And I recently spent some time in Japan with Ward Norrison who was the Secretary of that Interim committee. He and I reviewed a lot of these issues together. I get very upset when my friends today come around and tell me that it is time to get on with it, I agree with their bottom line. We don't want to do it again. I just had a book delivered to me today where there was a piece that I wrote on August 11, 1945. I said on the way home from Nagasaki we all hoped that we would never have to do it again. And there is no question--nobody wants to do that again. But let's don't run down everything that happened.

Question: The interesting thing, it seems to me, is what--again, people forget, we were dropping the bomb for one reason—to kill people to end the war.

Answer: Oh, and the other thing that McWilliams--oh, he let me have it. They didn't tell he was going to tailgate me in a radio thing that I did. And he did there and then again in writing. One of the reasons that prompted this cleanup this morning was I was looking for some clippings because I have to sit down and answer him. He talks about the fact that we bombed innocent civilians. He says the Japanese didn't bomb any civilians in the United States. Well, Christ, they couldn't. They didn't have the capability. But look what they did on Bataan and Pearl Harbor.

Question: What about Pearl Harbor?

Answer: Oh, he calls that a knee-jerk. Now, and he forgets that there was a national mental mood, a mindset. There was nothing too bad for the Japanese at that time.

Question: Let me back up. You have given me what I really came for. Was there any discussion, I would guess it would have to be after Hiroshima and Nagasaki, by riders {bomber crew members}? Your fellow riders on the airplane, that this was bad or that this--because it was so different that it should not have been done. Did you hear any?

Answer: Yes, Yes, First of all the thing that captured everybody's mind was the bizarre nature of this thing. One airplane, one bomb, just totally ruined the city. I never saw the intact city of Hiroshima. By the time I go there it was gone. See, I just saw this much and stuff, with new fires breaking out. I saw the fire- storm break out. The only guy at that point in time who really had any feeling about it, as I remember, was Morrie Jeppson. He came to me after we slept it off the effects of a beer party. We had a beer party for the whole outfit after the mission just to relieve the tensions. Morrie Jeppson said to me, "God I hope never again." He said, "I'm not sure we should have done that. And I said, "Well, Morrie, you don't have to worry about it. All you did was verify that the thing was right. He made a fortune in the nuclear instrumentation business afterwards. It didn't keep him out of that. In fact he built up and sold three businesses. But it did bother him.

Question: Well, it is one thing, it seems to me, to bother him on a personal level. It's another thing to—

Answer: Oh, I never heard him say, "Hey, we've just committed an atrocity," or whatnot.

Question: Did you fly practice missions over the Japanese Islands?

Answer: I made maybe a dozen flights.

Question: Did the Japanese send anybody up to intercept you?

Answer: On the third pass {over Kokura}, I detected them coming and notified our cockpit. The tail gunner also saw them, and said, "Here they come!" We made the third run and the fuel problem was getting very severe, and we were afraid we might not be able to make it back to even Iwo Jima if we didn't leave soon, so we decided then we were going on down to Nagasaki and — orders or no — if we couldn't see the target, we were going to bomb on radar. Then we were going to go up the coast and head in the direction of Okinawa —and hope we made if After the bombing, we told them where we were and they had the air-sea rescue alerted.

We started a radar run over Nagasaki, and in the last 15 to 20 seconds, there was a hole that opened up in the clouds. The bombardier shouted, "I see it! I got it! Bombs away!" —just like that. When the bomb went off, it was the same as before, except this the plane got three pretty good jolts! There was the main bang, the reflection from the ground under it and then off the hills on the side. Despite our scarcity of fuel Sweeney circled once, then headed for Okinawa. We broke radio silence to get a flight plan there, and that invited any enemy hornets who were in the area and who wanted to come in and get us to do so — but none did.

Question: Did you make those flights with Tibbets?

Answer: No. Tibbets did fly some of practice missions but not over the Empire. He was under strict orders not to go along on the flights over Japan. He knew too much for the United States to risk his capture. Other members of the 509th, who were not in the know, could and did fly practice runs over the Empire. They knew their mission was special; they knew the maneuvers they would have to carry out; but they knew little else. We all worked like a well-oiled machine.

Question: Other than yourself who flew on the *Enola Gay* on the Hiroshima mission?

Answer: Colonel Paul Tibbets was the pilot and aircraft commander. His navigator was Theodore van Kirk and Tom Ferebee was his bombardier. Both had flown with Paul on bombing missions over Europe. Other members of his crew were Bob Lewis, copilot; Wyatt Duzenbury, aircraft flight engineer; Bob Caron, tail gunner; Joseph Stiborik, radar operator; Dick Nelson, radio operator; and, Robert Shumard, assistant aircraft flight engineer. Navy captain William "Deak" Parsons was the weapons officer. His assistant was Morrie Jeppson who was the proximity fuse specialist.

Question: On the bombing raids do you think the Japanese knew you were coming?

Answer: I had what is called search receivers, radios that tuned various parts of the spectrum and whatever signals that might be there including radar and voice signals. I had the capability in my equipment to analyze these signals and see if there was any intelligence in them, and especially to see if they were close to where we were operating {the bomb radar proximity fuse}. The signal environment on August 6 was fairly active that day. About 300 miles off the coast I began to pick up their early warning radar signals. As we got closer the signals were no longer "whoosh-whooshing" by, but they were locked on us. At that point I knew that they knew we were coming. But what else would you expect? I was also able to monitor the Japanese {radio} command channels and while I didn't speak Japanese, I could tell the difference between ground and airborne chatter and tell if they were sending up fighters. As we cleared the coast on the way back from Hiroshima I was up front chatting with Parsons and Jeppson when the tail gunner announced that there was a Japanese fighter approaching. I suddenly realized that I had left my parachute back at my work-station. Tibbets said stay put for if we get a hole in the airplane the decompression would blow me out of the hole like a bullet. The fighter pulled along side; dropped his wheels and flaps to slow down; looked us over and did a slow rolled around us; and, sped away. The remainder of the flight was uneventful.

On the second mission it was a different story over Kokura. We made three passes over the target in the period of an hour from three different directions without success. On the third pass I detected Japanese fighters and notified the cockpit. The tail gunner also saw then and said "here they come." By this time the fuel situation was getting very severe and we had decided to go down to Nagasaki and, orders or not, we were going to make one pass over the target using radar and drop the bomb. Then we were going down the coast and head in the direction of Okinawa. After the bombing we told broke radio silence and told them {Tinian} where we were and they had the air-sea rescue alerted.

Question: There has been some discussion as to whether the bombs were armed on the ground or in flight. Do you know when they were armed?

Answer: The first bomb, Little Boy, the fuse was activated in flight. The bomb had been fully assembled when it was loaded into the aircraft. Sometime during the afternoon concern was express that if we did not make it off the runway there might be a remote possibility that would be a high order explosion on the end of the runway and maybe take out the whole airport so to allay those fears the bomb was partially disassembled. Early in the afternoon and for the rest of the day Adm. Parsons and Morrie Jeppson, who was the assistant weaponeer, went through considerable practice in reassembling the thing while it was in the bomb bay. Then about an hour after takeoff the airplane was cleaned up and we were at its cruising altitude they went down into the bomb bays and repeated this final assembly. This operation was not done on the Fat Man[35].

Incidentally on Hiroshima mission Morrie Jeppson had a Weapon Test Box which was used to indicate the health of the weapon. At one

---

[35] Fat Man was an implosion type device using plutonium as the fuel. Plutonium is chemically distinct from uranium and easily separated. But it naturally emits so many neutrons that even the gun-type bomb would be too slow to prevent pre-detonation. This problem was solved by using a symmetrical shell of about 5300 pounds of high explosives to squeeze a softball size sphere (sub-critical mass) of plutonium into a tennis ball size core of critical mass. The implosion instantly increases the plutonium's density, which traps the neutrons inside and causes an explosive chain reaction.

point in time the lights on his box lit up like a Christmas tree and for a moment we thought we had a sick weapon on our hands. In less than a minute the scare was over. I never did get all the details of this episode, or if I did I have forgotten them.

Question: What happened when the bomb exploded?

Answer: When the bombs were released I was busy doing other things but I did feel the release of the bombs. Then when the planed turned to the right, I was pinned to the floor by the force. When I got to the window it was all over. The cloud was up about 30,000 feet. I got to look at it when we leveled out at 29,000 thousand feet. We had been provided with dark glasses but I couldn't do my work and wear them. They had green liner over the windows anyway, so I figured it wouldn't hurt me. I did not hear any explosion from the blast but there was a big compression wave that came up which I thought was a nearby flak burst. You could also feel the plane get knocked around. It wasn't too bad at Hiroshima, but at Nagasaki it really got rocked where we got three jolts. We had expected two, one from the main bang and a second from echo reflected off the ground under the bomb. At Nagasaki we got a third jolt from an echo reflected off the nearby hills. This told us that we had not hit the briefed target.

Question: When you got to the window and looked down, what did you see?

Answer: It was like being at the seashore, stirring up the water and watching the sand billowing. I also saw a lot of fires breaking out around the periphery.

Question: Before dropping the bomb, had you given thought to the people on the target, or were they just the enemy?

Answer: Well, you always think about them. I felt no undue concern for their welfare. As far as I was concerned they were people down there who were doing their patriotic Japanese duty; working in their factories and mills; building their airplanes and ships; and, guns for killing our people. There was no doubt in my mind at the time that this was a war that they had asked for. Since then, I have gone back into some of the historical aspects of it, just wondering how much of it was by pre-arrangement on our parts?

Question: What do you mean?

Answer: Well, it's a hard thing to describe whether the war was something we needed, wanted, ask for or whether it was thrust upon us. It was, if you look at the sequence of events and they go way back, there may have been a possibility of averting this thing if we had taken a firm stand with Japan back in the 30's when she first began to branch out in Manchuria and China. Whether we consciously asked for it or not is hard to say. But darned little was done to try and avert it. We were talking peace out of one side of our mouth with them, and the junk dealers were sending them scrap iron to build up their war machine on the other, and as you know, not only with Japan, but the same thing with Germany. Those big red books here, are the transcripts of the German archives. I spent many an hour digging through there for several reasons. I am Jewish and I was quite interested in seeing for myself if some of the things that I had heard about really took place. The Jewish people in Germany during the early days of Hitler were used as tools and instruments of foreign policy. They were used more or less as hostages in exchange for capital goods. People were set free and allowed to leave the country. Then I got interested in the whole buildup of the extreme nationalistic National Socialism, its foundation and the part that Russia has had to do with it. This all gives me a little better understanding of the things that I deal with day to day. Russia wasn't innocent in all of this. She trained the German army on a rotating basis in the post Versailles years. They had a treaty and every year so many German officers and non-coms were rotated to Russia to maneuver with the Russian army. They instructed and built up the Soviet army at the same time they were exercising themselves. Well, this bothers me today, when we speak of planning our defensive posture on the basis of their intent. This was a well-camouflaged maneuver that they were pulling off then and we postulate five or ten years on this basis of intent. I am not sure in my own mind that our intelligent community has everything necessary to gauge that intent but we do have sufficient information to gauge their capabilities and we should plan accordingly. I think their intent will become clearer as time goes by.

Question: Do you have any feelings that the bomb shouldn't have been dropped?

Answer: None whatsoever. I think it should have been, and my one regret is that the bomb was not available for the final subjugation of Germany. I think the German people earned the right to that honor more than the Japanese people did. I say this because I have rubbed shoulders with a lot of Germans including men who worked at Pennamunda; scientist who worked in the laboratories for the big German companies;

204

and, others who worked for the German government ministries. By some strange coincidence they all said their jobs were all non-political--just scientists doing their job. As far as I am concerned they are a bunch of square-headed bastards. They knew what they were doing and why!

Question: What were your first thoughts?

Answer: Mine was "Thank God the worked after all this buildup we'd gotten!" The story is that Bob Lewis said. "My God! What have we done?" but what he really said was. "My God! Look at that sonofabitch go" He was Tibbets' copilot. I had installed a recorder at Tibbets' request on all stations to record everyone's impressions. I turned the tape over to Armed Forces Radio when we landed, and that was the last time I saw it. I know they used it, because I heard it that night.

Question: You've been on both of these raids. Have you ever given any thoughts to the casualties?

Answer: Not seriously. Beyond the extent that people get hurt in war. Wars are dangerous. Wars are basically immoral. Everything that goes along with war is immoral. It's a mode of operation that man has used for thousands of years but that still doesn't make it right. If you start worrying about things like that in the haste of battle then I think you are a psycho!

I don't know if you are aware of the fact or not but Nagasaki was our alternate target. Kokura was our other choice. We tried to get into Kokura but that city was all obscured by smoke from a fire bombing the night before. The actual raid was for Kokura the Pittsburgh of Japan. Nagasaki weather was bad. We pulled off Kokura and we couldn't get in there we went down to Nagasaki and we had problems galore. There was a lot of discussion about the problems of takeoff, or the others we became aware of over Kokura. We had 600 gal of gas in the bomb bay that we couldn't use. Chuck paddled around there {over Kokura} for almost an hour at full war power burning up the gas. I think were made three passes at Kokura. About that time they {the Japanese} were getting serious and started sending up fighters after us. But they never got to us before we pulled out of there! We had some close by flak bursts and things were getting a little hairy. That's when Ashworth and Sweeney decided that we would make one run on to Nagasaki since there was no sense trying to drag this thing {the bomb} home or dump it in the ocean.

So we went down to Nagasaki. The weather there was also bad with ten-ten cloud coverage. So we started the bomb run using radar. But in the last couple of seconds he {the bombardier} got a hole in the clouds and saw what he thought was his briefed aiming point. However it turned out we were a couple of miles off the briefed aiming point. The bomb hit up in the industrial valley instead of over on the other side of the ridge of hills into the city. Well, I look at that sometimes and I am sure not what you would call an overly devout person. I'm a religious person and I think the same God that was protecting us was also protecting many innocent Japanese on the ground. If we had hit the briefed aiming point, the casualty rate would have been higher. I got into an interesting discussion about this a few years ago with my rabbi and I.....well those discussions never came to any meaningful conclusions.

Question: I have heard that the Nagasaki trip was a pretty botched up trip all the way?

Answer: That's why I want to see what Ashworth is telling people because for a number of years they would come to me and I would say, "Go talk to Ashworth." And Ashworth would come in and say, "Go talk to Beser." Because he was still in the Navy.

Question: Well, Ashworth mentioned that it was a fouled up mission and that they had a problem with the fuel, just the standard story, and he made {the decision to drop by radar}.

Answer: I'll tell you the real story about that after you turn that thing {the tape recorder} off. As you know we left Tinian recognizing the possibility of a fuel transfer problem. While still over Kokura there was a fuel discussion between Sweeney and the flight engineer Sergeant Kuharek. After the "discussion" Kuharek was ordered to stop trying to transfer the reserve fuel. There were some comments by Sweeney as to who had responsibility for flying the airplane and making the safety decisions. We felt that Kuharek came out on the short end of that "discussion." It has been indicated to me on several occasions since, by both Captain Bock and Sergeant Clayton that if Sergeant Kuharek had been allowed to activate the transfer system and "just leave it on," the desired fuel transfer would have taken place. This was an undiagnosed gremlin in this airplane that caused the system to operate this way. A review of the Form 1 of the airplane, now on file at the United States Air Force Museum at Dayton, Ohio, reveals this to indeed be the case.[36]

---

[36] Editor's Note: My father told Jack Spangler on several occasions that he had documentation in a safe deposit box that would "blow the lid off" and correct some of the misinformation and myths being circulated about the events that took place prior to,

Question: Okay, who made the radar bomb run decision? Ashworth says that he along with Sweeney made the decision that they would drop it by radar rather than bring it back. But he {Ashworth} as the senior weapons officer would take the responsibility for making the decision.

Answer: Well what is the answer to that one? To a certain extent that's one thing that does bother me a hell of a lot because I had a big input to that decision. Turn that thing off {the tape recorder} and we will talk about it. That's what I was there for, I had the experience and I also had to evaluate the radar operator as well as the equipment.

Editor's Note (Jack Spangler): In later conversations, Jake expanded on this subject. The following is how I remember these conversations:

In World War II the conventional Army Air Corps aircraft mode of operation was for the pilot, or the aircraft commander, to have total responsibility for the conduct of a mission.   However the Atomic Bombing missions were a special case.   General Groves in his book "Now It Can Be Told" said:

"Because of the many technical details involved it was essential that there be no possible confusion as to responsibilities.

For this reason General Norstad, Chief of Staff, twentieth Air Force, had written to Genera! LeMay

"In actual delivery it is desired that the B-29 airplane which carries the bomb also carry two military officer specialists. The senior officer specialist will be qualified by familiarity with the design, development and tactical features of the bomb, to render final judgment in the event that an emergency requires deviation from the tactical plan."

It was Jake's opinion that this directive was actually written by General Groves. Groves wanted to be absolutely sure that the officer making the final judgments in any tactical situations that resulted from unforeseen emergencies, was of his choice and responsible directly to him for the success of the missions.

Navy Captain Parsons, Deputy Technical Director of the Los Alamos Laboratory and a recognized ordnance expert, was chosen for

---

during and after the Nagasaki mission. He further stated that this information had never been made public but he desired that it be released to the public at a future time but not before everyone named, including himself, had died.

the Hiroshima operation. Commander Fred Ashworth was assigned the Nagasaki operation. It was Captain Parsons who made up the title "Weaponeer."

A further important restriction was a directive from Washington that in case the delivery aircraft should reach the target and find visual bombing impossible, it should return to base with the bomb. The drop should be made with radar only if the plane could not otherwise return safely.

Therefore the ultimate responsibility for the successful bombing of Hiroshima and Nagasaki rested in the senior Weaponeers, Captain Parsons and Commander Ashworth. However the pilots and crews of the Enola Gay and the Bock's Car played an important part. Their responsibility was to get the weapon to the assigned target and the crew back home safely. It is also true that Colonel Paul Tibbets had the awesome responsibility of organizing and training the 509th Bomb Group and providing his technical expertise to modifications of the B-29s and his abilities as a superb combat pilot to the training the crews.

In addition to the Weaponeer and his assistant, Beser was another special case for these missions. He was not a member of any one aircraft crew. He was the 509th Composite Group staff Countermeasures Officer. He had worked with the Manhattan Project in developing the Radar Altimeter fuse. He was told early on that he would fly every mission until the Japs surrendered or he had seen enough destruction.

The proximity devices were modified radar sets an as such had some susceptibility to outside radar or radio interference. There was a remote possibility that such interference could prematurely detonate the bomb. Because of this possibility Beser had to know the workings of the altimeter fuse inside and out. His job was twofold. Number one, it was his responsibility to be absolutely sure that there were no interfering signals present that could prematurely detonate the bomb and number two he monitored the altimeter fuse telemetry to be sure that it was functioning properly on internal power. On the Nagasaki trip the bomb had armed four or five times prior to the drop. This operation required the removal and replacement of the red and green plugs each time. Based on his observations of the interference environment and internal health of the altimeter, he had the final responsibility of recommending whether to leave the altimeter fuse on or rely on one of the other fusing

208

mechanisms to detonate the bomb.

Question: You mean you evaluated the operator to determine whether he was getting it right?

Answer: And also whether he was the right guy to do it. These guys on this crew {Ashworth and the radar operator} hadn't done a hell of a lot of flying over the Empire. I had gone up there many times. Hiroshima was my 13th trip. I had more trips than anybody because every day the group {509th} flew, I moved all my junk {electronic equipment} onto another airplane because I wanted to be able to do my job right when the time came. And I wanted to get fairly familiar with the electronics {radio frequency environment} over Japan as well as the radar signatures of ground features. That's what I was there for. The geographic configuration of the port and the city of Nagasaki were such that the radar presentation was clear cut and obvious. I told them to let me know how they wanted to approach the target and I could get them there by radar. My inputs played an important role in getting us to and confirming that we were attacking the assigned target.

Question: Have you had any feelings of guilt about the thing, either one?

Answer: No! No sir. I saw enough of the war casualties. They were coming back to the states before I left. I had already known about much that had been going on in Asia when the Japanese were beating up on China. We still had a friendly government there, and a free press operating and we saw a lot of the results of their atrocities. The Japanese people, any people to my way of thinking, are fully responsible for their government's actions. I don't care whether it's a dictatorship or what. No people that refuse to be subjugated must be subjugated. A hundred million people can certainly overcome five or ten million soldiers. It might be bloody but there are ways of doing it. As long as they went along with it, they share the guilt and they were punished accordingly.

Question: How about the Japanese will to fight. Do you believe that the fire bombing raids in any way diminished their will to carry on the war?

Answer: I don't really think they had. This is a gruesome story which illustrates the point but I will tell it anyway.

As the American island hopping campaign came nearer to the Empire home islands the fighting became more fierce, their resistance stiffened to hold on at all costs. Okinawa is an example. One hardened veteran, a marine I think, told of a situation that developed when a Jap patrol was surrounded with no place to go and nothing to fight with. When offered the opportunity to surrender, four or five men gathered around their leader in a circle. It appeared that they may have been discussing what to do. Instead of surrendering, the leader knelt down, pulled the pin from a hand grenade and placed it on his head. Seconds later the grenade exploded and the entire group was killed instantly. I don't know if this was true or just a war story but in any case over 100,000 Japs died defending Okinawa and very few prisoners were taken.

Question: Al that lime, how many more bombs did we have the capability of building?

Answer: Four.

Question: Do you know where the other two would have been dropped?

Beser: Yes, Kokura and Nihama.

Question: So Tokyo wasn't considered?

Answer: No, it was a big barren plain —it was gone. You wouldn't believe what these huge cities looked like. . They were just burnt -- all gone!

Question: It's been said that the fire raids destroyed even more than the A-bombs.

Answer: Oh yes that is true.

Question: How do you feel if and when you do see pictures of Hiroshima victims?

Answer: Nothing particular. No strange sensations. I think it's one of the tragedies of war. I think all wars are tragic. All casualties are tragic. It hits home when it's your family. There is a certain detachment when its is someone else. It's true they are all fellow human beings, but the human animal chose this way of life by himself and I think he has to live with it.

Question: When you were on this mission, you knew that it would become historical and not just another run?

Answer: Oh Yes. And I have debated the issue many times, more than I can count. I have discussed it with members of the clergy of all faiths. I have debated the issue with members of congress and on public platforms. I have defended the entire operation and myself in the press and on radio. I am not averse to getting into open and free conversation with anyone about it, because I feel that it was something that definitely part and parcel of the whole war. When you get right down to it, it doesn't matter how you are going to die. If you are going to die in a war, these night fire-raids against Japan were far more horrifying experiences, due to the

210

length of them, the slowness with which they progressed, the uncertainty as to their progress. This thing {the atomic bomb} was instantaneous, it was merciful for those that got it immediately and sure there are scars left over.

I never turn down an invitation to speak to school and community groups about my war experiences. I always try to get the messages across that war itself is immoral as are all things done in pursuit of victory. I have personally seen the horror of atomic warfare. We as a people have also seen the horror of atomic warfare and cannot afford to let it recur, but in the perspective of the times, the dropping of the atomic bomb was the best decision that could have made. Yes, thousands of Japanese were killed at Hiroshima and Nagasaki, and that's a damn shame. They were, however, the enemy and they started it. The use of the atomic bombs, despite revisionist objections, shortened the war and saved both.

Question: Was Major Charles Sweeney or Colonel Paul Tibbets supposed to fly the first mission?

Answer: I have heard many times that my good friend Chuck Sweeney was the only man to fly both of the missions that dropped atomic bombs on Hiroshima and Nagasaki. Too many this implies that he was the pilot the strike aircraft for both missions which is a myth. It is true that Sweeney was the pilot of the *Great Artiste*, the instrumentation aircraft on the Hiroshima mission and the pilot of the *Bock's Car* that was the strike aircraft on the Nagasaki mission. But I was the only man to fly on the strike aircraft for both missions fly as a member of the crew. And to make it absolutely clear, one of my responsibilities was to monitor the workings of a radar proximity fuse-device that I had helped design. This device detonated the bombs when radar beams bounced off the ground indicated that the weapon had fallen to a precise altitude for an air burst of maximum destructiveness. My other job on both flights to and over the targets was to make sure that there were no enemy radar using the same operating frequency as the proximity fuse which could have set off the bomb prematurely. I had the final say so on whether to use the radar proximity fuse or not.

The B-29 assigned to carry the Hiroshima bomb was the *Enola Gay*. This airplane had been personally selected by Colonel Tibbets and assigned to Bob Lewis. In theory by being the 509th Composite Group Commander Tibbets did not officially have a plane and crew assigned to him. But, after he accepted the plane and "shook" it down we observed that he would let no one other than himself or Bob Lewis fly it. Neither would he let anyone but Sgt. Duzenbury, his flight engineer, nor his selected ground crew "put a wrench to it." Regardless of what others may say, I sat in on enough planning meetings to know that there is no question that there was ever any thought given to having anyone other than Colonel Tibbets fly the first mission. Also I might add after the numerous problems that developed on the second mission which was commanded by my good friend Major Chuck Sweeney, it is my opinion that if there were any additional missions, Colonel Tibbets would have been the pilot. Chuck Sweeney was a good friend but the bottom line is Chuck did not perform his duties and responsibilities as mission commander very well. In the vernacular "he screwed up." His mistakes could have cost his life and the lives of 12 others.

Question: Where and when did the atomic bomb final assembly occur?

Answer: We built the bombs up on Tinian. I was there and saw it. The First Ordinance Squadron, which was a part of our Group had this small complex that we built for them out on the island. That is where the thing {first atomic bomb} was put together. They did not risk flying the material {fissionable} over. Instead the USS Indianapolis brought it over and proceeded to get itself sunk about 24 hours later.

The second bomb I think Costello flew it out from the states. He had a hair-raising experience. Right at take-off the life raft door blew off and the raft fouled his elevator. As a result they had an emergency go-around and landing with a load of gas, twelve guys and the bomb onboard. It was at March Field, that this happened. He was a real interesting person. He very seldom showed any excitement when things were happening. But, to hear him tell about it later was a real comedy. That guy came close to having "it" right then and there. But he was a skilled pilot. He knew his B-29 and he knew what he could do with it. So he managed to stay airborne long enough. They kept him up there a couple of hours to lighten his load and then he maneuvered it in using mostly trim tabs because he had a fouled elevator.

Question: The bomb (and pumpkins) weighed between 5 and 10 thousand pounds. How did you load them on the airplane?"

Answer: Loading the bomb on the aircraft was not my responsibility but here is how they did it. The B-29 was so low slung airplane. These bombs because of their size could not fit under the plane, so a pit was provided to hold the bomb temporarily. The bomb loaded on a trailer that was pulled over the pit on two rails. Next a hoist would lift up the trailer and bomb far enough to pull out the rails. Then the trailer was spun on its axis and lowered into the pit until the wheels of the trailer rested on two concrete pads. The airplane then taxied up to the left side of the pit. With its right breaks set, the engines in the left wing were revved up, pivoting the plane around until the bomb bay doors were right above the pit. Then the bomb cradle was released from the trailer and hoisted up into the bomb bay where it was latched into place. The plane pulled away; the cradle was lowered back onto the trailer; and, the trailer was hoisted up and removed from the pit.

Question: Why is your name not stenciled on the nose of the *Enola Gay* along with the others?

Answer: Most people don't know the fact the *Enola Gay* had stenciled on its nose the names of just the nine normal crew members. But there were three others on board. Captain William S. Parsons, who was in military command of Los Alamos. He was the mission commander and weaponeer. Captain Parsons' assistance was Lieutenant Morrie Jeppson and I was the radar countermeasures officer.

Question: What happened when you got back from Hiroshima?

Answer: There was a big beer bust and barbecue for the whole group after we came out of the interrogation by the generals and admirals, such as Carl Spaatz and Nathan Twining.

Question: How did General Spaatz impress you?

Answer: I had a personal session with him. Tom Classen took me over to meet him, and he was a hell of a nice guy. He and I talked for about 15 minutes before the rest of the crowd got there. I also got to see him several times after I got back to the States at different dinners where he was speaking and I was a guest.

Question: How about Twining?

Answer: He asked very significant questions, of Tibbets in particular. I got to know Twining better when he was commander of SAC, the Strategic Air Command and I was then working for Westinghouse.

Question: Let's discuss some of the personalities involved with the bomb who you met at Los Alamos. What did you think of Drs. Edward Teller,J. Robert Oppenheimer, or Ashworth for instance?

Answer: Teller was very egotistical. Oppenheimer was pretty hard to judge, since he mumbled most of the time instead of talking. I knew

Ashworth very well and always felt accepted by him. This continued through his entire career after WWII. We were one of the Navy's prime suppliers of airborne radar and quite often he would come to the plant for high level meetings with our upper management, and without fail, he would insist upon seeing me before any of the day's business could begin. It got so that towards the end, I would be advised by the local VP to be at his office at the appointed hour so as not to delay the day's proceedings. He was wearing three stars by then. I found him to be a very Interesting person. I did not find out much about his background, but I was aware that he was an Annapolis graduate. My experience by that time had told me that both Annapolis and West Point graduates looked with disdain upon we lowly wartime issue GI officers. Their low serial numbers were a badge of distinction and they would never let you forget it.

Ashworth always treated me with respect for my professional abilities and never let any of the "trade school" mannerisms display themselves when we were together. He had been to the well in combat and had a full sense of mission; namely to do his damnedest to help end the war. He was a well trained professional carrying out his mission; he was there before the war began and intended to be there when it was over. I felt that he had adjusted to the wartime expansion of the service very well; more so than some of the others I served with. He regarded most of our types as rowdy's and for good reason. We were indeed a raunchy bunch, and those who should have moderated the mob led it. This seemed to be true of most of the fellows who had served in the Eighth Air Force. Some of it rubbed off from the RAF, and the rest of it was a release from the tension of the types of missions they flew. The Navy and the Air Force in the Pacific fought an entirely different type of war.

The Japs met them, fought them, and it was all over in a few minutes. You made it or you didn't make it. In the ETO there was repeated and prolonged hell for hours on end, and it was all conducted in a very hostile environment to begin with and at its peak became a daily nightmare. The number of fatigue cases in the ETO far surpassed the score in the Pacific.

Why am I defending all of this? I too found it to be a nuisance at times, but then again 1 more often as not joined in and became a part of it. I did it because I enjoyed raising hell.

Ashworth was a very competent person and I know from some of his writings, personal correspondence and otherwise, that inwardly he felt left out. His sponsor died suddenly and early on. His advancement to the top of his profession came as a result of hard work and dedication to duty. What was lacking, I think, was a public pat on the back. We all have some vanity, even if we don't fess up to it.

Question: What about Major General Leslie R. Groves, who was in overall command?

Answer: The story was that the program succeeded in spite of him! I don't believe that, and the people who talked like that were mostly civilians. Both Groves and Oppenheimer are dead. I saw Teller on TV just last week. Teller was the guy who later sold Truman on the hydrogen bomb, when the rest of the crowd was saying there was no need for it, and they were probably right.

Question: Was there any real fear that the Germans might beat us to the atomic bomb?

Answer: Yes, it was in the back of everyone's mind. There were two Allied commando raids made in Norway against German heavy water plants to prevent their getting the bomb first.

Question: You have raised so many interesting questions, and you obviously know so much more about it. But I asked Tibbets and it was on the basis of a very bad book that misquoted him completely, but the book says, he radioed back, "Mission Accomplished."

Answer: That's not true. Now, the strike report—before we ever left the ground Parsons was given an array of statements to make, depending on what he saw and the effects. And that is exactly what was passed to the radio operator for the strike report. I have forgotten the exact words but it was something like "dimples 82 over someplace and the sun shone beautifully" or words to that effect. This meant we had done everything we ever dreamed of doing. None of this "mission accomplished" stuff.

Question: What was the contingency plan, or was there a plan, in case the bomb didn't go off?

Answer: As far as I know there was no plan. However, wait a while. The probabilities that we are talking about here were so slight because we had to do our mission. We had the primary electronic fuse. The back up was a barometric fuse and if all else fails, we had a self-destruct, conventional impact nose and tail fusing and the whole God-damned thing cased in high explosives. So the probability of that {the bomb not going off} was so low that nobody even gave it a second thought. I wasn't aware of it. Paul {Tibbets} might have known if there was one. If he says no, I'd believe him.

Question: What was your reaction from when you saw it {explode}?

Answer: Well, I didn't see anything. I was very busy. I was very busy and very intent on what I was doing. Actually, I was watching simultaneously four different frequencies. I watched the fuses come on, I watched the function at the time the signal disappeared, all got real bright light and everything. When I got to the window he had pulled out of this tight turn, because I was pinned to the floor when he made his turn. And I forgot whether it was Joe Stuborak and I used words quite similar to what Lewis said. And that's what I heard. The younger guys were more emotional. They were more excitable and verbalized it more.

Question: I understand that the destruction below was very bad. What did the other people say?

Answer: This business of Bob Lewis saying, "My God, what have we done" is incorrect. What he really said was, "My God, look at that son of a bitch go." That was the language he used. The guy came off the streets of Paterson, New Jersey. He wasn't a holy man. He swore like a trooper, constantly.

Question: Did you hear him make that comment?

Answer: Yes and I recorded it.

Question: Were you at the Trinity test?

Answer: No, I was already on Tinian.

Question: Did you fly any training missions from Tinian before the Hiroshima mission?

Answer: I got out there and ran into a lot of guys from the old group who wanted to know what we were going to be doing, but I couldn't tell them anything. Actually, our unit, the 509th Composite Group, became the object of ridicule for awhile. We did fly some missions. We took the "pumpkin" version of the bomb without the nuclear component, but with normal high explosives instead and went in behind the big raids over the Empire to hit individual targets — stuff that had survived their raids. At the same lime, we were getting the Japanese used to seeing single B-29s on missions. We'd drop a single bomb, there'd be a big boom and then fly away. This was June-July 1945. We flew over many cities of the Empire.

Question: But didn't they show the movie?

Answer: They brought the movie. They had a projector but it didn't work. Parsons gave us a chalk talk and he drew the mushroom cloud and I remember he mentioned 20-kiloton yield. I tried to visualize that. The

216

only frame of reference I had was one pound blocks that we used to play with in training. I thought: how do you extrapolate that mentally to 20,000 tons of this stuff? You don't.

Question: But Hiroshima was really only 13 kilotons?

Answer: I'm aware of that. I am going to give a paper over at the Westinghouse Engineering Seminar the first of November, and I am to go through all those calculations for them. Somebody at Los Alamos sent me the whole sheet of these technical things.

Question: Let me ask a personal question of you. Did you feel any special significance or do you, for having been the only person on both planes? Did that give you a particular satisfaction?

Answer: Well, I will tell you how I got there. I was literally interviewed for the job and I got hired for it, Hal Brode looked me square in the eye and he says, "We have people that could do the job we want you to do, but they are too valuable to risk." So I thought, Jesus Christ, what am I getting into here? He asked me how did I feel about flying combat? I told him that's what I was trained for. I had wings and all that kind of stuff.

Question: I mean, you are a historical figure.

Answer: To an extent there was a degree of trust placed in my stability as a person, because they told me I would continue to go until I felt I'd had enough. Well, I didn't know they only had three bombs

Question: But you would have gone on the third one, too?

Answer: Yes.

Question: And you know Tibbets said he was going to fly the third one if there had been one?

Answer: Yes. I give Tibbets his due for the first one, but the second one should have been flown by a guy named Tom Classen but they sent him back to the States on a wild goose chase to get him out of there so that they could give it to Sweeney who was a buddy-buddy for the B-29 people.

Question: I asked Tibbets why Lewis didn't fly the second mission and he laughed and said he couldn't trust him as far as he could Sweeney. As you know Lewis is an independent person.

Answer: He was no goddamned good.

Question: Didn't Lewis fly to Japan with you on some of these training missions?

Answer: I never flew with Lewis. I think Lewis made one trip.

Question: But he thought he was going to fly the first mission, of course?

Answer: That's not true. He knew he wasn't going to fly that mission. There was never any doubt who was going to fly that mission. This all stems from a book called Look Up-Look Down. It's a piece of garbage. If I had known what the book author's true objectives were when he came to me, I would have never talked to the guy. He never presented himself to me as a psychologist and his interpretation of the data I gave him is all wrong.

One night in late July, I got a call from Associated Press. "Do you have any way of getting in touch with Kermet Beahan? We need to talk to him right away. Beahan was the bombardier on Nagasaki. "We understand he {Beahan} wrote a letter to the Mayor of Nagasaki and wants to come over and tell them how sorry he is and the Mayor turned him down."

Well, I almost dropped my teeth when I heard that. I couldn't see Beahan doing that for anything. I know that man too well. It wasn't until I was in Nagasaki and this damn guy comes up to me and tells me about Beahan and how much remorse he has and how badly he wanted to come {to Nagasaki} and the Mayor wouldn't let him. I ask him who wrote that letter? I can't see Beahan having done it. He said, "No, I did. Why do you ask?" I said, "Boy, don't you ever do that to me because if you do you are going to be in court so fast, and it shook him up." And I said, "When I get through talking to Beahan you are going to be in court, too."

So as soon as I got back to the States, I called Beahan. I couldn't get to him. He pulled his phone for three days because—he didn't know what was happening. The whole world descends on him. He didn't even know this idiot had done this. And I told him the whole story. I just sent him about a four-page letter detailing all the conversations I had with that idiot in Japan.

Question: Another interesting thing, when I was in Japan I talked to a couple or three Japanese, and they said that the Japanese never could understand why some people thought said it allowed them to save face.

Answer: Let me tell you something. They came up to me and they said, "You are not wrong for what you did. It was a war then. We didn't want the war. The militarists in Tokyo did, but we had to take what came with it." I told this one lady that was on Good Morning, America, with me. She was an English teacher, 80 years old, and we were sitting there talking. I asked her what were you doing forty years ago today when that thing {the atomic bomb} went off. She said, "Well, at eight o'clock I sat

218

down to eat my breakfast, because at 8:30 I go to work. At 8:15 you came and dropped your bomb. At 8:20 my neighbor pulled me out of my house, my house had fallen down on me, and my neighbor pulled me out. I didn't have a scratch. You, just scared me."

Question: It's funny how they, the Japanese, accept it as war.

Answer: Sure.

Question: There has been lots of stories about the crew of the *Enola Gay*. I have heard, like a lot of people in the country did, that the pilot out of his grief, remorse and guilt lost his mind - had a nervous breakdown. Apparently that is not true. As a matter there were stories that all of you guys had problems.

Answer: That is true. The use of the atomic bombs on Japan has been a fertile ground for revisionist historians and propagandists.

The remorse and guilt story began with the onset of the public awareness of the problems of one Major Eatherly. Major Eatherly was a member of our group and he flew the weather recon aircraft which preceded us over the city of Hiroshima by several hours and he radioed his weather report to us and he returned to Tinian in the Marianas. That was the extent of his participation to Hiroshima and to the decision making process whereby it was selected as the primary target. He informed us of the weather.

He was a very unusual person. No matter what he did, the guys couldn't stay upset at him. I liked him. He was a fun guy to be around, to have a beer with, and he always had an original tall tale to tell. He was probably the best pilot I have ever known and I knew a lot of them in WW II. He was a happy go lucky type of person who needed, and demanded, a lot of attention to himself. He had a weakness for women, liquor and gambling. He would often drive to Reno during off-duty hours at excessive speeds and accumulate lots of traffic violations in the process. When he did not get attention he always sought ways of attracting it to himself. He was very successful at the gambling tables and once remarked that he was going to make a ton of money off the atomic bombings after the war.

A little later in his career he was taking a course to be a meteorological officer and in the course of the final examination to get this rating, rather than studying the night before as everyone else had Eatherly probably engaged in a poker game or whatever else his normal evening past times were. {During the exam} he decided that his neighbor sitting next to him in the examination room probably had all the right answers and he would make liberal use of whatever information he could and cheating is not tolerated and he was dismissed from the service. From that point on it was downhill for Major Eatherly. He was first caught in New Orleans in the company of another Colonel Who had fallen on better days and they were running guns to Central America. They got caught by the federal agents and they were rather heavily fined, but they gained a lot of notoriety from it - national press coverage, radio and TV coverage. This sort of pleased Major Eatherly that he got all this attention and he figured some way that he could get the attention and not get confined. So he began holding up corner grocery stores and post offices. Once the money was transferred to him he would lay a toy gun which he carried and say "now call the police and the newspapers."

He is the one who fabricated the story that he had witnessed the dropping of the atomic bomb over Hiroshima and that seeing the blast made such an impact on him he went crazy. It was part of his successful insanity defense in federal court on the armed robbery charge. He beat the rap and gained notoriety for a while. If any reporters had bothered to check, they would have learned that Eatherly not only didn't witness the atomic blast, he had in fact, flown one of the weather planes on August 6 that was 250 miles away from Hiroshima at the time of the blast. The press, naturally, picked up his story without ever verifying it. But once the story was in print it begin a life of its own that persists to this day. And yes, eventually he was committed to a mental hospital.

In the summer of about 1964 I received a letter from a person in Czechoslovakia who was concerned about Major Eatherly's plight and wanted to engage in a three way written dialog with me and Eatherly. He felt that Eatherly was being abused by the government because of his opinion and actions. He believed Eatherly's story that he was having night mares about being over Hiroshima. This was converted to a book called "Burning Conscience" and it was the plight of Major Eatherly. Based on the book "Burning Conscience" a play was produced. I think it was in West Germany, in the summer of 1974 and it became a top play and of course it was ammunition for liberal propagandists in Europe and the rumor got worldwide attention.

The Book "Hiroshima Pilot" cast doubt on the Eatherly story. The author believes that pacifist and anti-nuclear activists created or exaggerated elements of Eatherly's story for propaganda purposes, and

220

that Eatherly cooperated in this myth making from desire for fame or attention. Some of this skepticism was refuted in the Book "Dark Star" by Ronnie Dugger. No other persons involved with the bombing of Hiroshima expressed guilt in the way that Eatherly did. Hiroshima pilot Paul Tibbets said that he couldn't understand why Eatherly felt so guilty, as he wasn't even there for the bombing.

Editor's Note: In 1959 Claude Eatherly wrote in a private correspondence:

"Throughout my adult life I have always been keenly interested in problems of human conduct.

Whilst in no sense, am I a religious or a political fanatic. I have for some time felt convinced that the crisis in which we are all involved is one calling for a thorough reexamination of our whole scheme of values and loyalties. In the past it has sometimes been possible for men to coast along without posing to themselves too many searching questions about the way they are accustom to think and act - but it is reasonably clear that we are rapidly approaching a situation in which we shall be compelled to reexamine our willingness to surrender responsibility for our thoughts and actions to some social institution such as the political party, trade union, church or state. None of these institutions are adequately equipped to offer infallible advice on moral issues, and their claim to offer such advice needs therefore to be challenged. It is, I fell in light of this situation that my personal experience needs to be studied, if its true significance, not only for myself, but for all men everywhere, is to be grasped.

My anti-social acts have been disastrous to my personal life, but I feel that in my efforts, in time my motives will succeed in bringing out my true convictions and philosophy."

Part 5
Back Home

Radio Interview 1962

Post War Years

Editor's Note: As previously stated I will continue with my father's words.

Before the year 1948 would be over, the most significant event of my entire life was to take place. Here again, just as in 1944 at Wendover Army Airfield, Utah. I happened to be in the right place at the right time. This time, unbeknownst to me, a certain young lady, who was about to graduate from the Towson Teachers College in Towson, Maryland, who had plans to go to Hawaii, was invited to dinner at her sisters house on Saturday evening the 29th of May for the purpose of possibly meeting "this interesting guy that my husband knows."

It just happened that this was Memorial Day weekend and I was one of the scheduled speakers at the National Cemetery in Catonsville, Maryland, and later at the Hebrew Friendship Cemetery in Baltimore where services were being held honoring Maryland's Jewish War Dead. For these reasons I had planned to stay in town for the weekend rather than visit a friend in Richmond, Virginia.

On Saturday I attended a Lacrosse Game at the University to watch several of my classmates perform. Upon returning home I had a telephone message inviting me for dinner at a friend's house. Not having any other plans for the evening, I accepted the invitation.

I no sooner arrived at the home of my hosts when it immediately became apparent to me that this was a "set-up" and I was there for the purpose of meeting the younger sister of my hostess. Under other circumstances I would have done one of two things: gotten a violent allergic headache and left as soon as possible, or, drink myself to oblivion. I never did appreciated being displayed as a "piece of meat." However, there was a certain gleam in the young lady's eye and she exhibited such a "joie de vivre" that I decided to behave myself and maybe I could even have a nice evening.

Before the evening was over it became apparent to me that this was no ordinary person that I was meeting but here was something special. My evening proved all too short so I invited the young lady to join me on the morrow as I performed my scheduled public duties and then spend the rest of the day with me getting better acquainted.

It was obvious to me that from the very moment I first laid eyes on her, Sylvia Rosen was the answer to completing the rest of my life plan. Three months later, to the day, on the 29th of August we were married. Four sons and eight grandchildren[37] have been the issue of this marriage. Now, over forty years later she still is my wife and lover, Mom to her daughter's-in-law, Grandma to the grand kids, 1st Mate on the boat, and most important, spends three days a week trying to retire from her job of the last twenty years as Director of Activities at the Jewish Convalescent and Nursing Home, where she brings some quality of life and enjoyment to the residents.

As I said earlier, I was discharged from the Army on 14 June 1946 and immediately went to work for Los Alamos Laboratories where I helped establish the Sandia Laboratories for the US Army Corps of Engineers. This organization later became a Bell Laboratories operated weapon facility of the US Atomic Energy Commission.

In 1948 I left Sandia Laboratories and returned to Johns Hopkins University where I spent about four years first as a student, and then as a research associate in the School of Medicine.

In 1951 I returned to private industry to work for AAI Corporation as a mechanical engineer building armored tanks for the US Army.

In 1956 I moved to the Air-Arm Division, Westinghouse Defense Electronic Center at the Baltimore-Washington International Airport as a mechanical engineer. In this capacity I assisted in program planning, preliminary design, and subcontractor management on several large airborne radar and ECM programs including the B-70 radar systems. Later as an advisory engineer reporting to the Engineering Manager, I performed advanced studies and system requirement analyses for future space and weapon systems.

In early 1966 I was assigned to a study team responsible for obtaining new business. At this time in our history, space business was in its infancy. The US Air Force was still a teenager and fighting a major war! Westinghouse was just beginning to become a player in the expanding space market areas. While Westinghouse was well known as a supplier of airborne weapon system electronics, we were not yet known as a principal supplier of space systems. It was a stated business goal of our Executive Management to expand the Westinghouse presence in the space sector and eventually win some large and highly classified space program contracts.

The opportunity came in 1966 when along with my senior partner Bill Parnell, made contacts with the Programs Planning Officer at the US

---

[37] Editor's Note: Number 9 grandchild, Jerome's daughter Jaclyn born in 1993, was named in memory of her grandfather.

Air Force Space and Missile Organization (SAMSO) in Los Angeles. We briefed this office on the capabilities of Westinghouse and in return they allow Bill and myself to have information on a sensor program known as Mission 2A that was being planned. By mid 1966 Westinghouse received a small study contract for this program that I led.

Editor's Note (Jack Spangler): In 1981, Jacob wrote a brief history for publication in the Westinghouse newspaper in which he said: "For several weeks, the Mission 2A team painstakingly analyzed a host of engineering alternatives and compiled comprehensive reports of their findings. A key part of this study was to do an end-to-end evaluation of a fully integrated system from a sensor in space to a set of data users on the ground specifically addressing ways to make the data user friendly. After a few weeks and all of a sudden without any advance notice, the study program was canceled. Needlessly to say, the team was disappointed. However all was not lost! Westinghouse had been introduced to the Air Force "space weenies.""

The SAMSO engineers and scientists were favorably impressed with the technical expertise exhibited in the presentations; the quality of the technical reports; and, the total system approach that Westinghouse had generated during the 2A studies. Shortly thereafter Westinghouse received a request for a proposal from the Air Force to study the requirements and propose a design for a new highly classified Weather Satellite System (later known as DMSP Block 5).

Editor's Note (Jack Spangler): Just prior to my retirement in 1994 as the Block 5 Program Manager, I was told that SAMSO knew nothing of the Westinghouse space capabilities and the Mission 2A contract had been a test which proved to them that Westinghouse did indeed have space capabilities.

The studies under the contract were initiated the first week of November 1966 and were to be completed by the end of the year. The study results were favorably received by the Air Force and by mid-June 1967 Westinghouse was under a fixed price development contract for the design and production systems. I was given the job of Deputy Program Manager for this new program.

As with most engineering endeavors, perfection comes with great difficulty and is seldom achieved. However for the case of space hardware the difference between failure and success is doing a thing almost right and doing it exactly right. As the program progressed through the design phase, some serious design, performance and contract problems developed.

Large subcontractors were brought into the program. As time progressed some fell seriously behind schedule and contractual issues developed. Breadboards of the electronic circuits, as well as mechanical, optical and thermal test models were built and tested solving the problems one by one but at the cost of time and money.

Editor's Note (Jack Spangler): In order to help solve these problems, Jacob was relieved of his responsibilities as Deputy Program Manager in order to allow him to devote his time, expertise and talents to solving engineering and contractual problems with the subcontractors. (Jewish Engineering as he called it!) As time went on the problems were identified and solved much like peeling an onion one layer at a time. Eventually the problems were solved and the program was recognized within some Government circles as the "best performing and the most cost effective program" in existence at that time. In fact the program at Northrop Grumman[38] is still a major contract some 40 years later.

Jacob continued in the capacity of Engineering Subcontracts Manager for the remainder of his career and retired in 1985.

Jacob Beser (left), Paul Kiefer (center) and Jack Spangler (right) celebrate 15 years of the Block 5 Program at Westinghouse November 1981

[38] Westinghouse Space Division was acquired by Northrop Grumman in 1996

The Raven

Editor's note: This chapter by Jack Spangler.

Jacob Beser was one of the very few to eyewitness the only two atomic bombs that have been used in warfare to date. He was the only person to have been a crewmember of both the airplanes that delivered the bombs on Hiroshima and Nagasaki. He had first hand knowledge of the results of the bombs. He was in total agreement the situation that existed in 1945 fully justified the use of the bombs and he was a willing participant in both missions. However he strongly believed that future international disputes must be resolved by peaceful means and such weapons should never again be used in warfare. He therefore felt that it was his responsibility, duty and post retirement mission to help educate others in the destructive capabilities of atomic bombs and the associated horrors.

When speaking of the use of atomic bombs Jacob would often use the phrase "Quote the Raven Nevermore"? For him there was a specific significance to that phrase. The color black has for centuries been associated with magic and mysterious situations. In the 1940s radar was a mystery to most people and electronic countermeasures to defeat radar was considered "black magic." In 1945 those trained in the art of electronic countermeasures were called "black birds, crows or ravens." Jacob was the "Raven" for the 509th Composite Group. Incidentally the word "black" is still associated with highly classified military programs or hardware. The once highly classified secret reconnaissance airplane the SR-71 is called the "Black Bird." Also there is an organizations of former electronic countermeasures veterans called "The Old Crows."

But getting back to the phrase "Quote the Raven Nevermore." It can be translated to mean, "Jacob Beser is saying he fervently hopes that atomic weapons will never again be used to resolve international conflicts."

From 1945 until his death in 1992, he seldom passed up an opportunity to speak to any group or individual or answer letters as the case might be to discuss what he witnessed on August 6 and 9 1945. He devoted many, many hours of his time lecturing to groups.

I can recall one lecture he gave at a Westinghouse Engineers

Seminar. Unfortunately there was no tape recording made of this lecture. It had been over 20 years since I heard him speak but I have tried to reconstruct here as best I can from memory the main points he made.

Recollections of the lecture:

The Hiroshima bomb, "Little Boy" was 120 inches long, 28 inches in diameter and weighed about 9000 pounds. It had an estimated explosive yield of between 12,500 and 20,000 tons of TNT. (The exact yield is still being debated.) The core temperature at the instant of detonation was estimated at 50,000,000 degrees Centigrade. Ten milliseconds after detonation a fire ball about 180 feet in diameter formed with an estimated core temperature of 300,000 degrees Centigrade. The shock wave produced by the explosion traveled at about 2.8 miles per second. A stationary firestorm developed around the epicenter that burned out 4.4 square miles. All wood structures within a 1 ¼-mile radius of the epicenter were almost instantaneously destroyed either by the blast or the firestorm. All concrete and steel structures were severely damaged and almost all collapsed. At 5 miles from the epicenter the paint on houses would melt and burn from the intense heat before the blast wave knock them down. Similarly glass windowpanes would soften and/or melt before being shattered by the blast. Fires broke out everywhere and windows were shattered within a 10-mile radius. Thirty-three miles from the epicenter, 10% of the houses were destroyed and 40% suffered severe damage. The shock wave reached out as far as 37 miles destroying cars, buses, trains and most minor structures. He made a point to say that these numbers are facts, not calculations.

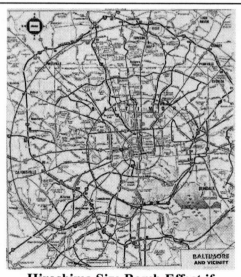

Hiroshima Size Bomb Effect if Exploded Over Baltimore MD

Jake went on to

illustrate his point by assuming a Hiroshima size bomb was exploded at an optimum altitude over the center of Baltimore City, Maryland using a map with circles drawn around the epicenter at 1 1/4, 5 and 10 miles. Since this lecture was given to Maryland residents, the map of local destruction really made the point as to why he often used the phrase "Quote the Raven Nevermore."

He went on to explain that the Hiroshima weapon was only 13 Kilotons in yield. The smaller circle represents a 1¼-mile radius from the epicenter of the explosion. At Hiroshima everything within this circle was destroyed with one exception. The Science and Industry Museum building at the very center of the blast (standing now as a memorial in Hiroshima) remained. Nothing was left and everyone instantly perished, leaving shadows burned on the pavement of where people once stood. A second circle on his map was drawn at a 5-mile radius. At Hiroshima everything within this circle was burned, but there were survivors non-the-less. Major damage occurred 25 miles away from the epicenter.

Now contrast this with today's weapon yield of 100 Megatons. If a single 100 Megaton bomb exploded over Ft. Meade, long considered a primary target, it would cause instant eradication of everything within a forty mile radius of the epicenter. This means that everything from Pikesville, Maryland to Falls Church Virginia would suddenly cease to exist. Damage would be 95 percent within a 100-mile radius, and those not killed immediately by the blast and firestorm would die from radiation. Casualties would be 100 percent.

The restored Enola Gay on display at the Smithsonian

The Enola Gay Smithsonian Exhibit Controversy

Editor's Note: This chapter by Jack Spangler.

The Smithsonian Institution accepted the *Enola Gay* in good condition in Chicago in 1949. It was eventually taken to Andrews Air Force Base where it was stored outside and unlocked from 1953 to 1960. For more than a half dozen years this B-29, a once proud war bird, had been subjected to abuse and neglect while it languished in a corner of Andrews Air Force Base open to the elements and souvenir hunters.

By 1960 it had become a decaying derelict. The tail gunner's station had been smashed. Significant parts were missing. Birds had not only used it as a bombing target, but they had also nested inside the plane's fuselage and virtually trashed it.

In a February 2, 1960 interview Jacob commented that he had seen the derelict *Enola Gay* the day before at Andrews AFB partially torn apart and wrapped in canvas and being readied for transportation to a storage warehouse for restoration by volunteers.

Following the lengthy restoration, it was proposed to use a portion of the aircraft at the Smithsonian's National Air and Space Museum in Washington as the centerpiece of an exhibit commemorating the fiftieth anniversary of its famous mission.

In the mid to late 1980s and early 1990s, antinuclear protesters and revisionists were attempting to rewrite our history with claims that Japan's invasion of Manchuria, the Marco Polo Bridge Incident, the bloody bombing of Shanghai, and the Rape of Nanking had never happened. Additionally they assert that the United States invited the attack on Pearl Harbor and that the Bataan Death March was a myth. There are even those who declare that the Holocaust never happened.

Some within these groups tried to hijack the proposed 50th anniversary *Enola Gay* Smithsonian exhibit and use it as a prop for a politically motivated propaganda show.

Jacob saw this as part of the cultural reinterpretation of history that was now appearing more and more frequently in the museum exhibits. He was especially concerned over the fact that the proposed exhibit would depict the Japanese more as innocent victims of an aggressor (the United States) motivated by vengeance and racism than as a ruthless aggressor

231

nation. Furthermore he was concerned that the proposed exhibit would inaccurately portrayed remorse by bomber crews that participated in the Hiroshima and Nagasaki raids.

Over the years Jacob had used his high level security clearances and political and media connections to collect documents; photos; film; audio and video tapes; eyewitness transcripts; government and media reports; and, personal correspondence that accurately and chronologically validated the historical *Enola Gay* and *Bock's Car's* missions.

With the increased fervor of the revisionist and antinuclear publications and the attempts of these groups to hijack the *Enola Gay* exhibit in the Smithsonian, he increased his efforts to document what really happened in 1945 and why it happened. In spite of his failing health, he increased his efforts to try and locate the in-flight recordings he made of the crew reactions made over Hiroshima as well as obtain additional documentation. Once these tasks were complete, he intended to accurately document his findings in a "tell all" book.

By 1992 his declining health severely limited his ability to finish his ambitious endeavors. His efforts to locate the in-flight recording proved unsuccessful in spite of a lifetime of searching. He did however collect a number of rare government reports and transcripts of eyewitness reports of many of the participants that he filed away in his personal archives. These archives along with his personal notes and an outline of his intentions provided enough information for someone to fill in the blanks at a later date.

The American image of Japan in the 1940's was much different than it was in 1990. In 1945 the American people were in no mood to make deals with the Japanese regime responsible for Pearl Harbor, the Bataan death march, the forced labor camps, habitual mistreatment of prisoners of war, and a fifteen-year history of atrocities from Manchuria to the East Indies.

In his radio address on August 9, 1945, President Truman said: *"The United States had used the atomic bomb against those who attacked us without warning at Pearl Harbor; against those who have starved and beaten and executed American prisoners of war; and, against those who have abandoned all pretense of obeying international laws of warfare. We have used it in order to shorten the agony of war, in order to save the lives of thousands and thousands of young Americans. We shall continue to use it until we completely destroy Japan's power to make*

232

war. Only a Japanese surrender will stop us." Later Winston Churchill wrote: "The historic fact remains, and must be judged in the after-time, that the decision whether or not to use the atomic bomb to compel the surrender of Japan was never an issue. There was unanimous, automatic, unquestioned agreement around our table (at Potsdam); nor did I ever hear the slightest suggestion that we should do otherwise."

Unfortunately the passage of time; the directed Japanese publicity campaigns; the repeated publication of pictures from Hiroshima and Nagasaki; the reliance on Japanese cars, televisions and other products; and, the desire not to offend the nation of Japan have provided aid and comfort to antinuclear and revisionist pseudo-intellectuals. More precisely they have helped to transformed Japan's image from the aggressor to that of the victim in World War II!

As for the proposed *Enola Gay* exhibit at the Smithsonian museum Jacob felt that any exhibit of the *Enola Gay* should honor the bravery of the World War II veterans in a patriotic manner that would instill pride in the viewer. In addition it should present a fair, balanced and accurate account of the historical and ethical nature of the events leading up to and during the war and why the use of the bomb was justified.

In the early 1990s Jacob became aware of what was being proposed for the exhibit to make it "politically correct." In his opinion the proposed exhibit did nothing to accurately preserve the past for the benefit of the future. Instead it would depict the Japanese as a proud nation in a desperate defense of their home islands saying little about what had made such a defense necessary. Furthermore it would depict the United States as a brutal, vindictive, and racially motivated aggressor nation. According to his information the exhibit would contain words such as: "For Americans it was a war of vengeance. For most Japanese, it was a war to defend their unique culture against Western imperialism." It would also depict the decision to use the atomic bomb as immoral, unethical, and criminal. It seemed to suggest that President Truman's decision to use the bomb was based on flawed information. Lastly, it was rumored that the proposed exhibit would grossly and inaccurately portray personal remorse by the bomber crews for participating in the Hiroshima and Nagasaki raids. These were fighting words for Jacob!

At this point it can be said that the proposed content of the *Enola Gay* exhibit rekindled the fire in this aging and sick warrior.

For over 45 years the Japanese had ignored their brutality and their sole responsibility for the war, the events that lead up to the war. An entire generation of Japanese citizens is totally ignorant of the part their parents played in the war. The *Enola Gay* exhibit as proposed would undoubtedly be viewed by millions of Americans as well as possibly a number of foreign visitors. They all would accept it as a factual representation of what happened in the final days of World War II.

Not only was Jacob outraged over the proposed exhibit content, he also felt that he and his fellow World War II veterans were being betrayed by "enlightened" historians and even the Smithsonian Institute, our national museum. He now joined the large group of veterans to lend his voice to the public outcry of disdain for the proposed exhibit. Their purpose was not to denigrate the Japanese people but to accurately preserve the facts. If the exhibit was allowed to exist as planned, he felt it was an attempt to distort and rewrite history in a very public place. It would not only aid and abet the revisionist but would also contribute additional fuel to the collective Japanese amnesia.

As the discontent and angry letters to the Smithsonian and influential politicians intensified, "sophisticated people" regarded them as merely an expression of crude emotions of the old warriors. But Jacob and the other World War II veterans felt that they had a more accurate understanding of the moral complexities that existed at the time and that they should not be ignored. They further recognized that the events of August 6, 1945 were not going to go away even though certain groups were attempting to do so by isolating it from the context of the war.

But what could he do to help defeat the proposed exhibit? After all he did have the distinction of being the only participant as a member of the strike aircraft crews that delivered the atomic bombs on Hiroshima and Nagasaki. Because of this participation, he had developed a number of contacts in influential military organizations as well as high level politicians. He made contacts with some of these people and let his opinions be known. However, his health was declining rapidly and his days were numbered. He was unable to continue as a vocal advocate for changes to the proposed exhibit. Fortunately, his opinion was shared by a vocal majority of veterans. Eventually the Smithsonian bowed to the pressure and scratched the original plans for the exhibit.

PART 6 Typhoon Louise

This could have happened to the US Invasion Fleet

Damage to the USS LCI(L)-641 USS LCI (Landing Craft Infantry) Buckner Bay Okinawa after being destroyed by Typhoon Louise October 1945. US Navy Photo

LSM 361 ran aground at Buckner Bay Okinawa during Typhoon Louise which devastated the Island on October 9, 1945

More destruction caused by Typhoon Louise at Buckner Bay, Okinawa October 1945

Epilogue

Editor's Note: This chapter by both Editors summarizes the naval historian's message:

The plan for the American invasion of Kyushu, Operation Coronet, was scheduled for November 1, 1945. The invasion fleet would consist of thousands of ships ranging in size from battleships to small amphibious landing craft sailing from Okinawa, the Philippines and the Marianas. They would put 14 divisions, over 500,000 soldiers and marines, on the southern, eastern and western shores of Kyushu. Army, Navy and Marine aircraft from the island of Okinawa would provide close air support.

Japan had never been successfully invaded in its history. American military planners knew that this invasion would be a difficult undertaking. But, because of the bombing of Hiroshima and Nagasaki on August 6 and 9th, the war had ended and the invasion plans of the Japanese homeland became obsolete and the invasion never occurred. Almost immediately thousands of American soldiers, sailors, and airmen were sent home.

However, had there been no bomb dropped or had it been simply delayed for only a matter of months, history might have repeated itself.

Following the surrender of Germany in the summer of 1945, the Allies were assembling a powerful armada. Millions of American soldiers, sailors, and airmen were being moved to the Pacific for the anticipated invasion of the Japanese homeland. The primary staging area for the invasion was Okinawa.

The Japanese people fervently believed that the American invaders would be repelled as the Mongols had been about six centuries earlier. They all seemed to share a mystical faith that their country could never be invaded successfully and again they would be saved by the "divine wind."

In October, Buckner Bay, on the east coast of Okinawa, was still jammed with vessels of all kinds, from victory ships to landing craft. On the island itself, 100,000 or more soldiers and marines were housed in "Tent Cities." All over the island, thousands of tons of food, equipment and supplies were stacked in huge piles and lay out in the open.

On October 4th, a typhoon was spotted developing in the Caroline Islands and tracked as it moved to the northwest. The storm had been expected to pass into the East China Sea, north of Formosa but unexpectedly, on the evening of October 8, the storm changed direction and abruptly veered to the east. That evening the storm slowed down and, just as it approached Okinawa, began to greatly increase in intensity. When it did, there was insufficient warning to allow ships in the harbor to get under way in order to escape to the open sea from the typhoon's terrible violence.

By late morning on the 9th, rain was coming down in torrents, the seas were rising, and visibility was zero. Winds of over 80 miles per hour blowing from the east and northeast and waves 30-35 feet high battered the ships and craft in the bay causing the small crafts in the bay to drag their anchors, collide with other vessels and in some cases to be beached.

By early afternoon, the wind had risen to over 100 miles per hour. The rain began coming in horizontally and was more salt than fresh, and even the larger vessels began dragging anchor under the pounding of 50 foot seas.

By mid afternoon, the typhoon had reached its raging peak with winds coming from the north and northeast blowing up to 150 miles per hour. Ships initially grounded by the storm were blown off the reefs and back across the bay to the south shore, dragging their anchors the entire way. More collisions occurred between the wind-blown ships and shattered hulks.

Gigantic waves swamped small vessels and engulfed larger ones. Liberty ships lost their propellers, while men in transports, destroyers and Victory ships were swept off the decks by 60-foot waves that reached the tops of the masts of their vessels.

As the winds continued to increase and the storm unleashed its fury, the entire bay became a scene of devastation. Ships dragging their anchors collided with one another and hundreds of vessels were blown ashore. Vessels in groups of two's and three's were washed ashore into masses of wreckage that began to accumulate on the beaches. Numerous ships had to be abandoned while their crews were precariously transferred between ships.

On shore, the typhoon was devastating the island. Twenty hours of torrential rain washed out roads and ruined the island's stores of rations and supplies. Aircraft were picked up and catapulted off the airfields, huge Quonset huts went sailing into the air, metal hangers were ripped to shreds, and the "Tent Cities" ceased to exist. Almost the entire food supply on the island was blown away. Americans on the island had nowhere to go but into caves, trenches and ditches in order to survive. All over the island were tents, boards, and sections of galvanized iron being hurled through the air at over 100 miles per hour.

The storm raged over the island for hours then slowly headed out to sea. Then it doubled back and two days later hit the island again.

After the typhoon roared out into the Sea of Japan and started to die, the bodies began to wash ashore. The dazed men on Okinawa crawled out of holes and caves to count the losses. The toll on ships was staggering. Almost 270 ships were sunk, grounded or damaged beyond repair. Fifty-three ships were badly damaged and were decommissioned, stripped and abandoned. Out of 90 ships that needed major repair, the Navy decided only 10 were even worthy of complete salvage, and so the remaining 80 were scrapped. Personnel casualties were 36 killed, 47 missing, and 100 seriously injured. Countless aircraft had been destroyed, all power was gone, and communications and supplies were nonexistent. Almost all the food, medical supplies and other stores were destroyed, over 80% of all housing and buildings knocked down, and all the military installations on the island were temporarily out of action.

According to Samuel Eliot Morrison, the famous Naval historian, "Typhoon Louise" was the most furious and lethal storm ever encountered by the United States Navy in its entire History.

If the war had not ended on September 2nd, this damage, especially the grounding and damage to 107 amphibious craft including the wrecking of four tank landing ships, two medium landing ships, a gunboat, and two infantry landing craft would likely have seriously impacted the planned invasion of Japan.

Had history been different, religious services and huge celebrations would have been held in the aftermath of this typhoon. A million Japanese voices would have been raised upward in thanksgiving. Everywhere tumultuous crowds would have gathered in delirious gratitude to pay homage to a "divine wind" which might once again protect their country from foreign invaders, a "divine wind" they had named centuries before, the "Kamikaze."

However, World War II is now history and few people concerned themselves with the invasion plans for Japan. Surprisingly few people have made the connection that an American invasion fleet of thousands of ships, planes and landing craft and a half million men might well have been in that exact place at that exact time. The typhoon, which struck Okinawa and the surrounding seas so severely, damaged the ships, planes, landing craft, and men poised to strike Japan that the invasion plans would have been crippled and would have required major revision while the resources were replenished. [39]

---

[39] Editor's Note: Information on Typhoon Louise was obtained from various Navy documents and newspaper reports.

End Notes

Editor's Note: This chapter by Jack Spangler.

Jacob Beser's unfinished manuscript and his archived documents for this book contained hundred's of pages of historical documents and other notes as well as audio and video tapes related to the atomic bomb missions. Some of his notes were handwritten and others were either typewritten or on computer disks. We have minimally edited his words and have not performed any extensive research to independently confirm the accuracy of what he had written. The Editors do not necessarily agree or disagree with the content of his manuscript, notes or his archived documents. What we have included is what he wrote or said. We have simply taken the outline for his unfinished book, supplement it with what he said in other writings; personal conversations and interviews; and, stitched them together to complete this book more or less in accordance with his original plan. It was interesting to note that in reviewing over 40 years of tape recordings, interview transcript, lecture notes, etc. he consistently used the same words and never deviated from his story.

While the Editors believe that all the information presented is factual, this book should be considered a historical essay and not as independently verified historical facts. Where we have reproduced documents they are either photo copies of the originals or verbatim transcripts.

While in the process of stitching together the information from his notes and transcripts of interviews, etc., we reviewed numerous books and papers by several authors. Among others, these included the books *Enola Gay* by Gordon Thomas and Max Morgan Witts; *Hiroshima and Nagasaki Revisited* by Jacob Beser; *The War's End* by Major General Charles Sweeney; and, *Return of the Enola Gay* by Paul W. Tibbets, Jr. While reviewing these documents and books it was obvious that in several cases they contained the same words, sentences, and identical or almost identical paragraphs as those appearing in Jacob's personal interviews; public and private correspondence; and, other notes. Some acknowledged Beser (or Cmdr. Ashworth) as their source. Others did not. Beser's documents were all written or recorded between 1945 and 1992. He had not annotated many of his notes with source data but his writings were all completed prior to June 1992. Plagiarism? Doubtful. We suspect these are good, no excellent, examples where different people who were eyewitness to the same spectacular events have described them with the same or similar words or combination of words.

Jacob Beser was my good friend and business colleague at Westinghouse for more than 20 years. Over that time period he and I had numerous conversations and I have heard the details of his wartime experiences many times. I have also read thousands of pages of his writings on this and other subjects and I am very familiar with his style of writing. The style of writing as well as the content of his personal manuscript and notes agrees with his writing style and my personal knowledge of his war experiences and his feelings on this subject. Therefore many of his notes as we found them have been included and unedited. However, should any reader have information that indicates other sources should be acknowledge, we will be more than happy to include the proper acknowledgments and credits in the next printing of this book.

Some readers may notice that there is sometime repetition of sentences and possibly paragraphs in the various chapters. The Editors are aware of this. As said earlier, Jacob was unable to finish this work but it was very clear on what he was trying to accomplish. In order to accomplish what he intended we were forced to supplement it with what he said in other writings; personal conversations and interviews; and, stitched them together to complete this book more or less in accordance with his original plan. Much of his writing, interviews, personal conversations, etc. took place at different times in his career. Early on in the preparation of this book we decided that that Jacob's spoken and written words would be included as far as possible in an unedited and original condition. This has resulted in the repetition that you may notice.

APPENDIX 1.

Myths and Facts

Editor's Note: The appendixes are compiled from recorded lectures presented to the US Naval Academy in early 1970.

For the purpose of today's lecture, I have tried to provide an engineering style executive summary some of the things relative to myths and facts that I have talked about in earlier chapters.

The use of the atomic bombs to effectively bring an end to World War II has been a fertile ground for peace activists, propagandist and left wing liberals every since the bombs were used in 1945. As a result there are lots of stories circulating – some true, some myths and some misconceptions. Since I was involved to some extent with the design of the weapon, the selection of targets and the deployment of both bombs I will try to set the record straight by summarizing some of the myths, report the facts and give a little insight into the reasoning behind using the bombs.

Over the years I have been regarded at various times an instant expert in Atomic Warfare, a National Hero, a Hired Killer, a Pariah, and even a War Criminal. I am none of these. War itself is the criminal. Yes there were possibly as many as 180,000 casualties at Hiroshima and Nagasaki in the two flashes of flame. But you have to trade this horrifying number off against the savings of unknown hundreds of thousands, if not millions, of lives that would have been lost had the alternative of allowing the war to continue and the inevitable invasion to occur. To me our leaders made the correct decisions. Revisionist historians and the liberal left wing can argue until Hell freezes over that Japan was already beaten and several more weeks of conventional bombings and the results would have been the same. While there is no denying that Japan had suffered terribly under the onslaught of the B-29s, they had previously demonstrated a will to fight to the death. This had occurred in each of the Island battles and there certainly was no reason to expect that they would do otherwise in resisting our invasion of their homeland. I was there and I witnessed first hand the "fight to the death" attitude of the Japanese soldiers and civilians.

This brings up a good point. It was obvious that Japan was defeated long before we ever bombed Hiroshima. The atomic bombs alone did not win the war. Most of the Japanese industrial capacity had been destroyed before we ever dropped the first atomic bomb. Any reasonable people would have given up and accepted the terms of unconditional surrender. The Jap leaders were not reasonable in any sense of the word.

As late as June 1945 following the horrible fire bombing of Tokyo the Japanese Cabinet issued this statement: "*With faith born of eternal loyalty as our inspiration, we shall--thanks to the advantages or our terrain and the unity of our nation--prosecute the war to the bitter end in order to uphold our national essence, protect the imperial land, and achieve our goals of conquest.*" Does a statement such as this indicate that the Japanese were ready to surrender? I don't think so. This statement which came from the top Japanese leadership says to me *"Hell no we will never give up the fight."* This one statement is proof to me that an invasion of the Japanese mainland was inevitable and President Truman had a very unpleasant decision to make.

It took a second atomic bombing followed up by the largest fire bombing raid of the war with over 1000 airplanes participating to convince the Japanese leadership that they had really lost the war should accept the terms of the unconditional surrender.

If the Japanese were already beaten then why did we drop the atomic bomb? And why should we have dropped the atomic bomb? We hear a lot of arguments about this from enlightened history professors, teachers, peace activists, and so on. Unfortunately many of these people were not even born in 1945 and simply just don't know what they are talking about to put it bluntly. The sad part is that many of them have not taken the time to even find out the facts. Expressing a personal opinion which differs from mine is fine as I said in an earlier chapter, but these people especially those in influential positions, should be familiar with all of the facts before expressing any opinion at all! It is understandable that a person cannot learn all the details about every single operation during World War II but unfortunately facts sometimes don't mean too much in an emotional or political discussion.

And now for some facts. As in any war, our goal was—as it should be—to win. The stakes were too high to equivocate. We had to do what was necessary!

In America, nothing is more natural in the time of war then for our leaders, which we elected to attempt to ensure victory with a minimum loss of life. For our armed forces the extravagant use of firepower was the approach to achieve the desired effect and had been employed from day one. Fire bombing raids on the Empire are good examples. Using the atomic bombs against Japan was simply the ultimate step in this approach. Some people may not want to believe it but it took those two bombs followed up by the largest single air raid of the war to finally convinced the Japanese leadership to surrender and end the Pacific conflict in short order.

Humane warfare is an oxymoron. War by definition is barbaric. To try and distinguish between an acceptable method of killing and an unacceptable method is ludicrous. In my mind, to suggest that one specific act of war is barbaric and thereby illegal is to imply that other forms of slaughter are acceptable and consequently legal! If you have to die in warfare, what is the difference of being killed by a bomb or a bullet?

First I would like to talk a little about the target selection process. The civilian population areas were not selected because of the population density and the desire to "kill more Japs" as some would like you to believe.

I sat in on some target committee meetings. What I heard there as well as historical documents that I have in hand show that at the highest levels of government President Truman and his top advisors agonized over the decision and the target selection for days before the use of the bombs were authorized. The decision was also discussed with the other world leaders at the Potsdam conference. They unanimously agreed that the bombs were necessary. President Truman's concerns were spelled out in his handwritten diary notes he made at Potsdam. He wanted to, and did, give the Japanese leaders one last chance to surrender or face the consequences. When his ultimatum was ignored he gave the orders to proceed but specifically directed that the bombs to be used only against targets of military significance.

Each potential target that was considered had significant military importance. Hiroshima was the headquarters for the southern command, responsible for the defense of Honshu in the event of an invasion. A large number of the people killed were soldiers and a part of the Japanese 2nd Army. They were the soldiers that would have been killing our people had an invasion occurred. We did not bomb Hiroshima simply to kill people. In addition the 2nd army headquarters, there were over 100 numbered military targets in the city of Hiroshima. But The most important of these that we wanted to get was the 2nd Army headquarters. This was where the battle-seasoned troops that would mount the initial defense were being assembled for the anticipated invasion. It was also where they would have direct the kamikazes and kaitens against the invading ships.

Nagasaki was an industrial center with two large Mitsubishi armaments factories. In both Hiroshima and Nagasaki, the Japanese had integrated these industries and troops right in the heart of each city. It is also true that these industries had a widely distributed source of supply of small parts and subassemblies from local cottage shop operations in nearby private homes.

I participated in both the Hiroshima and Nagasaki missions as a crew member. I can attest to the fact that we made sure that President Truman's orders were carried out as he intended them to be even though it required great personal risk especially to the crew of the *Bock's Car* on the Nagasaki mission.

On August 10 the Japanese Prime Minister offered to surrender. On August 12, the United States announced that it would accept the Japanese surrender, making clear in its statement that the emperor could remain in a purely ceremonial capacity only. Debate raged within the Japanese government over whether to accept the American terms or fight on. The fighting in the fields continued as well as the kamikaze raids. In response President Truman ordered fire-bombing raids to resume.

On August 13 over 1000 B-29s and other aircraft, carrying 6000 tons of explosive and incendiary bombs again visited Japan. It is not well known but that was the largest single air raid of the war on Japan. Just think of the number of Japanese civilians that were killed on that raid that nobody ever talks about! I suspect that almost as many people were killed on that raid as were killed at Hiroshima or Nagasaki. What is more, raids like that would have continued every day the weather was clear until the Japanese finally surrendered.

On August 15 Emperor Hirohito went on the Japanese radio and spoke to his people announcing that Japan had accepted the American surrender terms and appealed to the kamikazes to give in.

It is often heard that the effects of harmful radiation from the bomb were not considered. This is another myth. In reality the radiation effects were considered in selecting the altitude the bomb was set to explode. First and foremost we wanted to get the maximum destructive power from the bomb but we also wanted to minimize radiation at ground level. Since there was really no way to completely eliminate radiation at ground level and still achieve the desired blast effects on structures, the bombs were set to explode about 1850 feet above the ground. This kept strongest radiation well above ground level.

On the subject of remorse, guilt and insanity of the crews of the *Enola Gay* and *Bock's Car*. This is has been another fertile ground for myth-makers and propagandists. I personally knew all the men involved before, during and after the missions as well as during the post war years. They have let me know and I have quoted from interviews in earlier chapters of this book that none ever expressed any remorse and each and every man said that given the same conditions, he would do it again.

The remorse, guilt and insanity stories stem primarily from two incidents – the first being the statement "My God, what have we done" that Captain Bob Lewis, the *Enola Gay* co-pilot, wrote in his log a few minutes after the bomb exploded over Hiroshima. What he wrote and what he said are different. What he really said, and I recorded it, was "Look at that sonofabitch go."[40]

In an interview Bob said "I wrote down in my book, and this was a minute or two afterwards. Just a little letter I prepared, and whether {or not} I said it out loud but what I wrote down that I said {was} "My God, What have we done?" Meaning what has mankind done in designing and developing a bomb like this to destroy mankind. THAT IS WHAT I MEANT BY THAT {STATEMENT}. If you should quote "My God, What have we done?" explain and qualify the statement."

When ask did you think at that time when you saw this cloud coming up that this was it. This was the end of the war? Bob's answer was: "I'm sure that there was very little would have entered my mind that day other than this bomb and the delivering of it; the dropping of it; and, the getting away safe. Because dropping an atomic bomb was still untried from an airplane and our biggest thought naturally was our own survival. To get out of there and be able to get back {home} safely.

To me Bob's answer to these questions certainly did not express any guilt or remorse for what we had done as many revisionist historians have interpreted his written comment to mean.

The second part which relates to the insanity of the crew members began with the onset of the problems of Major Claude Eatherly. Claude

---

[40] Editor's Note: The recordings that Jacob made were lost for over 60 years but have been found. The recording confirms what Captain Lewis really said.

was a member of our group and he flew the weather recon aircraft which preceded us over the city of Hiroshima and radioed his weather report to us and returned to Tinian. That was the extent of his participation to Hiroshima and to the decision making process whereby Hiroshima was selected as the primary target. He informed us of the weather. Neither did he lead the bomber group to Hiroshima nor did he receive the Distinguished Flying Cross as has sometimes been reported.

Claude was a very unusual person. No matter what he did, the guys couldn't stay upset at him. I liked him and he was probably the best pilot I have ever known. He was a happy go lucky type of person who needed, and demanded, a lot of attention to himself. He had a weakness for women, liquor and gambling. While at Wendover he would often drive to Reno during off-duty hours at excessive speeds and accumulate lots of traffic violations in the process.

When Claude did not get attention he always sought ways of attracting it to himself. He was very successful at the gambling tables and once remarked that he was going to make a ton of money off the atomic bombings after the war. He was obviously disappointed that he and his crew did not participate in the tremendous amount of publicity that the *Enola Gay* crew received after the war.

At war's end, Claude wanted to stay in the Air Corps. In order to do so he opted to become a meteorological officer. In the course of the final examination to get this rating, rather than studying the night before as everyone else had, he probably engaged in a poker game or whatever else his normal evening past times were. During the exam he decided that his neighbor sitting next to him in the examination room probably had all the right answers and he would make liberal use of whatever information he could. This is called cheating. Cheating is not tolerated and he was dismissed from the Air Force. But, because of his war record he was allowed to resign his commission thus avoiding the disgrace of a dishonorable discharge.

From that point on it was downhill for Major Eatherly. He was first caught in New Orleans in the company of another Colonel who was down on his luck. They were caught by the federal authorities running guns to Central America. They were heavily fined, but they gained a lot of notoriety from it - national press coverage, radio and TV coverage. This pleased Major Eatherly that he got all this attention and he devised a scheme where by he could get the attention and not get confined. So he

248

began holding up corner grocery stores and post offices. Once the money was transferred to him he would lay a toy gun which he carried and say "now call the police and the newspapers." He later served some time in prison in New Orleans for forgery.

Eatherly, with the help of some liberal media people including the writer Gunther Anders, is the one who fabricated the story that he had witnessed the dropping of the atomic bomb over Hiroshima and that seeing the blast made such an impact on him he went crazy. It was part of his successful insanity defense in federal court on the armed robbery charge. He beat the rap and gained notoriety for a while. If any reporters had bothered to check, they would have learned that Eatherly not only didn't witness the atomic blast, he had in fact, flown one of the weather planes on August 3 that was 250 miles away from Hiroshima at the time of the blast. The press, naturally, picked up his story without ever verifying it. But once the story was in print it begin a life of its own that persists to this day. And yes, eventually he was committed to a mental hospital.

In the summer of about 1964 I received a letter from a person in Czechoslovakia who was concerned about Major Eatherly's plight and wanted to engage in a three way written dialog with me and Eatherly. He felt that Eatherly was being abused by the government because of his opinion and actions. He believed Eatherly's story that he was having night mares about being over Hiroshima. The following letters are a part of this three way dialog.

1

A Letter

Mr. Claude R. Eatherly   June 3rd, 1959
formerly Major A.F.
Veterans Administration Waco
Texas Hospital

Dear Mr. Eatherly,

The writer of these lines is unknown to you; you, however, are known to my friends and to me. No matter whether we are in New York, in Vienna or in Tokyo, we are anxiously watching the way you are trying to manage and master your condition. Not out of curiosity, nor because we are medically or psychologically interested in your 'case history'. We are neither medical men nor psychologists. But because full of burning concern, we have made it our daily task to push our way through the moral problems which are blocking the road of mankind today. The 'technification' of our being: the fact that today it is possible that unknowingly and indirectly, like screws in a machine, we can be used in actions, the effects of which are far beyond the horizon of our eyes and imagination, and of which, could we imagine them, we could not approve – this fact has changed the very foundations of our moral existence. Thus, we can become 'guiltlessly guilty', a condition which had not existed in the technically less advanced times of our fathers.

You understand what this has to do with you. After all, you are one of the first ones who have actually been caught in this new sort of guilt, in which everyone of us can be caught today or tomorrow. What could happen to us tomorrow, has actually happened to you. Therefore you are playing for us the great role of a crowning example, yes even that of a predecessor.

Probably you don't like that. You want your peace, your life is your business. We assure you that we despise indiscretion just as much as you do, and we ask for your forgiveness. In this case, however, indiscretion is, unfortunately, inevitable, even required. Since change (or however we may call the indisputable fact) wished to change you, the private individual Claude Eatherly, into a symbol of the future, your life has become our business too. Of course, it is not your fault that of all of the millions of your fellow men, just you have been sentenced to this symbolic function; but things are as they are.

And yet, please don't believe that you are the only one who has been sentenced in this way. For all of us have to live in this epoch in which we could slide into such a guilt; and as little as you have picked out your tragic function, so little have we picked out this tragic epoch. In this sense, we are all in the same boat, we are children of one and the same family. And it is this common fate which determines our attitude towards you. When thinking of your sufferings, we are doing it as brothers; as if you were a brother to whom the misfortune has actually

1)Claude Eatherly was one of the super pilots who had been chosen for the Hiroshima-Mission: for the bombing of Hiroshima. He sat in the cockpit of the B29 Straight Flush and gave the plane loaded with the bomb the go-ahead signal. After his release from the service Eatherly has twice attempted suicide and committed several 'normal' crimes such as forgery, breaking and entering etc; whereupon he was interned in one of the psychiatric wards established for former service men. Today he lives there. He feels persecited by the thousands of dead, which condition his doctors consider to be abnormal and only explainable by the Oedipus Complex. See Newsweek of May 25th, 1959 under 'Psychiatry'.

Gunther Anders' Letter to Claude Eatherly (page 1 of 4)

occurred to do that which each of us could be compelled to do t omorrow, as brothers who hope to avoid this calamity as you so terribly futilly hope that you could have avoided it. But at that time it wasn't possible. The machinery had functioned blamelessly, and you were young and lacking in insight. You have done it. But since you have done it, we can learn from you, and only from you, what would become of us if we had been you, if we would be you. You see, you are terribly important for us, even indispensable. So to say, our teacher.

Of course, you will reject this title. 'Everything but that', you will answer, 'for I just can't master my condition.'

You'll be surprised, but it is just this 'can't' which is decisive for us. And even consoling. I know that this statement must sound senseless at first. Therefore a few words of explanation.

I don't say: 'consoling for you'. Nothing lies further from my mind than to try to console you. The consoler always says: 'It's not as bad as all that', tries to belittle the pain or guilt or to talk it away. That is exactly what your doctors are trying to do. It is not difficult to see why they are doing it. After all, these men are employees of a military hospital to whom the moral condemnation of a generally respected, even glorified action, would not exactly be beneficial, to whom the possibility of such a damning may not occur; who, under all circumstances, must defend the purity of the deed which you so rightly feel as guilt. Therefore your doctors maintain: 'Hiroshima in itself is not enough to explain your behaviour' - which in a less indirect language means nothing else than 'Hiroshima wasn't really as bad as all that', therefore they confine themselves to criticizing your reaction to the deed instead of the deed itself (or the world condition in which such a deed is possible). Therefore they find it necessary to call your sufferings and expectation of punishment an illness ('classical guilt complex'), and therefore they must treat your act as a 'self imagined wrong'. Is it any wonder that men, who through their conformism and lack of moral backbone, in order to preserve the purity of your deed, must characterize your pangs of conscience as pathological - is it any wonder that men who work with such fraudulent suppositions have not exactly succeeded in reaching sensational results? I can imagine - if I am wrong please correct me - with what disbelief, with what suspicions, with what resistance you must face these men, since they only take your reaction seriously, not your action. Hiroshima - self imagined. Really! You know better. Not without reason do the screams of the wounded deafen your days, and not without reason do the shadows of the dead force their way into your dreams. You know that what has happened, has happened, and is not imagined. You are not taken in by those men, nor are we. We don't want to have anything to do with such sham consolation.

No, I say 'for us'. For us the fact that you cannot master what is done is consoling. Because it shows that now, afterwards, you are making the attempt to catch up with, to realize the magnitude of your acts, the effects of which you then had not realized; because this attempt, even if it fails, proves that you have been able to keep your conscience alert, although once you had functioned as a screw in a machine, even successfully so. And since you have been able to do this, you have proven that o n e is able to do this, that we must be able to do this. And to know that - and it is to you to whom we owe this knowledge - is consoling for us.

"Also if your attempt fails". For it must fail. Why?

Even if one has harmed but one fellow man - I am not speaking yet at all of killings - it is, although the deed can be seen at a glance, no easy task to 'digest' it. But here it is something else. You happen to have in left 200,000 dead behind you. And how should one be able to mobilize a pain which embraces 200,000? How should one repent 200,000? Not only you

Gunther Anders' Letter to Claude Eatherly (page 2 of 4)

cannot do it, not only we cannot do it, no one can do it. However desperately we may attempt it, pain and repentance remain inadequate. The
frustration of your efforts is not your fault, Eatherly. It is a consequence of what I previously had described as the decisive newness of our
situation. That we can produce more thank we can mentally reproduce; that
we are not made for the effects which we can make by means of our man-
made machines; that the effects are too big for your imagination and the
emotional forces at our disposal. Don't reproach yourself for this discre-
pancy. But although the repentance cannot succeed, you must daily experience the frustration of your efforts. For outside of this experience
of failure, there is nothing else which could replace the repentance, which
which could prevent us from having once again anything to do with such
a monstrous deed. That you, since your efforts cannot succeed, react
panically and uncoordinately, is comprehensible. One could almost say
that it is proof of your moral health. For your reactions prove that your
conscience is on guard.

The usual method of mastering what is too big consists of a mere sup-
pression-manoeuver; of going on in exactly the same way as before; of
sweeping the deed from the desk of life, as if the too big guilt were no
guilt at all. In order to master it, one makes no attempt to master it.
As, for instance, your buddy and compatriot Joe Stiborik, the former radar man on the Enola Gay, who, because he continues living as a 'regular guy', and because, in the best of spirits he explained, 'For me it
was just a bigger bomb', one loves to hold up to you as a shining example.
And even better illustration of this method is that 'resident who gave you
your go ahead signal, just as you gave the go ahead signal to the bomber;
who actually, therefore, finds himself in the same situation as you, if
not even in a worse one. But what you have done, he has failed to do. A
few years ago - I don't know whether you heard about it at the time - most
naively perverting all moral standards, he announced in a public interview,
that he felt not the least 'pangs of conscience' implying thereby, that
his innocence was proved; and recently on his 75th birthday as he sum-
med up his life, he named, as the only wrong worthy of his repentance,
that he didn't marry before his thirties. I can't imagine that you envy
this clean sheet. I am perfectly certain, however, that no common criminal could sell you his innocence by telling you that he doesn't feel any
pangs of conscience. Isn't a man who runs away from himself a ridiculous
figure? You, in any case, haven't done that, Eatherly. You are not a ridiculous figure. Even when you fail, you are doing what is humanly possible. You are trying to go on as the one who has done it. And that is
what consoles us. Although you, just because you have remained identical with your deed, have been changed by this deed.

Of course, you understand that I am referring to your forgery, robbery, breaking and entering, and God knows what other irregularities there
may have been. And also to your alleged demoralization. Don't believe that
I am an anarchist and in favour of breaking and entering and forgery, or
that I take such matters lightly. But in your case, these offenses have
another meaning than ordinarily. Theyare acts of despair. For to be as
guilty as you are and yet to be publicly classified as innocent, even to
be praised as a smiling hero on the 'strength' of this guilt - that must
be a situation which a decent person just cannot tolerate, and for the
ending of which he even takes recourse to indecent steps. Since the monstrous guilt which weighed and weighs on you was not understood, was not
permitted to be understood, and could not be made understandable, you had
to attempt to speak and to act in the language which is understandable
there, in the idiom of petty or big larceny, in the terms of the society
itself. Thus you have tried to prove your guilt by commiting acts which
at least are recognized as crimes. Yet even here you were frustrated.
Whatever you do, one continues classifying you as a sick man, not as a
guilty one, and for this reason, because the world is bebruding you this
guilt, you remain an unhappy man.

Last year I visited Hiroshima, and there I spoke with those, who are six

Gunther Anders' Letter to Claude Etherly (page 3 of 4)

still there after your visit to Hiroshima. You can be sure: Amongst
these people there is not one who would think of persecuting a man
who was nothing but a screw in the workings of a military machine
(that you were when you, as a twenty six year old, carried out your
'mission'); and no one who hates you.

But now you have proven that although at one time you had been
misused as a screw, you, contrary to the others, have remained a human being, or have become one anew.

And here is my suggestion:

Next August 6th, as every year, the population of Japan will celebrate the day on which ' it' happened. Why don't you send a message
to these people. which would arrive in time for the celebration? If
you would tell them: "At that time I knew not what I did, but now I
do know, and I know that this must never happen again. and that no human being ought to be allowed to demand such a thing of another human
being." And: "Your fight is my fight, your ' no more Hiroshima' is my
'no more Hiroshima', so, or in this way - you can be sure that with
such a message you would make this day of mourning a day of rejoicing,
and that the survivors of Hiroshima would receive you as a friend, as
one of them, and rightly so. Since also you, E„therly, are a Hiroshima
victim.

                                        With the deep esteem which I have
                                        for each and every Hiroshima victim
                                        I am

                                        Yours Sincerely,

                                        Gunther Anders

Gunther Anders' Letter to Claude Eatherly (page 4 of 4)

Mr. Günther Anders:

Dear Sir,

Many thanks for your letter which I received on Friday of last week.

After reading your letter several times, I decided that I would like to write you, perhaps carry on a correspondence with you to discuss matters of which, I think, we have a mutual understanding. I receive many letters, but I find it impossible to answer most of them, but to your letter I felt compelled to answer and give you some insight to how I feel towards matters which involve this world today.

Throughout my adult life I have always been keenly interested in problems of human conduct.

Whilst in no sense, I hope, either a religious or a political fanatic, I have for some time felt convinced that the crisis in which we are all involved is one calling for a thorough re-examination of our whole scheme of values and loyalties. In the past it has sometimes been possible for men to 'coast along' without posing to themselves too many searching questions about the way they are accustomed to think and to act – but it is reasonably clear now that our age is not one of these. On the contrary I believe that we are rapidly approaching a situation in which we shall be compelled to re-examine our willingness to surrender responsibility for our thoughts and actions to some social institution such as the political party, trade union, church or state. None of these institutions are adequately equipped to offer infallible advice on moral issues, and their claim to offer such advice needs therefore to be challenged. It is, I feel, in the light of this situation that my personal experience needs to be studied, if its true significance, not only for myself, but for all men everywhere, is to be grasped. If you feel that all this is relevant and more or less in accordance with your own thinking, what I would like to suggest is that we should together seek to work out its implications through a correspondence extended over a period of whatever time may be necessary.

I feel that you have an understanding about me that no one else, except my doctor and friend may have.

My anti social acts have been disastrous to my personal life, but I feel that in my efforts, in time my motives will succeed in bringing out my true convictions and philosophy.

Günther, it is a pleasure to write to you, and through our correspondence may we form a friendship of trust and understanding. Feel free to write of any problem, situation or activity that confronts us all. I in turn will give my viewpoint.

Thanks again for your letter
I remain

Sincerely

Claude R. Eatherly

Claude Eatherly's Response to Gunther Anders' Letter

Now for the myth that Major Sweeney was supposed to fly the Hiroshima mission instead of Colonel Tibbets. I knew Colonel Tibbets very well and Major Sweeney was a good friend. I sat in on enough planning meetings to know that there were no plans for anyone other than for Colonel Tibbets to fly the first mission. I truly believe that the reason Major Sweeney was selected to fly the second mission was not based on his experience but purely for political reasons. Major Sweeney was a good pilot but inexperienced in commanding a combat mission. In fact he was told by Colonel Tibbets just before taking off for the Nagasaki mission to talk with his bombardier if he needed any advice about what to do during the mission. Colonel Tom Classen was far more experienced but lacked the friendship connection with Colonel Tibbets.

Unfortunately Major Sweeney, because of his inexperience, did not exercise firm control and made some poor command decisions. I also noticed that it was not clear who was in command of the mission – Sweeney the airplane commander or Commander Ashworth the Weaponeer. But with luck we got the job done. I understand Colonel Tibbets considered a court martial for Major Sweeney for his actions or lack thereof during this mission. I also know for a fact that if any future atomic bombs had been needed Colonel Tibbets would have commanded the flights.

The Hiroshima mission was perfectly planned and executed. However this was not the case of the Nagasaki mission. We had troubles from the "get-go." Fuel transfer pump problems were noted before take off that caused a delay. One of the airplanes did now make the rendezvous as planned. In flight we had some serious personnel problems. Our commander, Major Sweeney, "waffled" when he had tough decisions to make. One of my fellow officers also commented it was not clear who was in command of the mission – Sweeney or Ashworth. We dwelled too long and used an excessive amount of fuel cruising around the rendezvous point waiting for a plane that did not show up. We made several bomb runs over the primary target again using lots of fuel and attracting Japanese fighter aircraft before making a decision to go to the secondary target of Nagasaki. Because of the dwindling fuel supply we had to fly over an area littered with Japanese fighter air bases. With Commander Ashworth assuming the responsibility of violating our special orders to bomb visually, we made a successful radar approach but released the bomb using the visual bombsight in accordance with our special orders.

We did not have enough fuel to make to our alternate base of Iwo Jima. We barely had enough fuel to make it to Okinawa. Our approach to the landing strip on Okinawa was not acknowledge by the control tower but being out of fuel Major Sweeney went in anyway. A B-24 pilot in the landing pattern noticed that we were in trouble and peeled off to allow us to land. The landing was hot and fast. Two engines quit as we touched down. At the end of the runway we were still going about 100 miles per hour. Major Sweeney made a 90-degree turn at the end of the runway without warning the crew to avoid going off the runway and into the ocean. The g-forces almost threw me through the side of the aircraft. But even with all the problems we accomplished our mission made it home safely. When we arrived back at Tinian, it was obvious that everyone, including our superior officers, were glad to see us, but not particularly well pleased with the performance of our mission.

Another myth, or maybe in this case a misconception, is that no leaflets were dropped on the Japanese cities warning the citizens to evacuate prior to dropping the bomb on Hiroshima.

In July of 1945, in an attempt to demoralize the Japanese citizens, our bombers dropped leaflets on a number of Japanese cities warning them that they could be next. The English translation of these leaflets read as follows: "In the next few days the military installations in some or all of the cities named on the photograph will be destroyed by American bombs. These cities contain military installations and workshops or factories that produce military goods. The American Air Force, which does not wish to injure innocent people, now gives you warning to evacuate the cities named and save your lives. America is not fighting the Japanese people, but is fighting the military clique which has enslaved the Japanese people. The peace, which America will bring, will free the people from the oppression of the military clique and mean the emergence of a new and better Japan. You can restore peace by demanding new and good leaders who will end the war. We cannot promise that only these cities will he among those attacked, but some or all will be. So heed this warning and evacuate these cities immediately."

In the next few days six of the cities were firebombed. Despite the warnings and thousands of civilian casualties, their military leaders wanted to keep fighting.

After the bombing of Hiroshima, thousands of leaflets were dropped on Japanese cities. Our leaders had hoped the Japanese people would evacuate their cities as instructed. This would not only save thousands of lives but would also disrupt war production in the factories that were concentrated in cities. Furthermore they hoped that a popular citizens revolution against continuing the war would take place and force the Tokyo officials to sue for peace according to requirements of the Potsdam Declaration.

Unfortunately time was too short for it to succeed. Moreover, Japanese military authorities controlled the government, and only another nuclear bombing, that of Nagasaki, enabled the emperor to prevail against them.

After Nagasaki was bombed additional thousands of leaflets were dropped on August 12 and 14th. I annotated one of these leaflets with the dates they were dropped and included a photo of it in an earlier chapter.

APPENDIX 2
Background Release of the Atomic Bomb

Marianas — Air groups
August 8, 1945

BACKGROUND RELEASE ON THE ATOMIC BOMB

The energy of the atom has been harnessed to produce the deadliest weapon ever devised, the atomic bomb, the War Department today announced shortly after the first of the aerial missiles cascaded upon a Japanese military target.

The initial combat use of the bomb culminated three years of intensive effort on the part of science and industry, working in cooperation with the Military. It is heralded as the greatest achievement of the combined efforts of science, industry, labor and the military in history.

President Truman and Secretary of War Henry L. Stimson made the first announcements of the new weapon, declaring that the atomic bomb has an explosive force such as to stagger the imagination. Improvements were revealed as forthcoming which will increase several fold the present effectiveness.

While the use in combat has permitted a slight relaxation in the security that has cloaked the project, the War Department declined for security reasons to disclose the exact methods by which the bombs are produced or the nature of their action and requested that the press and radio refrain from disclosing other information as well as all those connected with the Project.

In broad outline, the War Department made the following disclosures:

Late in 1939 the possibility of using atomic energy for military purposes was brought to the attention of President Roosevelt, who appointed a committee to survey the problem;

In June 1942 sufficient progress had been made to warrant a great expansion of the project and the assumption of its direction by the War Department with Major General Leslie R. Groves in executive charge;

By December 1942 a decision had been reached to proceed with plant construction on a large scale, two of which were located at the Clinton Engineer Works in Tennessee and a third at the Hanford Engineer Works in the State of Washington. A special laboratory to deal with the many technical problems involved was located in an isolated area in the vicinity of Santa Fe, New Mexico, under the direction of Dr. J. Robert Oppenheimer;

Certain other manufacturing plants much smaller in scale are located in the United States and Canada and the facilities of certain laboratories of the Universities of California, Chicago, Columbia, Iowa State College and at other schools as well as certain industrial laboratories were utilized;

Congress has appropriated up to June 30, 1945, a total of $1,950,000,000.00 for the operation of the huge project;

- 1 -

E-28

The atomic bomb has been developed with the full knowledge of and cooperation of the United Kingdom and substantial patent control has been accomplished in the United States, the United Kingdom and Canada;

Uranium is the essential ore in the production of the weapon and steps have been taken and will continue to be taken to insure adequate supplies of this mineral.

The series of discoveries which led to development of the atomic bomb started at the turn of the century when radio-activity became known to science. Prior to 1939 the scientific work in this field was world-wide, but more particularly so in the United States, the United Kingdom, Germany, France, Italy and Denmark. One of Denmark's great scientists, Dr. Niels Bohr, a Nobel prize winner, was whisked from the grasp of the Nazis in his occupied homeland and later assisted in developing the atomic bomb.

It is known that Germany worked desperately to solve the problem of controlling atomic energy.

Britain, suffering repeated air attacks early in the war, agreed to a concentration of the atomic bomb project in the United States and transferred many of her scientists to this Country to assist.

The attention of President Roosevelt was invited to the potentialities of the atomic bomb in 1939. Research which had been conducted on a small scale with Navy funds was put on a greatly expanded basis. At the end of 1941 progress had been sufficient to warrant additional expansion. In the meantime the project had been placed under the direction of the Office of Scientific Research and Development, with Dr. Vannevar Bush, Director of OSRD, in charge. At the same time the President appointed a General Policy Group, consisting of former Vice-President Henry A. Wallace, Secretary of War Henry L. Stinson, General George C. Marshall, Dr. James B. Conant, and Dr. Bush.

The General Policy Group recommended in June 1942 that the atomic bomb project be greatly expanded and placed under the direction of the War Department. This action was taken and Major General Groves, experienced and resourceful U. S. Army construction engineer, placed in complete control. At the same time, in addition to the General Policy Group, there was appointed a Military Policy Committee consisting of Dr. Bush as chairman with Dr. Conant as his alternate, Lt. General Wilhelm D. Styer, USA, and Rear Admiral William R. Purnell, USN.

The need for the weapon and its potential led to the decision in December 1942 to start the construction of an industrial empire that was to eventually consist of entire cities and employ upwards of 200,000.

Two of the plants were constructed on a 59,000-acre government reservation eighteen miles west of Knoxville, Tennessee. It assumed the name of Oak Ridge and became the fifth largest city in the State.

- 2 -

The third plant was erected at the Hanford Engineer Works on a 450,000-acre government tract fifteen miles northwest of Pasco, Washington. This became the city of Richland.

A special laboratory was established in an isolated area of New Mexico, about 30 miles northwest of Santa Fe.

The ramifications of the atomic bomb project reached such proportions that in August 1943 it was decided to establish a Combined Policy Committee, composed at the outset of Secretary of War Stimson, Dr. Bush, Dr. Conant for the United States, Field Marshal Sir John Dill and Colonel J. J. Llewellin, for the United Kingdom; and Mr. C. D. Howe for Canada. Col. Llewellin was later replaced by Sir Ronald I. Campbell who in turn was succeeded by the Earl of Halifax; the late Field Marshal Dill was succeeded by Field Marshal Sir Henry Maitland Wilson. The United States members have had as their scientific adviser, Dr. Richard C. Tolman; the British, Sir James Chadwick; and the Canadian, Dean C. J. Mackenzie.

The dropping of the first atomic bomb upon a Japanese Military target brings to first fruition a spectacular new discovery in the field of science. In its development, it appears that in the decades ahead there will ultimately flow multiple benefits for all mankind. To insure a study of the best use of the discovery, the Secretary of War has appointed an Interim Committee consisting of the following:

The Secretary of War, Chairman, Secretary of State James F. Byrnes, Ralph A. Bard, former Under-Secretary of the Navy, William L. Clayton, assistant Secretary of State, Dr. Bush, Dr. Conant, Dr. Karl T. Compton, President of the Massachusetts Institute of Technology, and George L. Harrison, special consultant to the Secretary of War and President of the New York Life Insurance Company. Assisting this group as a scientific panel are Dr. J. R. Oppenheimer, Dr. E. O. Lawrence, Dr. A. H. Compton and Dr. Enrico Fermi.

260

APPENDIX 3
FIELD ORDER 13

Mission Planning Summary

FIELD ORDER: #13

SPECIAL BOMBING MISSION: #13

MISSION EXECUTED: 6 August 1945

1. PRIMARY PURPOSE OF THE 509TH COMPOSITE GROUP

   Early in June, 1945, this headquarters was informed one Atomic Bomb would be available for use against the enemy on 6 August 1945. The primary limiting factor was production. By 5 August 1945, all was in readiness to initiate the first Atomic Bomb attack in the history of the world. The bomb was ready, weather was satisfactory, and the carefully selected crew was well trained. (See Report Number 1, 509th Composite Group, page 1, paragraph 1.)

2. TARGETS SELECTED FOR ATTACK

   A. Primary Target: 90.30 - Hiroshima Urban Industrial Area. AP 063096, AP Reference: XXI BomCom Litho Mosaic Hiroshima Area, No. 90.30 - Urban.

   B. Secondary Target: 90.34 - 168 Kokura Arsenal and City. AP 104082, AP Reference: XXI BomCom Litho Mosaic Kokura Arsenal, No. 90.34 - 168.

   C. Tertiary Target: 90.36 - Nagasaki Urban Area. AP 114061 AP Reference: XXI BomCom Litho Mosaic Nagasaki Area, Mitsubishi Steel and Arms Works, No. 90.36 - 546.

   Weather aircraft were dispatched to all three targets to relay strike-time weather forecast back to the strike force. However, since it was so desirable that the primary be hit if possible, rather than the other two assigned targets, instructions were given to the strike aircraft to pass close enough themselves to the primary target, regardless of the weather aircraft's broadcasts, to insure that a visual bombing opportunity on the primary was not missed. However, after that check, the strike aircraft were to proceed to either the secondary or tertiary, depending on the weather aircraft.

Although the bomb had a very extensive MBA, because it was so expensive and because the important areas of the urban targets were so concentrated, it was essential that visual bombing be accomplished to make the attack efficient. Radar was to be used as an aid, but if a visual check on the target-sighting operation could not be made with the Norden bombsight, the crew was to bring the bomb back to base. To permit the crew additional chance of obtaining a visual sighting operation, two targets, in addition to the primary, were assigned.

3. REASONS FOR TARGET SELECTION

Of the four cities set aside for Atomic Bomb attack, Niigata was discarded because it was so poorly laid out for this sort of an attack - the industrial concentration and the residential-small factory areas were relatively widely separated. Of the other three, Nagasaki was the poorest of the layouts, and it had a prisoner-of war camp nearby; so, it was made tertiary. The other two - Hiroshima and Kokura were well laid out and relatively important, but Kokura had a prisoner of war camp and Hiroshima had none to our knowledge; so Hiroshima was made the primary.

As for the target itself, Hiroshima was highly important as an industrial target. Prior to this attack, Hiroshima ranked as the largest city in the Japanese homeland (except Kyoto) which remained undamaged following a wave of B-29 incendiary strikes. The city had a population of 344,000 in 1940.

It is an army city - headquarters of the 5th Division and a primary port of embarkation. The entire northeastern and eastern sides of the city are military

262

zones. Prominent in the north-central part of the city are the Army Division Headquarters marked by the Hiroshima Castle, numerous barracks, administration buildings and ordnance store houses. In addition, there are the following important military targets:

    A. Army Reception Center

    B. Large Military Airport

    C. Army Ordnance Depot

    D. Army Clothing Depot

    E. Army Food Depot

    F. Large Port and Dock Area

    G. Several Ship Yards and Ship Building Companies

    H. Japan Steel Company

    I. Railroad Marshalling Yards

    J. Numerous Aircraft Component Parts Factories

The fact that Hiroshima was undamaged made it an ideal target. This was deemed necessary to assess correctly the damage which could be inflicted by the Atomic Bomb. The size of Hiroshima was another important factor in the selection. According to preliminary data, it was believed that the radius of damage which could be inflicted by the Atomic Bomb was 7,500 feet. By placing the aiming point in the center of the city, the circle of prospective damage covered almost the entire area of Hiroshima with the exception of the dock area to the south.

4. MUNITIONS

One (1) Atomic Bomb.

5. NAVIGATORS PLAN
(See Report Number 1, 509th Composite Group, page 6, paragraph 1.)

263

6. **BOMBARDIERS PLAN** have the attack go off on time as planned in spite
   (See Report Number 1, 509th Composite Group, Page 6, paragraph 2.)

7. **RADAR PLAN**
   (See Report Number 1, 509th Composite Group, page 7, paragraph 2.)

8. **FLIGHT ENGINEERS PLAN**
   (See Report Number 1, 509th Composite Group, page 7, paragraph 4.)

9. **R.C.M.**
   None

10. **FIGHTER ESCORT**
    None

11. **AIR SEA RESCUE**

    Normally this function is arranged by Wing Headquarters, but due to the
    importance of this operation, 20th Air Force Headquarters made arrangements for
    this mission. Every precaution was taken to provide complete air sea rescue
    facilities so that any untoward incident would not jeopardize the safe return
    of all witnesses.

12. **STRIKING FORCE**

    3 A/C - one bombing, 2 observing.

13. **SPECIAL PLANNING OPERATIONS**

    A. In order to prevent interference with the attack all friendly aircraft
    were instructed to stay at least 50 miles away from target areas for four hours
    prior to strike time. And in order to protect friendly aircraft from the
    almost infinite amount of radio activity in the immediate area above the explo-
    sion, they were restricted from entering the 50-mile area for six hours after
    the attack. The post-strike photo aircraft were permitted in the area four
    hours after the attack, because they had had special briefing.

B. In order to have the attack go off on the day planned in spite of possible abort of the bombing airplane, a spare ship was stationed at Iwo Jima, where there was also a pit for unloading and reloading the Atomic Bomb.

C. Weather: Three aircraft which will be dispatched one to each target at such a time as to be able to relay, from their assigned target, the target weather forecast for strike time, broadcasting the message between 060845K and 060915K. This will enable strike force to select either the secondary or tertiary target in the event the primary is found to be covered by clouds. Each weather aircraft will have aboard a weather observer furnished by the 313th Wing.

D. Post Strike Photography: C.O., 509th Group, will be responsible for briefing and dispatching two F-13 A/C. These aircraft will not enter target area until four hours after bombs away. To insure this schedule is maintained regardless of whether the strike force has to make use of the spare aircraft at Iwo Jima or not, the photo aircraft will be required to check in with the ground stations at both Tinian and Iwo Jima to obtain clearance to proceed past Iwo Jima. If these photo aircraft do not receive notification of which target has been bombed, they will photograph all three targets.

265

Pencil sketch by the love of Jacob Beser's life, his wife Sylvia, on one of their cruises in their sailboat No Dod II (Hebrew for wanderer)

References

This is a collection of books and periodicals related to the subject and reflects opinions on both sides of the a-bombing controversy. When reading some of these references please keep in mind that the bombings of Hiroshima and Nagasaki has proved to be a fertile ground for propagandists.

Anders, Gunther, *Burning Conscience*, New York Monthly Review Press, 1962

Anders, Roger, *The President and the Atomic Bomb: Who Approved the Trinity Nuclear Test?*, Prologue, Winter 1988

Baldwin, Hanson, *How the Decision To Drop the Bomb Was Made: 'Little Boy's' Long, Long Journey*, New York Times Magazine, 8/1/65

Bainbridge, Kenneth T., *Prelude to Trinity*, Bulletin of the Atomic Scientists, April 1975.

Bamett, Lincoln, *J. Robert Oppenheimer*, Life, 10/10/49.

Bernstein, Barton, *Triumph and Tragedy: Hiroshima and Nagasaki - 30 Years Later*, Intellect, Dec. 1975.

Bernstein, Barton, *Leo Szilard: Giving Peace a Chance in the Nuclear Age*, Physics Today, Sept. 1987

Cary, Otis, *Atomic Bomb Targeting - Myths and Realities*, Japan Quarterly, Oct.-Dec. 1979.

Beser, Jacob, *Hiroshima and Nagasaki Revisited* - Global Press 1988.

Byrnes, James, *Byrnes Answers Truman*, Collier's, 4/26/52.

de Vore, Robert, *The Man Who Made Manhattan*, Collier's, 10/13/45.

Fermi, Enrico, *The Development of the First Chain Reacting Pile*, Proceedings of the American Philosophical Society, vol. 90, no. 1, Jan. 1946 bomb

Finney, Nat, *How F.D.R. Planned to Use the A-Bomb*, Look, 3/14/50

Groves, Leslie, *Some Recollections of July 16, 1945*, Bulletin of the Atomic Scientists, June 1970.

Groves, Leslie, *The Story of the Atomic Bomb,* Think, Nov. 1945

Groves, Leslie,   The Atom General Answers His Critics, Saturday Evening Post, 6/19/48

Groves, Leslie, *The Atomic Bomb Project,* The Military Engineer, Dec. 1945

Groves, Leslie, *Development of the Atomic Bomb,* The Military Engineer, June 1946

Knebel, Fletcher and Bailey, Charles, *The Fight Over the A-Bomb,* Look, 8/13/63.

Knox, Ralph M. *The Emperor's Angry Guest: A World War II Prisoner of the Japanese Speaks Out*

Kosakai, Yoshiteru (Compiler), *A-Bomb: A City Tells its Story*

Laurence, William L., *The Story of the Atomic Bomb.* New York Times, 1946

Laurence, William L., *Dawn Over Zero* 1972

Laurence, William *Would You Make the Bomb Again?,* New York Times Magazine, 8/1/65

Lewis, Robert L. *How We Dropped the Bomb,* Popular Science, vol 171, no 2, August 1957

Oppenheimer, Robert *Atomic Weapons,* Proceedings of the American Philosophical Society, vol. 90, no. 1, Jan. 1946.

Oppenheimer, Robert, *Letters,* Science, Dec. 4, 1959.

Oppenheimer, Robert, *Secretary Stimson and the Atomic Bomb,* The Andover Bulletin, Spring 1961

Paterson, Thomas, *Potsdam, the Atomic Bomb, and the Cold War: A Discussion With James F. Byrnes,* Pacific Historical Review, May 1972

Shils, Edward, *Leo Szilard: A Memoir,* Encounter, Dec. 1964

Sigal, Leon, *Bureaucratic Politics and Tactical Use of Committees: the Interim Committee and the Decision to Drop the Atomic Bomb,* Polity, Spring 1978.

Smith, Alice Kimball, *Behind the Decision to Use the Atomic Bomb: Chicago 1944-45,* Bulletin of the Atomic Scientists, Oct. 1958

Smith, Alice Kimball, *Los Alamos Focus of an Age,* Bulletin of the Atomic Scientists, June 1970.

Stem, Alfred, *Interview With Einstein,* Contemporary Jewish Record, June 1945.

Stimson, Henry, *The Bomb and the Opportunity,* Harper's, March 1946.

Stimson, Henry, *The Decision To Use the Atomic Bomb,* Harper's, February 1947

Sweeney Charles, War's End: An Eyewitness Account of America's Last Atomic Mission

Thomas, Gordon and Witts, Max Morgan, *Enola Gay*: 1977

Tibbets Paul W., *Return of the Enola Gay*

Truman, Harry S., *Year of Decision*

Villa, Brian, *The U.S. Army, Unconditional Surrender, and the Potsdam Proclamation,* Journal of American History, June 1976.

Wilson, Robert, *The Conscience of a Physicist,* Bulletin of the Atomic Scientists, June 1970.

Fifteen Years Later - The Men Who Bombed Hiroshima. Coronet, Vol 48, no 4 August 1960.

U.S. Strategic Bombing Survey, *Atomic Bomb: First Official Report On Damage to Japan,* U.S. News and World Report, July 5, 1946

GI's in Pacific Go Wild With Joy; 'Let Em Keep Emperor,' They Say, New York Times, 8/11/45, pg. 1,4

Truman, in Letter to Hiroshima Defends His Atom Bomb Order, New York Times, 3/15/58, pg. 1, 5

Hiroshima's protest of Truman's earlier defense of the a-bombings NY Times, 2/14/58, pg. 2

War Was Really Won Before We Used, We Were Anxious to Get the War Over -interview with James Byrnes, U.S. News and World Report, 8/15/60.

My Father

T'was in June of '92, a tired old soldier,
In agony and great pain on his deathbed lay,
Waiting for the Heavenly Shepherd of Mercy,
To arrive and take him on his way.

As he lay there his mind ran rampant with nostalgic scenes,
Thinking back to the history making events of long ago,
Reliving again the forgotten memories of his days in the Army,
And recalling fond memories of friends he used to know.

There was Tibbets, van Kirk, Ferebee, Lewis, Duzenbury, Caron,
Stiborik, Shumard, Nelson, Jeppson, Parsons and about 1800 more,
Some have gone on but others still await their special orders
From the higher command to prepare to soar.

The Heavenly Shepherd of Mercy arrived later that day,
And said "St. Peter is waiting for you on the pearly way,"
As He took my father tenderly by the hand he heard him say,
You and your buddies will fly again as a crew some day.

Jerome Beser

270

INDEX

272

275

ABOUT THE EDITORS

Jerome Beser is Jacob Beser's youngest son.

In 2004 the Jacob Beser family home was sold. In the process of relocating, his family discovered a vast archive of historical documents. These documents included hundreds of unpublished lecture notes, private correspondence, interview recordings, eyewitness debriefing transcripts as well as a number of private photos and films from crewmembers and government sources. All of these were related to the *Enola Gay* and *Bock's Car* atomic bomb missions.

In an interview Jerome said: "Reviewing my father's document collection revived my memories of our many conversations about his wartime experiences and I took on the challenge to complete his book. However my journey to complete his work has not been easy. In 2005 I was diagnosed with a large cell tumor mass that, due to its late discovery and pain, caused me to come very close to ending my quest to finish his work. But, when my health failed friends like Jack Spangler and Robbie Jacobson stepped forward to pick up the torch working by my side as my health deteriorated and taking over when it all became too painful for me

During the process of compiling this book using Dad's archives and other sources as reference material I became deeply involved in other projects including the search for and returning soldiers and sailors still missing in action from World War II and Korea. It was then that I decided to continue and expand my efforts by bringing together a team of highly skilled individuals to create *The Beser Foundation for Archival Research and Preservation*.

The mission of the Beser Foundation is to encourage others to become more engaged in locating, cataloging and preserving the records of the past. It is hoped that with my efforts and the efforts of the others with similar interests, we will be able to obtain and preserve materials that accurately validate historical events from the past up to the current times. Simply stated the Foundation mission is to preserve the past for the benefit of the future."

Jack Spangler and Jacob Beser were friends and business colleagues at Westinghouse for over 25 years.

During an interview Mr. Spangler said: "In August of 2005 there appeared in a local newspaper a column and number of letters to the editor from antiwar activists. In some of these letters the writers expressed their opinion that the use of the atomic bombs in 1945 was not justified and a criminal act on the part of those that participated. I responded with a letter to the newspaper editor taking issue with the column and the letters."

Shortly thereafter Jerome called Mr. Spangler and said that they should get together and talk as soon as possible and discuss a book project his father had started. In a couple of days they met and discussed his project to complete his father's book. At this point Jerome was seriously ill and felt that he would be unable to finish the task alone.

Mr. Spangler continues: "Jacob had been my Subcontracts Manager at Westinghouse. He and I did a lot of traveling together and we spent lots of time on airplanes, in hotel lobbies and at Vandenberg Air Force Base. Our conversation were often related to his wartime experiences and I had heard his stories many times. So I offered to help Jerome finish the work his father started.

Jerome immediately provided me with many of his father's papers and a few days later he was put in an extended medical coma. At this point I continued with the book project. In particular it was my objective to take Jacob's writings and conversational information from his radio, TV and private interviews, etc. and stitch them together as if we were sitting in a hotel lobby and talking about the events of 1945. Of course I had to generate the "connectivity" required to make the subject matter flow together with some semblance of order. The material I had to work with was generated at various points in Jacob's career, some as early as 1945. The ground rules I set up was to include his writing and words (as well as the words of others from interview recordings and transcripts) as far as possible in an unedited form following the outline that he had made before his death. This book is the result of our combined efforts."

"I, for one, to this day cannot forget the impression the Japanese made on me as a youth and at Pearl Harbor and Bataan and Shanghai. I felt then as I do today, in the context of 1945, that the Japanese, like the Germans, earned everything they received."

Jacob Beser

Printed in the United States
86002LV00005B/140/A